PALACE EXTRAORDINARY

CHARLES GRAVES

Palace Extraordinary

THE STORY OF ST JAMES'S

CASSELL · LONDON

CASSELL & COMPANY LTD
35 Red Lion Square · London WC1
and at
MELBOURNE · SYDNEY · TORONTO
JOHANNESBURG · CAPE TOWN · AUCKLAND

———

Printed in Great Britain
by Ebenezer Baylis and Son Limited
The Trinity Press, Worcester, and London
F.763

Contents

Illustrations

vii

ILLUSTRATIONS

Radio Times Hulton Picture Library

1. A bribe for Anne Boleyn

Myne awne sweetheart, this shall be to advertise you of the great ellingness that I find here since your departing, for I assure you, methinketh the tyme longer since your departing now last then I was wont to do a whole fortnight; I think your kindness and my fervence of love causeth it, for otherwise I would not thought it possible, that for so little a while it should have grieved me, but now that I am coming towards you, methinketh my pains been half released, and also I am right well comforted, insomuch that my book maketh substantially for my matter, in writing whereof I have spent about iiii hours this day, which caused me now to write the shorter letter to you at this tyme, because of some payne in my head, wishing myself (especially an evening) in my sweetheart's armes whose pretty duckys I trust shortly to kysse. Written with the hand of him that was, is, and shall be yours by his will.

HENRY VIII's infatuation for Anne Boleyn, expressed in a series of passionate love letters still in existence, was directly responsible for the erection of St James's Palace by order of the King. He was of course still married to the saintly Katharine of Aragon but already had an illegitimate son, the Duke of Richmond, and had made Mary Boleyn, Anne's elder sister, one of his mistresses.

Anne herself had been deeply in love with Lord Henry Percy, eldest son of the Earl of Northumberland, who returned her affection, but was frightened out of his secret engagement by Henry VIII.

Anne had lived for some years in France at the gay courts of Louis XII (as maid-of-honour to Henry's sister, Mary, Queen of France), of Francis I and of the Queen of Navarre. She was,

1

therefore, highly sophisticated, used to luxury and versed in intrigue, and her dark beauty drove Henry VIII into paroxysms of emotion, in spite of the large mole on her throat and her malformed left hand which had the stump of a sixth finger on it. For a long time she kept him at arm's length. As a final bribe Henry built St James's Palace specially for her, and divorced poor Katharine.

At that time he was living in Whitehall Palace; the ground on which St James's Palace was to be built being occupied by a large nunnery originally designed as a leper house. This was the property of Eton College, the Provost of which, Roger Lupton, was forced to dispose of it to him under an indenture, covenanting:

> that the King shall have the site, etc. of the house of St James' in the Field, with 185½ acres, between Charing Cross and Aye Hill, of which there are 64 acres on the south side of the highway between these places, 96 acres in the Northfield upon the north side of the same highway, and 18 acres in two closes at Knightsbridge, 5 acres in a meadow called Temes Mede, half an acre in Chelsey Mede, and 2 acres at Fulham, with reservation of the lands called Chalcotes and Wyldes, in the parish of Hamsted, and all lands in London and Westminster not mentioned in a schedule annexed. In exchange for which the college shall have the manor of Baudewyns near Dertford, Kent, and lands called Brokes in Dertford, the advowson of Newington church, and a pasture ground in Luddenham Marsh, Kent, the manor of Chatesham, Suff. with the Advowson of the church.

This indenture was confirmed on 24 December 1531, when Lupton made a grant to Henry VIII, 'of the hospital and lands of St James's by Westminster, which they had by patent 30 Oct. 28 Hen. VI; with reservations of Chalcolts and Wilds, in the parishes of Hendon, Finchley and Hampstead, and a tenement called the White Bere, in the parishes of St Mary Magdalene and All Saints, in Westcheap and Bread St, London, now in the tenure of Agnes Cavendish, widow, and another messuage in Westminster, in which Thos. Brightman now dwells'.

Henry's first action was to despatch one of his King's Messengers, the aptly named Thomas Swallowe, all over the kingdom to find the finest craftsmen to build the palace. Swallowe's expenses, incidentally, were 12d. a day. Samwelle bricks were supplied by the Vicar of Kingston-on-Thames at 2s. 8d. a thousand. Caen stone was brought over from Normandy at the price of 4s. 6d. a ton. Plaster of Paris also came across the Channel at a price of 4s. per 30 cwt. Some idea of the splendour of the palace may be gained from the fact that William Southwood of London, a goldbeater, supplied 300 ounces of fine gold, which Henry used for gilding the initials 'H' and 'A' entwined into every possible device. (The adherents of Queen Katharine derided them by reading them as 'ha ha'.)

It is said that Holbein, recently settled in England, was responsible for the design, though the palace was built under the direction of Thomas Cromwell. Altogether, 211 workmen were employed with six clerks to oversee them and it took them eighteen months to complete the palace, together with its bowling alleys and tennis courts.

In the meantime, the marshy land surrounding it had been drained and fenced in to form part of the present St James's Park.

One of the most significant entries in the book of payments for building the palace was the load of green birch and willow for 'refreshing' it 'against our Sovereign Lord's coming thither'. Water closets are first mentioned in the St James's Palace documents in 1720. In those days, the big houses and palaces were maintained in indescribable filth—human excrement, dog turds, garbage of all sorts. It was for this reason that reigning royalty always had several palaces in which to stay so that each could be cleaned after a visit of, say, six weeks. True, Henry VIII refused to allow any mastiffs, hounds or other dogs in the palace except for a few spaniels for the ladies. Nevertheless, dogs abounded.

In those days, indeed right up to the reign of Queen Mary, cleanliness was conspicuous by its absence. Floors were neither swept nor washed. All that happened was that fresh rushes were strewed on them from time to time, 'just like the littering of a farmyard when it is newly spread with straw for the accommodation of the cows and pigs', and the old surface remained a fomenting mass beneath. These layers of rushes accumulated on top of each other, covering up bones, fragments of food and

3

other horrors. If it was decided to dance, all this layer was heaped up around the walls, leaving a small circle in the middle. Imagination boggles at the horrible smells which the newly disturbed compost must have created.

Erasmus, not used to such filth in his native Rotterdam, rightly attributed the various diseases which plagued England to these revolting habits. In a letter to his friend, Dr Francis, he wrote, 'The floors are usually made of clay, covered with rushes. These are so little disturbed that the lower mass sometimes remains for twenty years together, and in it a collection of every kind of filth. Hence upon a change of weather, a vapour is exhaled most pernicious to the human body.' He added that the nobles' houses were no cleaner than those of the country gentry, but as they usually had several seats, 'they indulged in the luxury of removing from one to another when the nuisance cherished by their dirty customs became inconvenient. These progresses were usually termed "going to sweeten" '.

Henry's secret marriage to Anne Boleyn, which had taken place on 25 January 1533 in an attic at Whitehall Palace, was declared valid in May of that year.

After the Coronation and pageantry, which had its climax in Westminster Hall, Anne drank spiced wines and other aphrodisiacs. She then 'went in her barge secretly to the king in his manor of Westminster (St James's) where she rested that night'. From that moment onwards, she spent most of her time at the palace, described at the time as a magnificent and goodly house, where the favourite diversions of Anne and Henry seem to have been cards and dice. Henry's losses at games were considerable. Sums of £9 6s. 8d., £18 13s. 4d. and £11 13s. 4d. occur frequently in Henry's Privy Purse expenses and each time the winner seems to have been Anne Boleyn. Another game they played was a kind of Happy Families, except that the various points in the game were Matrimony, Intrigue, Pope Julius and similar allusions to the current situation.

The amount of time, however, spent solely in eating must have been prodigious. In the palace records, there are a number of specimen menus for the royal couple and also for the members of the Court, one of whose perquisites was to have all their meals free. Thus, on a fish day:

4

DYNNER

Cheat Bread and Manchett (White bread)	Playce or Gurnard
Ale & Beare (6 galls.)	Sea Bream or Soalles
Wyne (1 sexter)	Congers, Door
Herring	Porpose, Seale
Pottage	Carpe, Troute
Organe Lyng	Crabbs, Lobsters
Poudred Eales or Lamprons	Custard
Pyke	Rascalls or Flage
Calver Salmon	Tarte closed
Whyting	Fritter
Haddocks, Mullets or Base	Fruite

Second Course

Second Pottage	Crevez
Sturgion pr. vel. r.	Shrympes
Byrt or other dish	Tarte
Tench	Frytter
Perch or other dish	Fruite
Eles with Lampreys rost	Baked Pepins, Oranges
Chynes of Salmon broyled	Butter & Eggs

and on a meat day:

DYNNER

Cheat Bread & Manchett	Mutton
Beare & Ale (6 galls.)	Carpes or yong Veale in arm farced
Wyne (1 sext.)	Swanne, gr. goose, storke or Capons of gr.
Flesh for Pottage	
Chines of Beef	
Rammuners in stew or cap	Conyes of gr.
Venison in brewz or mult	Fryanders, baked carpe
Pestells of Red Deere	Custard Varnished or Fritters

Second Course

Jelly, Ipocras, Creame of Almonds	Larkes or Rabbetts
Pheasant, Herne, Bitterne, Shovelard	Shyters, Pullets or Chickens
	Venison in fine paste
Partridges, Quailes or Mewz	Tarts
Cocks, Plovers or Gulles	Fritters
Kydd, Lambe or Pigeons	Fruit, with powder or piscards
	Butter & Egges

Details are also extant of an order taken before Sir John Gage,

Knight, Comptroller of the King's most Honorable Household, and other officers of the Green Cloth for 'washing and Cleane keeping of the napery which shall serve for the King's own Table as hereafter followeth:

First it is ordered that there shall be delivered for the King's Highnesse into the hands of Anne Harris, the Kings laundresse in Fine Diaper, in Damascue worke, for great pieces 28 long breakfast clothes, 28 short ones of 3 yards the piece, 28 hand Towels and 12 dozen of napkins to be by her washed and sweet kept and to be delivered weekly to the serjeant, or yeoman of the King's mouth of the Ewry in the manner following, that is to say:

The said Anne shall weekly wash 7 long breakfast clothes, 7 short ones, 8 Towells, 3 dozen of napkins and Pieces as need should require: and of the same shall dayly deliver as much to the said officers, as shall be necessary to serve the King's Majesty withall: and the said residue of the said Diaper to remaine still in the hands of the said Anne, to be kept sweet here untill it shall be occupied. Furthermore the said Anne shall not faile dayly upon the delivery of the said cleane stuff to take with her the stuff which was occupied the day before, to wash again, discreetly perusing and viewing the stuff how it hath been used and ordered: and in case she shall find and thinke it hath not been very well ordered or used, that then she shall immediately bring the same to some of the officers of the Compting House to see the same, that remedy may be for the amendment thereof.

Item:—The said Anne shall have two standard Chestes delivered unto her for the keeping of the said Diaper—the one to keep the cleane stuff and the other to keep the stuff that hath been occupied.

Item.—The said Anne shall provide as much sweet powder, sweet Herbes and other sweet things, as shall be necessary to be occupied for the sweet keeping of the said stuff, and she to be allowed in the Compting House.

Item.—The said Anne shall be allowed, for her paines for washing and keeping of the said stuff yearly £10, to be paid to her out of the Compting House quarterly, without any further charge, or allowances of wood, sope or other thing.

Anne Boleyn was soon at the height of her power and persuaded Henry to marry his illegitimate ten-year-old son, Henry Fitzroy, Duke of Richmond, to her cousin, Lady Mary Howard.

In the meantime, Henry had her initial, 'A', crowned and associated with his own regal 'H' on the gold and silver coins struck after their marriage. He was the first and last monarch to offer this compliment to his consorts and it was a dearly purchased honour for some of these unhappy ladies.

Anne had become pregnant and Henry VIII, in his usual conceited way, took for granted that the child would be a boy. As it turned out, on 7 September 1533, after a very bad time Anne gave birth to a daughter, the future Queen Elizabeth I. To have her baby, she had temporarily left St James's Palace for Greenwich, choosing an apartment called the 'Chamber of the Virgins' because the tapestry with which it was hung illustrated the parable of the Foolish Virgins. In spite of her pain, Anne tried with ready wit to point out how felicitous it was for a princess to be born in the Chamber of the Virgins. This, however, did nothing to assuage Henry's disappointment and almost pathological anger. He had been so certain of having a son that in a circular sent out to the nobility announcing the birth of the child, the word 'Prince' was written in the first instance. An 's' had to be added when the truth became known. Henry, in revenge, refused to allow Anne to feed her own baby. He gave as his reason the probability that his rest would be broken and that the frequent presence of the infant princess in the bedroom might be inconvenient to him.

Two years later, Anne became pregnant again and felt certain that she would have a boy. She had regained Henry's affection; she had won the great political game against Sir Thomas More and now changed her way of life, spending much of her time in needlework, with her ladies of the bedchamber. (Much of the tapestry at Hampton Court was woven by them.) She also distributed £14,000 in alms and arranged for a number of promising youths to be sent to Oxford at her expense.

'Now I am indeed a Queen,' she exclaimed when she heard of Katharine's death. It was said that she was washing her hands in a costly basin when Sir Richard Southwell brought her the news; whereupon she instantly gave him the basin and its rich cover as a reward.

On the day of Queen Katharine's funeral, she not only disobeyed Henry's order which required Court mourning, she flouted good taste by appearing in yellow and making her ladies of the bedchamber do the same.

B

It was now, of course, Anne Boleyn's turn to be *trompée*. It was poetic justice that just as she, as lady-in-waiting, had stolen Henry VIII from Katharine of Aragon, Jane Seymour, one of her own ladies-in-waiting, should steal Henry VIII from her. According to Agnes Strickland, Anne had not the slightest idea of Jane's intimate relations with the King until, just before she was expecting her next baby, she found Jane sitting on Henry's knee and *in flagrante delicto*. It was so unexpected that Anne collapsed on the floor.

Henry VIII, desperately afraid that Anne Boleyn might have a miscarriage, jumped up, saying, 'Be at peace, sweetheart, and all shall be well with thee.' Unfortunately, the shock brought on premature labour and after several hours of acute agony, during which she nearly died, she gave birth to a still-born boy. Henry, instead of showing the slightest sympathy when he heard of the tragedy, burst into her apartment and blamed her furiously for the loss of his son and heir. Anne Boleyn retorted angrily that he had no one to blame but himself. It had been caused solely by her distress about 'that wench, Jane Seymour'. Whereupon Henry turned sullenly away, muttering as he left that she should have no more boys by him.

So determined was he to prevent any discussion of his amours by his subjects that even the conversation of a married woman in Watlington had been solemnly investigated by the local Justices of the Peace. They were told that the woman, after complimenting a midwife on her skill, added that she was worthy of being midwife to the Queen of England, provided it had been Queen Katharine, but that she was far too good for Anne Boleyn, of whom she spoke in such scurrilous terms that the ungrateful midwife laid an information against her. The wretched woman denied the charge and tried to divert attention herself by saying that one of her neighbours had declared that 'it was never merry in England when there were three Queens in it'; whereupon the midwife had said that there would be fewer shortly. At the trial, everybody denied everything and magistrates transmitted the depositions to the Privy Council. No doubt if any three noblemen had been accused of these charges, they would have been executed. But even Henry VIII decided it was beneath his dignity to punish such common women and they were all acquitted. Incidentally, the reference to the third Queen showed that Henry VIII's infatuation with Jane Seymour was common knowledge.

Anne Boleyn slowly recovered her health, but not her spirits. She knew her husband only too well and realized that her influence was terminated for ever. On finding that she could not succeed in having Jane Seymour dismissed from the royal household, she left St James's Palace and went to Greenwich, where she sat for hours in silence without even the consolation of having her infant daughter with her. Her inconsistencies had much to do with the final tragedy of her life. Her love of admiration had allowed her to accept passionate compliments from members of her household, including Mark Smeaton, one of the Court musicians. In addition, Sir Francis Weston and Messrs Brereton and Norris were accused of having been her lovers in St James's Palace. Worse still, she was also accused of incestuous relations with her brother George, who had been made Viscount Rochford. It was actually Lady Rochford who was responsible for this appalling accusation. Very soon afterwards, a secret committee of the Privy Council was opened to inquire into the charges. The first result was that William Brereton was committed to the Tower.

Three days later, on 1 May 1536, Anne Boleyn appeared for the last time in public with Henry VIII at the Greenwich jousts. Her brother was the chief challenger. Henry Norris was one of those who accepted the challenge. In the midst of the pageant, Henry VIII left abruptly, followed by six of his chief henchmen.

The tournament came to a sudden halt. Rochford and Norris were arrested on a charge of high treason. Sir Francis Weston was also taken into custody which naturally terrified Anne. That night she sat down to dinner at the usual hour, but was further alarmed when the King's waiter did not pass on Henry's usual, if dubious, compliment, 'Much good may it do you.' Before dessert was served, the Duke of Norfolk and others appeared and took her to the Tower by barge, where she was told that her lovers had confessed their guilt. Anne protested her innocence vehemently, asking to see the King. This was refused. She was then subjected to a series of insults by two ladies-in-waiting who never left her by day or night, sleeping at the foot of her bed and reporting all her delirious ravings to the Privy Council.

There were times when she could not believe that Henry really intended to harm her and thought that she might at worst be exiled to the Continent. Yet within the week, she and her alleged lovers were charged with high treason. Smeaton tried to save his life by pleading guilty. The others resolutely maintained their innocence and that of Anne. However, they were all condemned to death. Incidentally, there are no records of the trial.

Anne and her brother were the next to be brought to 'justice'. Lady Rochford continued to outrage all decency by appearing as a hostile witness against her husband. The records of this trial also were carefully destroyed. Anne was condemned to be burnt or beheaded at the King's pleasure, and Henry cheerfully signed the death-warrant. Smeaton, being of low birth, was hanged. The others were beheaded.

Anne now prepared herself for death, Henry having decreed out of the kindness of his heart that she should be beheaded and not burnt on Tower Green. It was a case without precedent in English annals. Never before had a woman been beheaded. Anne awoke at 2 a.m. and received the Sacrament. Kingston, the Governor of the Tower, told her that death by beheading would hardly hurt. She replied, 'I have heard say the executioner is very good and I have a little neck'; then put her hands about it, laughing wildly. For her final appearance on earth she wore a robe of black damask with a white cape falling from it on to her shoulders. Eye-witnesses say that her cheeks were flushed and she appeared in a 'fearful beauty'. On the scaffold, she said, 'Good Christian people, I am come hither to die according to law, for by the law I am judged to die and therefore I will speak nothing against it. . . .'

Then with her own hands she removed her cape and covered her hair with a little linen cap, but refused to allow her eyes to be covered. The result was that when the executioner approached her (he had been summoned specially from Calais) he was completely put off when he saw her brilliant glances. Finally, taking off his shoes, he beckoned to one of his assistants to advance on one side while he subtly approached on the other.

Anne, deceived by this subterfuge, turned her eyes in the direction of the assistant as the executioner struck her head off with one blow of the notorious Calais sword. One of the bystanders noted that her eyes and lips were still moving when her head was held up by the executioner. It was also said that, before they dimmed, they seemed for one instant sorrowfully to regard her bleeding corpse as it fell to the ground. In a matter of minutes her 'warm and almost palpitating body' was conveyed in an old elm chest, normally used for keeping arrows, to St Peter's Church and thrust into a grave prepared for her alongside her brother.

Henry VIII waited on the outskirts of London until the report of the signal gun, booming faintly from Tower Hill, announced the joyful tidings that he had been made a widower. He thereupon rode at full speed to his bridal orgies with Jane Seymour.

Not surprisingly, the latter showed no inclination to live in St James's Palace. Instead, Henry VIII installed Henry Fitzroy, his illegitimate son by Elizabeth Blount (another of Katharine of Aragon's ladies-in-waiting). He, however, lasted barely a month, the first of many people of royal blood to die in St James's Palace—not without suspicion of having been poisoned. His death was duly recorded in the *London Chronicle* as follows: 'Then dyid the Kyngge's bastard son, Douke of Rechemonde, at St. Jamys beyond Charyng Cross.'

This was a major blow to Henry, who had been prepared to acknowledge the Duke as his successor in the event of having no legitimate male issue.

Possibly, it was the knowledge that both monks and nuns had put curses on various monasteries and nunneries acquired by Henry VIII which gave him, not unnaturally, a superstitious fear about his immediate family living there. Whatever the reasons, he lent St James's Palace to Thomas Cromwell, his Lord Treasurer. Cromwell was the next victim of the curse (if any) for shortly afterwards, he was taken to the scaffold on Tower Hill, where his head was literally hacked off.

* * *

A few months later, Henry decided to refurnish St James's

Palace. Furthermore, he held King's Maundy there. This consisted of washing the feet of twelve beggars and then giving them meat, money and clothes. For the ceremony of 1543, a warrant was issued to Lord Windsor, Master of the Great Wardrobe,

> to deliver to Richard Scyssell, yeoman of the Wardrobe of Robes, for the use of the King's Maundy, the following parcels, viz: One gown of violet in graigne cloth furred with martrons; 53 gowns of russet cloth for 53 poor men; 53 pairs of singled soled shoes; 256 ells of linen cloth; 30 ells of linent cloth of ell quarter broad, for the Wardrobe of the Robes; 20 pair of bearing sheets of $2\frac{1}{2}$ breadths and $2\frac{1}{2}$ ells long; 12 press sheets for 3 presses in the Wardrobe of the Tower and 2 breadths and 4 ells long each; 2 doz. diaper napkins for the Wardrobe of Robes, 2 bags of linen cloth an ell each, drawn with laces, to carry stuff for the laundry, with canvas and cord to truss the same stuff in. Also to pay for their carriage to the manor of St James's.

Another use to which St James's was put was the assembly of the Privy Council, many meetings being held there while Henry VIII was King. In 1545, an investiture of Knights of the Garter also took place.

More importantly, the Board of Green Cloth, inaugurated in the reign of Richard II, was established in St James's Palace where it remained until 1850; after which it was transferred to Buckingham Palace. The jurisdiction of this Board, 'held in the Counting-house of the King's household for taking cognizance of all matters of government and justice within the King's Court Royal; and for correcting all the servants that shall offend', extended over what was called 'The verge of Court', or twelve miles around the residence of the sovereign; while all offences were tried within what was called 'The Sessions of Verges', committals being made to the Marshalsea. To the Board alone belonged the right of arresting within the limits and jurisdictions of the palace.

In 1541

> Sir Edmund Knevet of Norfolk, Knight, was arraigned before the officers of the Green-Cloth, for striking one Master Cleer of Norfolk, within the Tennis Court of the King's House; being

found guilty he had judgment to lose his right hand, and to forfeit all his lands and goods; whereupon there was called to do
execution, first the Serjeant Surgeon, with his Instruments per-
taining to his office, then the Serjeant of the Wood-Yard, with a
mallet and block to lay the hand upon, then the King's Master-
Cook with a knife to cut off the hand, then the Serjeant of the
Larder to set the knife right on the joint, then the Serjeant Ferrier
with searing irons to sear the veins, then the Serjeant of the Poul-
try with a Cock, which Cock should have his head smitten off
upon the same block and with the same knife, then the Yeoman of
the Chandry with Sear-Cloths, then the Yeoman of the Scullery,
with a pan of fire to heat the irons, a chafer of water to cool the
ends of the irons, and two forms for all officers to set their stuff
on, then the Serjeant of the Cellar with Wine, Ale and Beer, then
the Serjeant of the Ewry, with Bason, Ewre, and Towels: all
things being thus prepared, Sir William Pickering, Knight Marshal, was commanded to bring in his prisoner, Sir Edmund
Knevet, to whom the Chief-Justice declared his offence, which the
said Knevet confessed, and humbly submitted himself to the King's
mercy; only he desired that the King would spare his right hand
and take his left, because (said he) 'if my right hand be spared,
I may live to do the King good service'; at whose submission
and reason of his suit, when the King was informed, he granted
him to lose neither of his hands, and pardoned him also all his
lands and goods.

2. Two brief reigns

POOR little Edward VI had been born at Hampton Court in 1537. His mother, Jane Seymour, died of puerperal fever less than a fortnight later, largely due to the stupid and arduous ceremonies to which she was subjected in connexion with the royal christening. From the start Edward VI was a sickly child, in spite of every possible precaution being taken by Henry VIII to keep strangers from him and to prevent any kind of infection. His food was elaborately tested to avert risk of poison; no member of his establishment was allowed to approach London during the summer; beggars were horsewhipped if they came nearer than the regulation distance from the gates for the reception of alms.

At first, the future king lived mostly at Hampton Court. On the death of his father, who had, incidentally, failed to make him Prince of Wales, he became more closely associated with St James's Palace and stayed there frequently. Here, at the age of nine, he developed galloping consumption. Perhaps it was this consciousness of the importance of health that caused him to restore St Thomas's Hospital after it had lain derelict for eleven years. An official extract from the Patent Rolls (translated into more modern English) states:

> In view of the sick and infirm poor men lying begging in the public streets and places of London and its suburbs to the infection and annoyance of the King's subjects using these streets and places: Grant to the Mayor and commonalty and citizens of London of the house and site of the late hospital of Thomas Becket in Southwarke, of late called the hospitall of Saynt Thomas in Southwarke, Surr., with the church, steeple, church-yard and

14

all buildings, barns, stables, dove-houses, ponds, yards, orchards, gardens and ground within the said site; also the rectory of Thomas Becket, lately called the parsonage of St Thomas in Southwarke; the yearly fair (nundinas) in Southwarke which belonged to the said hospitall, and all possessions of the said hospitall in the parish of the said Thomas Becket also the messuages, land etc. . . . to the yearly value of £154 17s 1d.

Grant, further, that the said hospitall of Southwarke should in future be the place and house for relieving and sustaining the poor there and shall be called the poorhouse in Southwarke next London of the King's foundation.

The number of people for whom the hospital would have to provide is rather instructive:

Of ffatherles children	300
Of sore and sick persons	200
Of poore men overburdened with children	350
Of aged persons	400
Of decayed householders	650
Of ydell vagabondes	200

Edward VI, in spite of his illness, was a real Tudor. Young though he was, plans for his marriage were soon put forward—a common practice in royal circles at that time. The idea was to marry him to his cousin, Mary Stuart, the maiden Queen of Scotland.

In the meantime, his uncle Thomas Seymour, the Lord High Admiral, was trying to marry Katharine Parr, the Dowager Queen of England. Somerset and Northumberland made it impossible for Seymour to see the Prince personally, so he tried to contact him secretly through John Fowler, one of Edward VI's personal servants. Seymour himself had apartments in St James's Palace. One day, he sent for Fowler and inquired about the state of Edward VI's health. Fowler told him that he was very well. The Admiral asked whether Edward VI needed anything. Fowler told him 'nothing'. The Admiral inquired whether the King ever asked for him. Fowler replied that he sometimes did.

'Does he ever ask why I have not married?' 'Never,' replied Fowler. After a brief pause, the Admiral asked Fowler to find out whether he would like him (Seymour) to marry and if so,

15

whom he would like him to marry. Fowler, who had been bribed, said to the King that evening, 'An please your grace, a marvel my Lord Admiral marrieth not.' Since Edward VI made no reply, Fowler put the question bluntly to him, 'Could your grace be contented he should marry?'

'Yea, very well,' replied Edward.

'Who would your grace like him to marry?' inquired Fowler.

Edward VI innocently named Anne of Cleves; then after a pause said, 'Nay, nay, I wot I would he married my sister Mary.'

Next day, Seymour waylaid Fowler in the gallery of St James's Palace and was told what had transpired. Laughingly, he asked whether it would be approved if he married Anne of Cleves. Fowler evidently arranged a private interview between uncle and nephew next day. What they said to each other is not in the records but the result is well-known. During the negotiations, Seymour had actually married Katharine Parr in secret and then persuaded sad young Edward VI to write a letter to her pleading his cause. So everything was above board.

Although later on he did not use St James's Palace much except for state occasions, Edward VI often put up relatives there, among them Katharine Parr and her new husband, and his half-sister, the future Bloody Mary. The only restriction he made was that no musical instruments were to be played in the palace. So even Mary did not dare play the virginals or the lute, which were her favourite instruments. His other half-sister, Princess Elizabeth, the future Elizabeth I, was also a frequent visitor to St James's Palace, for which she had a decided liking.

One splendid addition to the palace was the royal library which he founded. Edward VI was also responsible for the permanent choir at the Chapel Royal—the boys actually being conscripted for this purpose.

Edward died just before reaching his sixteenth birthday. In the meantime, however, Northumberland, having realized that if Mary, that fanatical Catholic, came to the throne, his days would be numbered, had hurriedly married his son to Lady Jane Grey, and before Edward VI was cold in his grave succeeded in having her proclaimed Queen of England.

During this dramatic coup, the then Princess Mary, rightful heir to the throne, was in Hertfordshire and Edward VI's death was kept secret for two days to enable Northumberland to inveigle her into his hands. A message from the Privy Council was sent to say that her brother, who was very ill, begged her to go to him because he strongly desired the comfort of her presence.

Princess Mary nearly succumbed to this request. But fortunately for her, if not for the hundreds of Protestants whom she afterwards had butchered, a mysterious messenger—a goldsmith sent by Sir Nicholas Throckmorton—warned her at Hoddesdon.

So she decided to make for Suffolk, where she stayed the night at Sawston Hall. Next morning, very early, she made for Kenninghall in Norfolk. Scarcely had she set out when Sawston Hall burst into flames, a deliberate case of arson on the part of her political opponents. She gazed at the flaming building calmly. 'Let it blaze,' she said, 'I will build a better.' She kept her word. The present Sawston was built by her order and at her expense.

At Bury St Edmunds she was received loyally, perhaps because the news of the death of Edward VI had not yet arrived. The same evening, she arrived safely at Kenninghall. From here, she sent a message to the Privy Council, regretting the death of Edward VI, and offering an amnesty if they proclaimed her as sovereign in London. Instead, the following day, the Privy Council proclaimed Lady Jane Grey as Queen (actually Lady Jane Dudley since her marriage to Lord Guildford Dudley) and, branding Mary with illegitimacy in gross terms, advised her to submit to her sovereign lady, Queen Jane.

It was a devious route which Mary had to take to reach St James's Palace, her ultimate destination. From Kenninghall, she rode on horseback to Framlingham.

At that moment she had neither money, soldiers nor advisers. Only Sir Thomas Wharton and her ladies-in-waiting were with her until Sir Henry Jerningham and Sir Henry Bedingfeld brought their yeomen to her aid.

Within five days of her arrival at Framlingham, six men-o'-war were seen sailing past in the direction of Yarmouth. They had been sent by the Privy Council to carry cannon and ammunition to attack her headquarters and/or to intercept her if she tried to leave the country. Whereupon Sir Henry Jerningham boldly went out in a boat to halt the Fleet, which had come close to the harbour under the pretence that the weather had driven them inshore; upon which 'the sea-soldiers' asked what he wanted. 'Your captains,' replied Sir Henry—'Your captains, who are rebels to their lawful Queen, Mary.' 'If they are,' was the reply, 'we will throw them into the sea, for we are her true subjects.' At which the captains immediately surrendered themselves and Sir Henry and the men of Yarmouth took possession of the ships.

Simultaneously, Sir Edward Hastings, who had raised four thousand men in the name of Jane, switched horses, and proclaimed Mary as his rightful Queen. This turned the trick. Northumberland, who was leading his troops at Cambridge, learned suddenly of the wind of change and proclaimed Mary as Queen in the Cambridge market-place. But it was too late. Sir John Gates, one of his most guilty henchmen, arrested him when he was personally helpless, with his boots half on and half off.

On 31 July, Mary started her triumphant march to London, from where her sister Elizabeth met her, at the head of a cavalcade one thousand strong. Mary's first stop was the Tower of London, where she liberated a number of her adherents and remained in privacy until after the funeral of Edward VI. This having been completed with great magnificence, she made straight for St James's Palace.

The trial of Northumberland and his fellow conspirators took place six weeks later. Eleven were condemned to death, but only three were executed. . . .

One light-hearted aspect of this phase at St James's Palace was when the Queen showed her gratitude to the Earl of Sussex for having sided against Northumberland. Lord Sussex was a hypochondriac so frightened of head colds that he petitioned Mary for permission to wear his nightcap in her royal presence. The Queen not only gave him leave to wear one, but two nightcaps if he pleased. His patent for this royal privilege is perhaps unique in royal annals. It reads, 'Know ye, that we do give to our well-beloved and trusty cousin and councillor, Henry Earl of Sussex, Viscount Fitzwalter and Lord of Egremond and Burnell, licence and pardon to wear his cap and coiff or nightcap as well in our Royal presence as in the presence of any other person or persons within this our realm or any other place in our dominions wheresoever during his life; and these our letters shall be sufficient warrant in his behalf.' The Queen's seal, with the order surrounding it, was affixed to this singular grant.

By contrast, Lord Kingsale inherited this privilege (of keeping his hat on in the presence of his sovereign) from an ancestor in the reign of King John. It is a pleasant story. The ancestor, Sir John de Courcy, had been sentenced to life imprisonment in the Tower of London on a trumped-up political charge. A year later the ownership of the Duchy of Normandy became a matter of international dispute between King John and the King of France. Somewhat on the lines of the Battle of the Thirty later on, it was decided not to go to war but to pick a champion to fight a duel or duels with the decision, in both senses of the word, going to the winning side.

Sir John de Courcy was the best swordsman in England and, on hearing this story, requested permission to represent King John. This was granted. So the day for the duel was fixed, the two men met face to face, but just as the duel was about to start, the Frenchman, who had heard of Sir John's reputation, panicked and ran. The King of France kept his word. The Duchy of Normandy remained under the English Crown. The matter having been settled, the King of France expressed a wish to see Sir John perform one of his famous feats of strength. The English King commanded de Courcy to do so. Whereupon de Courcy severed a heavy helmet with a single blow of his sword. For this feat King John gave him back all his property which had been confiscated and invited him to ask for anything else which he might like. De Courcy replied that he was not interested in titles but asked for permission for himself and his successors to have the privilege of appearing covered in the presence of the sovereign.

After his death, his elder son became Lord Kingsale and from time to time the Kingsale of the day presented himself in the presence of royalty without taking off his hat. This privilege was, for example, exerted right down to the days of Queen Victoria. When William III expressed surprise at the behaviour of the current Lord Kingsale, the latter replied, 'Sir, my name is de Courcy, I am Lord of Kingsale in Your Majesty's Kingdom of Ireland, and the reason for my appearing covered in Your Majesty's presence is to maintain the ancient privilege of my family granted to John de Courcy by John, King of England.' William III immediately acknowledged the claim and gave his hand to Lord Kingsale to kiss. George III, who knew of the privilege, was angry when the Kingsale of the day appeared wearing his hat. 'Lord Kingsale, I do not dispute your right of standing covered in my Presence,' he said, 'but, my lord, there is the Queen!' to whom he pointed. History does not relate what took place on that occasion, but in 1859 at a levee held at St James's Palace, the thirtieth Lord Kingsale endeavoured to assert his hereditary right. The moment, however, that he entered the throne-room there was a loud exclamation from the Queen. The offending hat would at once have been removed by the Gentleman Usher in Waiting if Sir Spencer Ponsonby Fane had not prevented a scene in Her Majesty's presence. Standing in front of her, Lord Kingsale took off his hat—an old-fashioned Deputy-Lieutenant's affair decorated with cocks' feathers—made a low bow, put it on again and moved on. A few days later the Lord Chamberlain wrote to him to say that the Queen did not dispute the privilege which his predecessors had exercised on former occasions, but that whenever Lord Kingsale considered it important in the maintenance of his right to adopt this unusual course previous notice should be sent to the Lord Chamberlain to prevent any misunderstanding on the part of the Officers of the Court on duty. Lord Kingsale in his reply expressed much regret at his behaviour and promised that he would give notice in future if and when he planned to remain with his hat on in the presence of the monarch. . . .

To return to Mary—she now concentrated all her attention on her approaching Coronation. There was no precedent for a Queen as sole monarch, as opposed to consort. However, the Bishop of Winchester crowned her at Whitehall where she had gone for the ceremony from St James's Palace, after the citizens of London had voted £20,000 towards the cost of the pageantry and festivities.

The next two problems which she had to solve were connected with her forthcoming marriage to Philip of Spain and the forcible removal of Lady Jane Grey. Insurrections started all over the country on behalf of the puppet queen and against Mary's marriage. The most dangerous of them was led by 23-year-old Sir Thomas Wyatt who marched from Kent all the way to Deptford at the head of 15,000 men; Mary remained resolutely at St James's Palace.

Her ladies-in-waiting, certain that their fate was sealed, 'made the greatest lamentations that night'. They wailed and wrung their hands. 'Alack, alack,' they cried, 'we shall all be destroyed this night.' Mary alone kept her presence of mind even when the Earl of Devonshire showed the white feather and ran back to the palace having said that all was lost.

The rebels meanwhile were not sure whether Mary was at Whitehall or St James's Palace. The royal troops were posted at selected strong-points between Charing Cross and St James's with a battery of cannon at the top of St James's Street.

Coming through the Park, one rebel brigade attacked the back of St James's Palace, another attacked Whitehall Palace, while the third made for Piccadilly. Sir Henry Jerningham beat off the attack on St James's, but Whitehall Palace very nearly fell and with it Queen Mary, who had moved there overnight. After fierce fighting at Charing Cross, however, Sir Thomas Wyatt surrendered and next day Mary signed the death-warrant of Lady Jane and her husband Dudley. The Spanish Ambassador did his best to persuade her to sign that of her half-sister, the future Queen Elizabeth, as well. Instead she was committed to the Tower until the troubles blew over. Nevertheless, a forged warrant for her execution was only detected in the nick of time and she had to be removed to Woodstock under armed guard.

At long last Philip of Spain, to whom Mary had allowed herself to be affianced for state security, arrived at Southampton with the combined French and Spanish fleets. In appearance he was no beauty, with small, blue weak eyes, sandy scanty hair, a yellowish complexion and a receding forehead. They were married in Winchester on St James's day, 25 July. After honeymooning at Windsor Castle and entertaining publicly at Whitehall Palace, they held court at St James's Palace. Among the courtiers was Alva the Terrible, as he became known later,

21

earning his infamous reputation for his suppression of Pro-
testantism in the Netherlands, of which he became Governor-
General and Regent. It was an odd coincidence that his two
chief victims, Count Egmont and Count Horn, also attended
Mary's court in St James's Palace at the time of her marriage to
Philip of Spain. Both men, having been imprisoned for a year,
were executed after being sentenced by the Council of Blood.
William of Orange tried to save the situation but was defeated
and Alva the Terrible boasted that 18,000 civilians were executed (in other words murdered) in addition to those killed in
action.

When the exiles regrouped themselves and four of the
Northern Provinces declared for the Prince of Orange, Alva
sacked every major town, Catholic and Protestant alike, including Haarlem and Naarden. Finally he returned to Spain, the
last major city he sacked being Lisbon.

Against the biblical prophecy, he did not perish by the sword
but died in bed at the age of seventy-four. Meantime, there he
was at St James's Palace, exchanging pleasantries with his future
victims, taking part in tournaments, going to the play and having the usual intrigues with ladies of the Court—which was enjoying a splendour never previously surpassed until the Queen
fell ill. (She thought she was going to have a baby; in fact, she
had dropsy.) It was during this period at St James's Palace that
she initiated the appalling persecution of the Protestants which
gave her the name of Bloody Mary for all time.

Philip of Spain was still reluctantly alternating between
Hampton Court and St James's Palace. One day he saw Lady
Magdalen Dacre, one of the ladies-in-waiting, putting on her
clothes. So he opened the window with a view to gaining access.
However, Lady Magdalen took up a stick which stood in the
corner and hit his arm so hard that he was glad to make a
speedy retreat. When he found that the other ladies-in-waiting
were equally respectable, he consorted with prostitutes.

According to John Bradford, the martyr, the Court at St
James's Palace now degenerated into something more like a
'hostelry or tavern than a noble house' until news was received
at the Palace that Philip's father, the Emperor Charles V, had
abdicated, partly because of gout and partly because of the

22

strain of sovereignty. In 1555, therefore, Philip left for Spain. The year following, Mary once more appeared in public, pale as a corpse, and looking ten years older than when she was last seen.

Promptly a new series of plots and insurrections broke out, mostly on behalf of Elizabeth. But, in spite of Philip's request either to put Elizabeth to death or to marry her to his friend, Prince Philip the Warlike of Savoy, Mary refused. Philip returned to St James's Palace for a few days in 1557. Shortly afterwards the Duke of Guise captured Calais. 'When do you English intend to visit France again?' a French cavalryman asked an English veteran. 'When your national crimes exceed ours' was the admirable reply.

The recapture of Calais proved the final blow to Mary who, as has been recorded so often, said, 'If my breast were opened, Calais would be found written on my heart.' At that moment she was staying at Hampton Court.

Throughout her reign the summers had been cold and wet and the Jesuits had not yet discovered the virtues of quinine made from Peruvian bark. So little was known about malaria in those days that she moved back to St James's Palace—the marshiest place in London—where she died on 17 November 1558.

3. The ill-fated Prince Henry

Queen elizabeth was more hygienically minded than Mary. She moved from palace to palace at much shorter intervals, to allow the apartments to be sweetened. Thus it was that she would spend only a few days at St James's Palace before moving to Greenwich or Hampton Court, Richmond Palace, Nonsuch or the palace at Croydon.

Her chief aim, once she ascended the throne, was to establish a great, prosperous and, above all, peaceful England. With this object in mind she let nothing and no one stand in her way—including her more personal inclinations. That her policy began early to bear fruit is apparent from the following, which concerns the notorious St James's Fair—still celebrated annually despite the conversion of the convent into a manor-house. So quickly had trade begun to expand that, in 1560, 'the XXV day of July, Saint James fayer by Westminster was so great that a man could not have a pygg for money, and the beare wiffes hadd nother meate nor drinck before iij of ye cloke in the same day. And the chese went very well away for 1d of the pounde. Besides the great and mighti armie of beggares and baudes that ther were.'

In Elizabeth's reign occurs the first real description of the palace for many years:

> Not far from the glorious hall (Whitehall) another of her Highness's houses descryeth itself, of a quadrate forme, erected of brick the exterior shape whereof although it appear without any sumptuous or superfluous devices, yet in the plot verie princelye, and the same with art contrived within and without. It standeth from other buildings about two furlongs, having a farmehouse opposite

to its North gate. But the seituation is pleasand, indued with a good ayre and pleasant prospects. On the East, London offereth itself in view. In the South, the stately buildings of Westminster, with the pleasant park, and the delights thereof. On the North the green fields.

In September 1561, Elizabeth made one of her sensational 'progresses' from Enfield to St James's Palace, during which every preparation was made for the smooth completion of her journey—to the extent of cutting down all the hedges and filling up all the ditches from Islington to the door of St James's.

* * *

Later on, Elizabeth was at least as Bloody as Mary. 'Good Queen Bess' indeed! Babington and six others who were conspiring to rescue Mary, Queen of Scots, were hanged, drawn and quartered—quartered while they were still alive. It was Elizabeth's own idea that 'some new device' should be adopted whereby the victim's sentence might be made more acute and more calculated to strike terror into the spectators. A faint picture of the horrible scene is provided by the poet Campbell more than two hundred years later:

> Life flutters convulsed in each quivering limb,
> And his blood-streaming eye-balls in agony swim;
> Accursed be the embers that blaze at his feet,
> Where his heart shall be cast ere it ceases to beat,
> With the smoke of its ashes to poison the gale.

The bystanders were so horrified by this revolting spectacle that Queen Elizabeth had to issue a special order from St James's Palace that the remainder of the conspirators should be dealt with more mercifully. They were, therefore, strangled before being drawn and quartered.

The inevitable corollary to the plot was the murder of Mary, Queen of Scots. Immediately after the news reached Elizabeth she wrote from St James's Palace to King James VI. 'I would you knew (though not felt) the extreme dolour that overwhelms my mind for that miserable accident which, far contrary to my meaning, hath befallen. I beseech you—that as God and many more know how innocent I am in this case—so you will believe me that if I had bid aught, I would have abided by it.'

It was once again St James's Palace which Queen Elizabeth made her headquarters when the Spanish Armada set sail. The first news about it was that a storm had forced the fleet into Corunna for repairs. This was reported in England as the entire destruction of the Armada. Elizabeth, with her usual economy, sent orders to Lord Howard of Effingham to put four of the largest warships into dry dock to save money. Lord Howard, however, promised to pay for their upkeep out of his own pocket and kept them at the ready. It was just as well; for the real battle did not start until two months later. Many people may have forgotten the coded message sent to Queen Elizabeth at St James's Palace by Lord Howard. It was 'Cantharides' (The Spanish Fly), then used as an aphrodisiac at the Court.

The defeat of the Spanish must have given Elizabeth particular pleasure in view of Philip of Spain's reception at his Court of a man named Robert Dudley who claimed to be a son of hers and the Earl of Leicester. According to Dudley, he did not know the secret of his birth until he was in his twenties and was then advised by Sir John Ashley and Sir John Dure to keep his mouth shut and to go to the Continent. Philip clearly believed his story; at any rate he treated him as minor royalty and gave him a daily allowance of six golden crowns. History does not relate what ultimately happened to him.

*　　*　　*

Unlike many royalty, Elizabeth disliked dwarfs and other freaks as being unlucky. On the other hand, she was very fond of singing birds, apes, spaniels and bull-baiting. The last-named 'sport', which could be so easily witnessed at St James's Palace, was in keeping with the pedigree of cruelty inherited from her father, Henry VIII.

Indeed, the tremendous number of executions for treason during the last years of Elizabeth's reign had hardened her heart and must surely have made her familiar with the most revolting details of torture and not-so-sudden death. Among her victims was, of course, her reputed lover Essex. The story of the ring which she had given him in a moment of fondness as a pledge of her affection with a remark that 'if you ever forfeit my favour and send it back to me the sight of the ring will ensure my forgiveness', is well documented. Unfortunately for Essex, when he lay under sentence of death, the ring never reached Elizabeth. Knowing he was surrounded by enemies, he did not dare trust it to anyone in attendance on him. Then one day, looking out of his window, he saw a boy whom he induced by a bribe to carry the ring, which he threw down from above, to his cousin, Lady Scrope. By mistake, the boy gave it to Lady Scrope's sister, the Countess of Nottingham, who took it to her husband, Essex's deadliest enemy. He told her to do nothing. Elizabeth, unaware of what had happened, waited in angry suspense for the token to arrive. When it failed to do she decided that Essex was too proud to appeal to her tenderness and ordered the execution to proceed.

Two years later, Lady Nottingham felt that she could not die in peace until she had told the Queen the truth about the ring. Elizabeth, in a mixture of grief and fury, struck the dying woman, shouting, 'God may forgive you, but I never can.'

Meantime, more executions for high treason took place and horrible it must have been to see these relics from day to day,

> While darkly they faded
> Through all the dread stages of Nature's decay.

It was actually possible at one moment to count on London Bridge the heads of no fewer than three hundred people who had been executed for high treason.

Ultimately, Fate was very good to Elizabeth, for she died in her sleep.

* * *

James I, the next to inherit St James's Palace as one of the appurtenances of the Crown, was conceited, violently opposed to tobacco, weak, erudite, metaphysical, a witch-hunter, and a lover of pretty boys. He never washed his right hand, because he wished to keep it soft—merely moistened the ends of the fingers with a damp cloth. This was the hand with which he fondled the cheeks and smoothed the clothes of such as Robert

Carr, who broke a leg while tilting. Fair-haired, with a pink and white complexion, Carr became the King's love and was soon given the Earldom of Somerset. Next, George Villiers appeared on the scene. This beautiful youth was soon made a gentleman-of-the-bedchamber. His hands and feet were described as 'specially effeminate and curious'. But, like Lord Hervey later on, he was undoubtedly epicene and in record time he became Duke of Buckingham. James called him Steenie as a diminutive of St Stephen because of his angelic face.

Alarmed at his success and growing power, the Earl of Nottingham and Lord Knollys produced a new pretty boy, the nephew of Sir Thomas Monson. He was made to wash his face every day with posset curds, dressed in the most effeminate clothes and sent to receive Communion from the Archbishop. But for some reason King James did not fall in love with him and both Nottingham and Knollys were forced to leave the Court.

James it was who appointed William Shakespeare as one of his Grooms of the Chamber when he waited on the Constable of Castile at St James's Palace at a fee of £14 8s. 0d. for eighteen days. James, too, was the man to whom we are indebted for the Authorized Version, who survived the Gunpowder Plot, who ordered Sir Walter Raleigh to be executed, and was the father of not only Charles I but also of the brilliant Prince Henry. Since he never stayed at St James's Palace, the rest of his career is of no consequence to this history, except as the father of Prince Henry.

* * *

If the next occupant of St James's Palace had survived, the whole course of English history might have been changed. Certainly there would have been no Oliver Cromwell, and quite possibly no Hanoverian dynasty. For Prince Henry, elder son of King James I, proved to be, during his all too brief life, one of the most remarkable characters in English history. Yet, if the superstitious are to be believed, he was never destined to reign. When the stuttering, tongue-tied, sickly Prince Charles was two and a half years old, a Scottish laird saw him with his elder brother, Prince Henry, and immediately saluted the younger boy. James I remonstrated with him for his behaviour. 'Nay, nay, Sire,' said the old man. 'I ken my future king, for this wee prince shall succeed ye.'

Incidentally, the number of Princes of Wales who were never crowned is remarkably high.

Henry was personally coached in kingship from his sixth year by his fantastic father, who composed his Golden Book, a three-decker of which the first volume was religious, the second dealt with his future kingly duties and the third told him how to behave generally. From the start he was also coached in French and Latin. When he was seven, he wrote his father a letter in Latin for his birthday. When he was nine, he wrote again in Latin to say that he had read Terence's *Hecyra*, the third book of Phaedrus's fables and two books of Cicero's select epistles— all in the original. In the meantime, he was being coached in horsemanship, singing, dancing, high jumping, shooting with bow and gun, tossing the pike and the general use of small arms. No wonder that James I was intensely proud of the child and gave him a private establishment at Oatlands with his sister, the Princess Elizabeth. Here, when he was still only ten years old, the staff consisted of seventy servants. A few weeks later they rose to 104. By the end of the year they numbered 141.

Prince Henry now developed an interest in ships and a 28-footer was built for him at Chatham. His erudition was extraordinary. In 1604, we find him writing letters to the Doge of Venice in Latin, to the Landgrave of Hesse in the same tongue, another in Latin to his uncle, the King of Denmark, one in French to the Duke of Savoy and still more in Latin to the Duke of Brunswick and the Prince of Poland. That year, James I decided to hand over St James's Palace to him. As a result, the Earl of Worcester, then Master of the Horse, sent the following instructions:

> Whereas St Jameses howse is appoynted by his Majestie for the Prince to lye at, unto the which there is neyther barne nor stable belonginge, the wch wante of necessitie must be supplyed; Theise are therefore to praye you to draw a warrant unto the Ld: Heighe Treasurer to gyve his directions unto the Officers of His Maties woorkes for the buildinge of such conveniente stablinge and barne

roome as shall there bee founde needfull for the Prince's service.
Whitehall the 14th day of July 1604.

Yor Lovinge ffreind

(*Signed*) E. Worcester.

To the Right Worl Sir Thom. Lake, Knight, One of the Clarkes
of His Maties Signett.

Inigo Jones was appointed surveyor of the works and made
various alterations and improvements to the interior. These
included suitable surroundings for Lord Lumley's library,
which was bought by James I and transferred to St James's
Palace.

Prince Henry, technically the Duke of Cornwall, though not
actually benefiting financially from the Duchy, now decided
to take advantage of the title, and also of his right to be invested
as Prince of Wales. He was prompted to this action by the
tremendous debts which his household, so swollen by his father,
was incurring. This was readily agreed by King and Parliament
and very considerably increased his income. To celebrate it, he
delivered a challenge to all the knights of Great Britain to
attend a military tournament. During the preparations, he
feasted the earls, barons, knights assailants and combatants at
his own apartments in St James's Palace, until the night when
the great feat of arms was to be performed at the Palace of
Whitehall, in the presence of the King and Queen, the Ambassadors of Spain and Venice and the whole aristocracy.

Here, Prince Henry maintained the barriers against all
comers, being assisted only by the Duke of Lennox, the Earls
of Arundel and Southampton and four others. Against them came
fifty-five opponents—earls, barons and knights. Each challenger
fought with eight different opponents, two duels of single
sword and push of pike. Prince Henry gave and received thirty-
two pushes of pike and 360 strokes of sword, to the admiration
of everyone.

This feat of arms began at 10 p.m. and continued until three
the next morning. Later that same day, the precocious Prince
conducted the King to St James's Palace where he had invited him and the whole Court, except the Queen, to supper.
This lasted until 10 p.m. Next, they saw a play, and then returned to a set banquet which continued again until 3 a.m. All

ANNE BOLEYN

HENRY VIII

EDWARD VI

MARY I

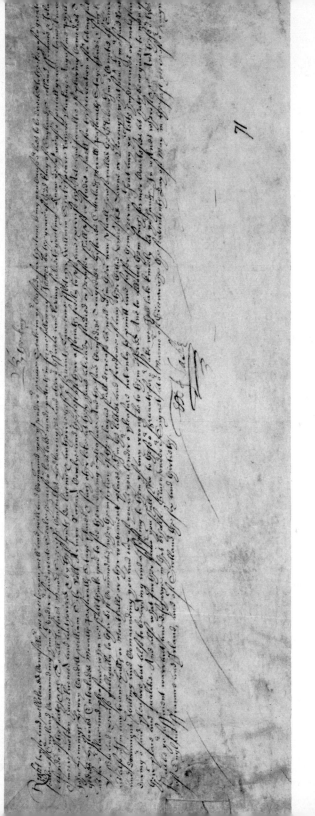

SHAKESPEARE: ARTICLE OF EMPLOYMENT

PRINCE HENRY, SON OF JAMES I

these high jinks cost the Prince £100 a day, a fabulous sum by modern standards.

From his earliest years, his fearlessness was outstanding. As a child, he never cried. One day, watching a stag hunt and being asked whether he liked it or not, he replied, 'Yes, but I love another kind of hunting better.' Asked what it was, he replied, 'Hunting of thieves and rebels with brave men and horses.' And turning to one of the pages descended from Highland parents who were reported to be thieves, he added, 'And such thieves as I take shall be hanged, great ones higher than the rest. And you, sir, if you be a thief, highest of all.'

He had been scarcely ten when he decided to mount a very spirited stallion, refused any assistance, climbed on its back from the top of a bank, spurred the animal to full gallop and brought it back at a gentle walk, asking, as he dismounted, 'How long shall I continue to be a child in your opinion?'

At his Court, he collected a number of young men of spirit and entered into correspondence with the most celebrated military leaders in Upper and Lower Germany. He learned to swim, not such a common accomplishment in those days, and walked fast and far to accustom himself to long route marches when he was old enough to join the army. But his favourite sport was tennis, which he often played three or four hours non-stop. Sometimes he amused himself by playing chess, billiards or cards, though the latter only for amusement. When he won it is said that his expression remained unchanged, but he used to laugh when he was losing.

His clothes were normally very simple, except on state occasions. He had developed a royal memory at a tender age and could quote Virgil at great length. He could also speak Italian, studied military history and geography, encouraged poets, was a tremendous admirer of Sir Walter Raleigh (still in prison) and was always able to keep secrets entrusted to him. He knew his entire staff by name, although they had now increased to 426. He paid close attention to his house books which he balanced with his annual revenue (following his emoluments as Prince of Wales and Duke of Cornwall) and managed to save some thousands of pounds a year 'for contingent and occasional exigencies'.

By this economy, he was saved the necessity of raising the rents of his tenants or taking advantage of forfeitures.

He was also unusually hygienic. In his Orders to be observed by all gentlemen and officers of his household, the ushers had authority to visit all the rooms of St James's Palace and if they found any uncleanliness which might breed infection or other disease, they were to take immediate steps to remove it. Further, if anyone in the courtyards or anywhere else where the Prince might wish to walk 'do by any uncleanly means, such as making water etc. make them unsweet after warning given, they shall be thought unfit to be entertained in the Prince's house and whoever shall wilfully visit any sick person whose disease may be contagious or such as come from those that are supposed to be infectious or receive cloathes or other things from them whereby infection may be taken, he shall be forbidden to come near the house for the space of a month at least'.

Prince Henry also forbade any gaming at the palace, and fined anyone who was blasphemous or who swore. The fines were placed in a box kept in St James's Palace and the takings subsequently doled out to the poor. He was such an exemplary prince and so popular with the Court that his levees were attended more fully than those of King James, who once said, not unreasonably, 'Will he bury me alive?' With those of the general public who came in any kind of contact with him he became more and more popular, in contrast to his father with his exaggerated ideas about the Divine Right of Kings, his defiance of Parliament and his brutal treatment of the rapidly increasing Puritan element.

Prince Henry was 5 ft. 8 in. tall, had a strong, athletic body, was broad-shouldered, auburn-haired, with aquiline features, wide forehead, a delightful smile and 'a terrible frown'. He could not, it must be repeated, tolerate blasphemy. Indeed, he once said, 'All the pleasure in the world is not worth an oath.' His passion for keeping clean caused him to swim in the Thames at Richmond, frequently after a hard game of tennis. Another passion was eating grapes in unlimited quantities. It may have been some contagion at St James's Palace which caused him, when he was eighteen and a half, to grow daily more pale and emaciated.

Now and then he complained of a 'cold, lazy drowsiness' in his head. This caused him to ask the nature of and cure for the current epidemic, known as 'the disease'. Just as in 1918 the virus which killed so many millions of people was supposed to have emanated from Spain and was given the name 'Spanish 'flu', this earlier epidemic was supposed by doctors to have been brought from Hungary. Or so his physician, Dr John Hammond, told him. In October 1612, he became more and more listless.

On Saturday, 10 October 1612, he had two shivering fits which kept him indoors and caused him to summon Dr Hammond. Two or three days later, he had violent diarrhoea. At that moment he was staying in his Palace at Richmond. He then made the fatal decision to go to St James's Palace to receive the Elector Palatine and Count Henry de Nassau (later Prince of Orange). He was particularly fond of the Count and played tennis with him on several occasions in the St James's Palace courts. Very unwisely, in view of his weak state of health and the cold weather, he played in his shirt-sleeves. After the final game, he once again complained of pains in his head.

Next day, although feeling drowsy and ill, he went to hear a sermon given by one of the royal chaplains on the very topical thesis 'Man that is born of woman is of short continuance and full of trouble'. He then took luncheon with King James. His appetite seemed reasonable but 'the hollow ghastliness' of his eyes was very noticeable. Once again, he was seized with a shivering fit, accompanied by a high fever and headache, which from that moment never left him.

There is no doubt that a modern physician would by this time have diagnosed typhoid. As it was, he was obliged to leave suddenly and go back to bed in St James's Palace. He grew more and more ill; his mouth was dry; he was continually thirsty. The royal surgeon, Mr Nasmith, was sent to him by King James. Dr Mayerne, another royal specialist, prescribed bleeding, but the other physicians in attendance opposed this treatment strongly. Yet another physician, Dr William Butler, was summoned. The latter could not make out what was the matter with the unfortunate Prince but realized that his condition was very serious. So much so that he refused to stay with him for more than one hour every morning and another in the afternoon for consultation with his colleagues.

A month after the day he was first taken ill, Prince Henry became giddy; his ears tingled; he had a series of small convulsions. Dr Butler advised enemas and a strong tonic. Yet another physician, Dr Henry Atkyns, was brought in and diagnosed a 'putrid fever' under the liver. The Prince's delirium increased. He suddenly called out for his clothes and rapier, saying he must be gone. As an example of how backward the best English doctors were in those days, a cockerel split in half was applied to the soles of his feet; needless to say without any result.

In the meantime, Sir Walter Raleigh, imprisoned in the Tower, had heard of the Prince's illness and sent him a special tonic which he said could cure him of any disease unless he had actually been poisoned. It needed the permission of the Lords of the Council for it to be given. The result was that it threw him into a sweat which gave him some relief; but this did not last long. He died on 16 November, at the age of eighteen years, eight months and seventeen days.

On the Monday after his death, the Lords of the Privy Council came to St James's Palace to make arrangements for a state funeral. His body was embalmed and put in a lead coffin. The Guard Chamber, the Privy Chamber and the Bed Chamber were all hung with black velvet. In the middle of this, a canopy of black velvet was erected under which the coffin was placed on trestles. On the head of the coffin was laid a cushion of black velvet with the Prince's cap of state and coronet on it, together with his robes and sword. There it remained until three days before the funeral, constantly watched day and night by seventy of his staff.

The funeral took place on 7 December. The night before, a dummy of the Prince, made at short notice but looking exactly like him, wearing his personal clothes, his garter and collar, and with his golden staff in his right hand, was placed on top of the coffin. The funeral was attended by two thousand mourners in black, the chief mourner being young Prince Charles, later Charles I. It is noticeable that neither King James I nor the Queen attended the funeral, perhaps through fear of infection. Neither of them had seen the Prince throughout his final weeks of illness.

A month later, the Prince's household at St James's Palace was dismissed.

4. A royal prisoner

WITHIN three months of the death of Prince Henry, his younger brother Charles was moved into the palace, where he spent a lonely time while his father searched the Courts of Europe to find him a wife. Nothing happened for four years. At last, at the instigation of Steenie, Duke of Buckingham, he decided to take matters into his own hands and with him went to Madrid, where they wore false beards and travelled incognito as Tom Smith and John Brown. The object was to woo the Infanta Maria, the sister of Philip IV of Spain. At first it seemed as if he were going to be successful, and orders were sent to prepare St James's Palace for her, while the Spanish Ambassador demanded that a new chapel be built to the design of Inigo Jones.

So popular were the Spaniards at the time that according to a current account, their camels and elephants were taken daily to feed in St James's Park.

After six months at Madrid, however, Charles found that the prospect of this marriage was as remote as ever, and returned to England; at which point Louis XIII of France agreed to allow his sister Henrietta Maria to marry him. The chapel was eventually completed for her use.

Within the year James died.

The final anecdote about him concerned his walking in the gardens surrounding St James's Palace with his chaplain, Dr Mountain. James said that he did not know to whom to give the vacant bishopric of London. 'If Your Majesty had such faith as a grain of mustard seed,' his chaplain replied, 'you might say to this Mountain, be thou removed and be thou cast into that

See.' At which King James laughed and agreed to his chaplain's promotion.

* * *

Shortly afterwards, Charles married Henrietta Maria, who was still only fifteen, a year younger than the present age of consent, therefore. Her immediate preference was for St James's Palace so, although Charles had moved to Whitehall on coming to the throne, he agreed to move back. With her had come no fewer than 440 attendants, including a young bishop and twenty-nine priests. Her chief attendant, Madame St George, particularly irritated Charles because she tried to insist on riding with the King and Queen in their own coach. In every way she behaved extremely rudely. This, together with the cost of maintaining the huge foreign retinue, finally forced Charles's hand and he expelled them from the palace. Until that moment the establishment required:

86 tables, well furnished each meal, whereof the King's table had 28 dishes, the Queen's 25; four other tables had 16 dishes each; three others 10 dishes each; 12 others had 7 dishes each; 17 other tables had each of them 5 dishes; 3 others had 4 each; 32 other tables had each 3 dishes, and 13 others had each two dishes—in all about 500 dishes each meal, with beer, wine, and all other things necessary.

There was spent yearly in the King's House, of gross meat, 1500 oxen, 7000 sheep, 1200 veals, 300 porkers, 400 shards and young beef, 6800 lambs, 300 flitches of bacon, and 25 boars; also 140 of geese, 250 dozen of capons, 470 dozen of hens, 750 dozen of pullets, 1470 dozen of chickens; for bread, 3600 bushels of wheat, and for drink, 600 tuns of wine and 1700 tuns of beer. Moreover, of butter, 46,640 pounds, together with fish, fowl, venison and fruit, and spice proportionally.

The total cost of upkeep was nearly £1,700 a week, a fantastic sum in those days. In addition, many of the senior staff invented bills to the tune of £10,000 which they pretended had been incurred on the Queen's behalf. One was an apothecary's bill for £800 worth of drugs; another for £150 was for the 'Bishop's unholy water'. Charles was finally compelled to turn the Queen's attendants out of Somerset House, to which he had moved them from St James's Palace, and sent them home. The cost of all this was another £50,000.

The housekeeper at St James's Palace was particularly delighted at their departure. According to her, the French servants 'had so defiled the house, as a week's work would not make it clean'.

Henrietta Maria was furious and actually broke a number of windows in the palace when Charles tried to drag her to her apartment. . . .

In spite of financial troubles, Charles now granted a warrant to pay Thomas Hooker, the Keeper of the tennis court at St James's Palace, the sum of £798 3s. 2d. for provision of tennis balls and the money he had won from him at tennis.

The arrival of Marie de Medici, his mother-in-law, involved Charles in extra expenses. The meeting between her and Henrietta Maria was a touching one since they had not seen one another for thirteen years. Historians must be grateful to this visit because the Sieur de la Serre, the French writer, was in the French retinue and left an exact description of the palace as it was at the time.

This place [he wrote], is situated in the same suburb as that wherein the castle of Whitehall stands, from which it is distant only the extent of a park that divides them. Near its avenues is a large meadow, always green, in which the ladies walk in summer. Its great gate has a long street in front, reaching almost out of sight, seemingly joining to the fields. That castle is very magnificent and extremely convenient. It is built with brick, according to the fashion of the country, having the roof covered with lead in form of a floor surrounded on all sides with crenelled eaves which serve for an ornament to the whole body of the building. Its first court, or entrance, is very extensive; from it is the ascent to the great Guard Chamber.

This first hall was decorated with tapestry, the beauty and invention were still admirable, and shewed its former value as a piece of furniture of a house truly royal. The second hall, of the same size, having a canopy, was ornamented with a new suit of tapestry which forcibly excited the admiration of the most curious. . . .

A picture of the Fainting of the Virgin by the Chevalier Vandheich (Vandyke) attracts the admiration of even the most incurious; and in truth the painter has in this work represented death so beautiful, and sorrow so reasonable, that this object equally disposes the heart of the wisest to sigh, and the mind of the most timid to despise life.

The scene of Tintoret has its place in the public esteem, and truly he represents the Feast of Grace, where souls are fed rather than bodies, the minds are much more satisfied than the eyes in admiration of him, considering the wonders of this work in the virtu of the pencil of him who did it.

There is also an infinite number of paintings which cannot have been bought, according to their value, but by a great monarch. At one of the ends of the three-sided gallery, there is a portrait of the king in armour, and on horseback, by the hand of the Chevalier Vandheich; and, not to lie, his pencil, in preserving the majesty of this great monarch, has by his industry so animated him, that if the eyes alone were to be believed, they would boldly assert that he lived in this portrait.

To express the great number of chambers, all covered with tapestry, and superbly garnished with all sorts of furniture, where the Court was to be lodged, without reckoning the other apartments which were reserved and of which Mr le Visc de Fabroni had one of the principal, would be impossible. You shall only know that the Sieur Labat, who continued to execute the office of quarter-master, had liberty to mark with his chalk fifty separate chambers of entire apartments, and the whole were furnished by the particular commands of the Queen of Great Britain, who seemed to convert all her ordinary diversions into continual cares and attention and give all sorts of satisfaction to the Queen her mother; and this vast expense on so great a quantity of rich furniture, shewed anew the riches and power of a great monarch, since in only one of his pleasure houses there was sufficient room to lodge commodiously the greatest queen in the whole world, with her whole court.

Soon Marie de Medici proved so unpopular that Parliament voted her the sum of £10,000 on condition that she left the country, a sum said to have been doubled by Charles himself; but the bribe was cheap, for her stay in England was costing £3,000 a month and she had no option but to leave.

* * *

One of the more fascinating habitués of St James's Palace during the reign of Charles I was Sir Jeffrey Hudson, the famous midget, 'the least man in the least county'. He was born at Oakham, the county town of Rutland, where his father kept baiting-bulls for the Duke of Buckingham. Both his parents were of ordinary height and so were all the other children. Jeffrey, however, was only eighteen inches tall at the age of nineteen and, according to eye-witnesses of the day, was not really a dwarf at all, being perfectly proportioned. It was while Charles and Henrietta Maria were being entertained at Burleigh, the Duke of Buckingham's estate, that Jeffrey was served up at the table in a cold pie, wearing full armour.

Henrietta Maria immediately asked if she might have him and was promptly granted her request. The ladies of the Court became very fond of him but he was always being teased by the staff and especially by the giant porter, William Evans. On one occasion, during a game of charades, Evans brought a long loaf out of one pocket and Jeffrey Hudson, instead of a hunk of cheese, from the other. It is said that on another occasion, when he was washing his face and hands in his basin, Jeffrey was nearly drowned. On yet another occasion only a bush saved him from being blown into the Thames.

According to his own statement, he remained eighteen inches tall until he was thirty. (In the meantime he had been knighted by King Charles in a whimsical moment.) Nevertheless, he was frequently sent on important diplomatic missions. When he was only twenty-one, he was despatched to France to fetch a midwife for Henrietta Maria. On his return with her and Her Majesty's dancing master and many rich presents for the Queen from Marie de Medici, he was captured at sea by privateers from Dunkirk. Not only did he lose the property of his royal mistress but also valuables of his own to the tune of £2,500. Though stripped of his belongings, he was fortunately able to return to England. Another time he was captured by Turkish pirates and sold into slavery on the Barbary coast. Ultimately his ransom was paid and he returned to England.

Later, at the start of the Civil War, he was made a Captain of Horse and was largely instrumental in saving Henrietta Maria from the Roundheads at Exeter. In the Queen's retinue at that time, besides Sir Jeffrey Hudson were her confessor and one lady-in-waiting. They hid in a hut for two days without food under a heap of litter and could hear the parliamentary soldiers defiling each side of the hut.

It was largely thanks to the midget that the Queen was able to escape from Pendennis Castle in Cornwall to France. She spent the autumn at Nevers where Sir Jeffrey was still in attendance on her. Having proved himself at least as brave as and more intelligent than the other members of the royal household during the Civil War, he objected to jeering stories about his nearly having been killed by a turkey-cock. He announced that he would fight a duel with the next man who insulted him. Whereupon Mr Croft, the brother of Lord Croft, lost no time in provoking a challenge. The duel, only intended for fun, was arranged in the nearby park. The terms were to fight each other with pistols on horseback.

Croft took no firearms—merely a giant squirt with which he intended to extinguish his small opponent and the powder in his pistol. Sir Jeffrey, however, managed to avoid the squirts of water and shot dead his grinning adversary. To save the midget's life, Queen Henrietta wrote to Cardinal Mazarin to explain what had happened and to say that she had asked the Queen of France to give her power to pardon the little man. His life was spared, but after a brief term of imprisonment he was expelled from the Court, ultimately returning to England where he subsisted on a pension given him by the Duke of Buckingham. He lived to the age of sixty-two, possibly the most remarkable mannikin of all time.

*　　*　　*

Although the Commonwealth was not proclaimed until 1649, St James's Palace had been involved with the Parliamentarians from the moment that Charles had left London before the start of the Civil War. He had taken with him his two elder sons, the future Charles II and James II, both of whom had been born in the palace, but Elizabeth and Henry, Duke of Gloucester, were imprisoned in St James's Palace. So, too, was Princess Henrietta, who had been put in the charge of Lady Dalkeith under the overall supervision of the Earl of Northumberland.

The courageous Lady Dalkeith decided to escape with

Princess Henrietta as soon as possible. One night she disguised herself as a hideous hunch-back and dressed the Princess as a boy in equally disreputable clothes. They set off for Dover, Lady Dalkeith being careful to call Henrietta by the name of Pierre and describing the child as her son. Unfortunately, the Princess, being a true Stuart, nearly caused disaster by announcing angrily that the clothes were not her own, that she was not Pierre, and in fact that she was Princess Henrietta. Luckily, Lady Dalkeith succeeded in persuading people that the child was romancing and in due course they safely reached Holland.

Much more dramatic was the escape of the future James II, when, after the battle of Edgehill, he was handed over to the Parliamentarians and locked up in the palace. Charles made two attempts to have him rescued, without success. On the third occasion he was successful. Anne, Lady Halkett, tells the thrilling story of what happened.

At this time Colonel Bampfield had frequent letters from the King, who employed him in several affairs, but that of the greatest concern which he was employed in was to contrive the Duke of York's escape out of St James (where his Highness and the Duke of Gloucester and the Princess Elizabeth lived under the care of the Earl of Northumberland and his lady). The difficulties were represented by Col. B.; but his Majesty still pressed it and I remember this expression was in one of his letters: 'I believe it will be difficult, and if he miscarry in the attempt it will be the greatest affliction that can arrive to me; but I look upon James' escape as Charles's preservation, and nothing can content me more, therefore be careful what you do.'

This letter, amongst others, he showed me, and where the King approved of his choice of me to intrust with it, for to get the Duke's clothes made, and to dress him in his disguise. So now all C.B.'s business and care was how to manage this business of so important a concern, which could not be performed without several persons' concurrence in it, for he being generally known as one whose stay at London was in order to serve the King, few of those who were intrusted by the Parliament in public concerns durst own converse or hardly civility to him, lest they should have been suspected by their party, which made it difficult for him to get access to the Duke; but (to be short) having communicated the design to a gentleman attending his Highness, who

42

was full of honour and fidelity, by this means he had private access to the Duke, to whom he presented the King's letter and order to His Highness for consenting to act what C.B. should contrive for his escape, which was so cheerfully entertained and so readily obeyed, that being once designed there was nothing more to do than to prepare all things for execution.

I had desired him to take a ribbon with him and bring me the bigness of the Duke's waist and his length, to have clothes made to fit for him. In the meantime, C.B. was to provide money for all necessary expense, which was furnished by an honest citizen. When I gave the measure to my tailor to enquire how much mohaire would serve to make a petticoat and waistcoat to a young gentlewoman of that bigness and stature, he considered it a long time, and said he had made many gowns and suits, but he had never made any to such a person in his life. I thought he was in the right; but his meaning was, he had never seen any woman of so low a stature have so big a waist; however, he made it as exactly fit as if he had taken the measure himself. It was a mixed mohaire of a light hair colour and black, and the under-petticoat was scarlet.

All things being now ready, upon the 20th of April, 1648, in the evening, was the time resolved on for the Duke's escape. And in order to achieve that, it was designed for a week before every night, as soon as the Duke had supped he and those servants that attended His Highness (till the Earl of Northumberland and the rest of the house had supped) went and played Hide and Seek, and sometimes he would hide himself so well that in half an hour's time they could not find him. His Highness had so used them to this, that when he went really away they thought he was but at the usual sport. A little before the Duke went to supper that night he called to the gardener, who alone had a treble key besides that which the Duke had, and bid him give him that key till his own was mended, which he did. And after His Highness had supped, he immediately called to go to the play, and went down the privy stairs to the garden, and opened the gate that goes into the park, treble-locking all the doors behind him. And at the garden gate C.B. waited for His Highness, and putting on a cloak and periwig hurried him away to the water side, and, taking the boat that was appointed for that service, they rowed to the stairs next the bridge, where I and Miriam waited in a private house hard by that C.B. had prepared for dressing His Highness, where all things were in readiness.

But I had many fears, for C.B. had desired me if they came not there precisely by ten o'clock, to shift for myself, for then I might conclude they were discovered, and so my stay there could do no good, but prejudice myself. Yet this did not make me leave the house, though ten o'clock did strike, and he that was entrusted often went to the landing place and saw no boat coming was much discouraged, and asked me what I would do. I told him I came there with a resolution to serve His Highness, and I was fully determined not to leave that place till I was out of hopes of doing what I came there for, and would take my hazard. He left me to go again to the water side, and while I was fortifying myself against what might arrive to me, I heard a great noise of many as I thought coming up stairs, which expected to be soldiers to take me, but it was a pleasing disappointment, for the first that came in was the Duke, who with much joy I took in my arms and gave God thanks for his safe arrival.

His Highness called 'Quickly, quickly, dress me', and putting off his clothes, I dressed him in the woman's habit that was prepared, which fitted His Highness very well, and he was very pretty in it. After he had eaten something I made ready while I was idle, lest his Highness should be hungry, and having sent for a Woodstreet cake (which I knew he loved) to take in the barge, with as much haste as he could be His Highness went across the bridge to the stairs where the barge lay, C.B. leading him; and immediately the boatmen plied the oar so well that they were soon out of sight, having both wind and tide with them. But I afterwards heard the wind changed and was so contrary that C.B. told me he was terribly afraid they should have been blown back again. And the Duke said 'Do anything with me rather than let me go back again', which put C.B. to seek help where it was only to be had and after he had most fervently supplicated assistance from God, presently the wind blew fair, and they came safely to their intended landing place. But I heard there was some difficulty before they got to the ship at Graves-End which had like to have discovered them had not Colonel Washington's lady assisted them.

After the Duke's barge was out of sight of the bridge, I and Miriam went where I had appointed the coach to stay for me, and made drive as fast as the coachman could to my brother's house, where I stayed. I met none in the way that gave me any apprehension that the design was discovered, nor was it noised abroad till the next day, for (as I related before) the Duke having used to play at hide and seek, and to conceal himself a long time when they missed him at the same play, thought he would have discovered himself as formerly when they had given over seeking him. But a much longer time being passed than usually was spent in that divertisement, some began to apprehend that his Highness was gone in earnest past their finding, which made the Earl of Northumberland (to whose care he was committed) after strict search made in the house of St James' and all thereabouts to no purpose, to send and acquaint the Speaker of the House of Commons that the Duke was gone, how or by what means he knew not, but desired that there might be orders sent to the Cinque Ports for stopping all ships going out till the passengers were examined and search made in all suspected places where his Highness might be concealed. Though this was gone about with all the vigilancy imaginable yet it pleased God to disappoint them of their intention by so infatuating those several persons who were employed for writing orders that none of them were able to write one right, but ten or twelve of them were cast by before one was according to their mind. This account I had from McN. who was mace-bearer to the Speaker of that time and a witness of it. This disorder of the clerks contributed much to the Duke's safety, for he was at sea before any of the orders came to the ports, and so was free from what was designed if they had taken his Highness.

In point of fact, the plot nearly went wrong at the last minute. While Colonel Bampfield and James were on their way to Tilbury, the master of the barge looked into the cabin at the very moment when 'Mr Andrews' (Colonel Bampfield) was tying up the garter of his 'sister', who had 'her' legs stretched out in a most unladylike manner. Frightened at what he saw, the bargemaster started to insist on returning to London. It took Colonel Bampfield some time both with threats and promises to persuade the bargemaster to carry on to Tilbury and from there to the Continent and safety.

* * *

The history of Charles I's military downfall is too well-known to recapitulate here, especially as he did not set foot in St James's Palace from 1642 until 1648 when he was brought there as a prisoner. The previous month the Parliamentarians had decided to try him for high treason and he was installed in St James's Palace, still full of the countless treasures, both statues and paintings, which he had collected from all over the Continent, notably from Mantua.

Sir Thomas Herbert and Sir Philip Warwick both wrote of his last days. For the first fortnight things were not so intolerable, it seems. He dined regularly in public in the Presence Chamber and was served at meal times with the regal protocol of carvers, cup-bearers and gentlemen ushers in attendance. His wines and dishes were presented, as usual, on bended knee. Then the army officers gave instructions that all the usual respect to him should be discontinued. His meals were brought in by ordinary soldiers and all the other royal rituals ceased. This caused Charles to say, 'Is there anything more contemptible than a despised prince?' and he decided that the best course of action was to eat only a few dishes and those in private.

In the meantime, he had been taken to Westminster under a strong guard of infantry to stand his trial. Plans for his escape had been made, but according to a letter he wrote to Lord Ashburnham, he decided that he would not try to escape unless Henrietta Maria advised him to do so. While the case continued he spent each night at the house of Sir Robert Cotton and it was not until sentence was passed that he returned to St James's. Just before he was convicted he cried out in desperation, 'Where is there in all the world that Court in which no place is left for reason?' To this the President replied naïvely, 'Sir, you shall find that this very Court is such a one.'

According to Sir Philip Warwick,

> The King's deportment before and after sentence was very majestic and steady, and though his tongue usually hesitated, yet he was very free at this time; for, as he confessed himself to the Bishop of London, that attended him, one action shocked him very much; for while he was leaning upon his staff (in the Court) which had an head of gold, its head broke off on a sudden; he took it up, but seemed unconcerned, yet told the Bishop it really made a great impression upon him, and to this hour (says he) 'I know not possibly how it should come'. It was all an accident, I confess. I myself have often thought on it and cannot imagine how it came about, unless Hugh Peters (who was truly and really his jailer,

46

for at St James's nobody went to him but by Peters's leave) had artificially tampered upon his staff—but such conjectures are of no use.

Though he was brought up to St James's by Saturday noon, and though the Bishop of London was in town, yet they admitted him not till Sunday evening, though they murdered him on Tuesday. The Bishop himself told me the manner of his reception. As soon as he came in, the King very open-facedly and cheerfully received him; the Bishop began to make some condolement. 'Leave off this,' says he, 'my lord, we have not time for it. Let us think of our great work and prepare to meet the Great God, to whom ere long I am to give an account of myself, and I hope I shall do it with peace, and that you will assist me therein. We will not talk,' says he, 'of those rogues' (that was his term) 'in whose hands I am. . . . They thirst after my blood, and they will have it, and God's will be done. . . . I thank God, I heartily forgive them, and I will talk of them no more.'

And so for two or three hours they confessed together, and though they shut the door, a soldier would open it once in half a quarter of an hour and see if the King was there, and so shut it again; and then the next day, which was Monday, they spent much of their time together in like manner, and then they parted late that night, the murder being to be committed the next day. I have this comfort, that of himself without occasion to move him into the discourses 'My Lord' (says he), 'I must remember one that hath had relation to you and myself. Tell Charles—for so he was pleased to call the Prince—he hath been a useful and honest man unto me.

In a French History of England published in 1652, the following passage shows what was thought in other countries of insults offered to the unfortunate King: 'I am asked to report to you the indignities which the insolent attendants committed in his presence. They slept in his bedroom, laughing and shouting, which made it impossible for him to go to sleep, and because they knew he particularly disliked the smell of tobacco, which he begged them not to smoke, these infamous characters told him that they were not there to obey him and it was not for him to object to their pleasures. They spat in his face and pulled off his bed-clothes. It was like a troup of devils in the cell of St Anthony.'

From Sir Thomas Herbert we learn that Charles took a ring from his finger and gave it to him to take to Lady Wheeler, the King's laundress. He did so and in return was given a small cabinet covered with three seals. Next morning, after prayers by Bishop Juxon, Charles broke open the seals and showed the contents—diamonds and jewels—which he gave his small children, the Princess Elizabeth and the Duke of Gloucester, who came to bid their last farewell. All he kept was the one piece of personal jewellery which he wore round his neck.

The Princess Elizabeth gives a touching third-person account of this final scene:

He told her he was glad she had come, for though he had not time to say much, yet somewhat he wished to say to her which he could not to another, and he feared the cruelty was too great to permit his writing. 'But, sweetheart,' he added, 'thou wilt forget what I tell thee.' Then the Princess, shedding an abundance of tears, told him that she would write down all he said to her. He wished her, he said, not to grieve and torment herself for him, for it was a glorious death he should die—it being for the laws and religion of the land. He told her, moreover, what books to read against Popery. He said that he had forgiven all his enemies, and he hoped God would forgive them also. Above all, he bade her tell her Mother 'that his thoughts had never strayed from her, and that his love for her would be the same to the last'.

Withal, he commanded the Princess and her brother to love their mother and be obedient to her. He desired the Princess not to grieve for him, for he should die a martyr, and that he doubted not but God would restore the throne to his son, and that they would be all happier than they could possibly have been had he lived; then, taking the Duke of Gloucester on his knee, he said, 'Sweetheart, now will they cut off thy Father's head?' Upon which words the child looked very earnestly and steadfastly at him. 'Mark, child, what I say,' continued the King. 'They will cut off my head, and perhaps make thee a king; but mark me, thou must not be a king so long as thy brothers Charles and James do live, for they will cut off thy brothers' heads when they can catch them, and cut off thy head at last, too; and therefore I charge thee, don't be made a king by them,' at which the child said earnestly, 'I will be torn in pieces first'—which ready reply from so young an infant filled the King's eyes with tears of admiration and pleasure.

On the night before his execution, Charles had asked Sir Thomas Herbert to lie by his bedside on a pallet. Sir Thomas found it almost impossible to sleep. Charles, however, managed to do so for four hours. Two hours before daylight he arranged with Sir Thomas what clothes he would wear, adding that he wanted 'one shirt on more than ordinary, by reason the season is sharp as probably may make me shake, which some observers will imagine proceeds from fear. I would have no such interpretation. I fear not Death; Death is not terrible to me. I bless my God, I am prepared.'

The day of the execution happened to be remarkably cold, with a heavy frost on the ground; so much so that the King was induced to take a glass of claret and a piece of bread after the Holy Communion in the Chapel Royal as a further protection against shivering 'which would by his enemies be attributed to fear'. He was wearing a rich red, striped, silk brocaded waistcoat on top of his other clothes. After he had taken Holy Communion, Colonel Hacker, his personal jailer, knocked on the door and told him that it was time to go to Whitehall. He then walked on foot through St James's Park guarded by a battalion of infantry to the scaffold at Whitehall, where he was beheaded at 2 p.m.

After embalming, his head was sewn on and the coffin removed to St James's where it was on view for some days. While it lay there, a tall figure, enveloped in a cloak and with his face covered, walked into the room one night, paced solemnly round the coffin and on departing was heard to say, 'Dreadful necessity.' It is generally assumed that this was Oliver Cromwell.

Among the curiosities exhibited in London in 1889 at an Exhibition of Relics belonging to the Royal House of Stuart, were the Communion cup from which Charles I received Holy Communion on the day of execution; one of the shirts worn at his execution still bearing faded blood-stains; one of his gloves; and the lace collar and the cap he wore at the time of his execution, embroidered with scrolls of gold thread. The gold ring with the portrait of Charles I given by him to Bishop Juxon just before his execution was also on view.

*   *   *

After Charles's execution, St James's Palace became the prison for his loyal supporters, the Duke of Hamilton, the Earl of Holland, the Earl of Norwich, Lord Capel and Sir John Owen. They were all sentenced to the block, at which Sir John Owen made a deep bow and humbly thanked the Court. Upon being asked what he meant by thanks, he said, 'It is a very great honour for a poor gentleman of Wales to lose his head with such noble lords. I had been afraid that you would have hanged me.'

This strange gratitude saved his life. He and the Earl of Norwich were pardoned, though the others were beheaded.

The next action of the Parliamentarians was to sell the King's private property for the benefit of the State. This included Charles's splendid collection of art treasures, perhaps the best ever amassed before or afterwards. These were sold at the following ridiculous prices:

		£	s.
1.	St George (Raphael) appraised at and sold for	150	
2.	The Burial of Christ (Isaac Oliver)	100	
3.	The Marquis of Mantua's head (Raphael)	200	
4.	Albert Dürer's Father and himself (Raphael)	100	
5.	Frobernius and Erasmus, 2 Pictures (Holbein)	200	
6.	Christ, Mary, and others (Old Palma) appraised at £200 sold for	225	
7.	Three figures (Titian)	100	
8.	A man in black (Holbein)	100	
9.	M. Parnassus in a case (Indeluago) appraised at £100, sold for	117	
10.	Lucretia, standing by herself, in ebony frame (Titian)	200	
11.	St John (L. da Vinci)	140	
12.	A piece (Titian) appraised at £150, sold for	174	
13.	Charles V, full length (Titian)	150	
14.	St Jerome (by Romano)	200	
15.	Twelve Emperors (Titian)	1,200	
16.	Eleven Emperors (G. Romano)	1,100	
17.	A courtesan, holding a looking-glass (Portinensis)	150	
18.	Titian's Picture with a Senator (Titian) sold for	112	
19.	A satyr head (Correggio)	1,000	
20.	Another of the same (Correggio)	1,000	

		£	s.
21.	Three pieces of San Sebastian (Lucas von Leyden)		
	appraised at £100, sold for	101	
22.	Conversion of St Paul (Palma)	100	
23.	David meeting Saul with Goliath's head (Palma)	100	
24.	Dorcas lying dead (Michael Angelo Caravaggio),		
	appraised at £150, sold for	170	
25.	Family of the Queen of Bohemia	100	
26.	History of Queen Esther (Tintoretto)	120	
27.	A family with divers figures	100	
28.	King on horseback	105	
29.	Hercules (Guido Bolognese)	400	
	'Peace and Plenty' (Rubens)	100	
	'Venus attired by the Graces' (Guido)	200	
	'Christ, the Virgin, and many angels dancing'		
	(Vandyck) valued at	140	
	King Edward III, with a great curtain before it	4	10
	Portrait of Buchanan	3	10
	Queen Elizabeth in her Robes	1	
	The Queen's Mother in mourning	3	
	The King, when a boy	2	

One picture escaped this fate. It was the triple portrait of Charles I which had been sent to the sculptor Bellini in Rome to enable him to carve a statue. It is said that when Bellini saw the picture (by Vandyke) he said he hoped that the emissary who was bringing it to him was no relation of the sitter, because it was clear from his expression he was soon doomed to sudden death.

Most of the pictures and treasures sold by Cromwell were bought by foreigners. The King of Spain acquired so many that it took eighteen mules to transfer them from Corunna to Madrid. Queen Christina of Sweden bought medals, jewels and pictures. The King of France, through Cardinal Mazarin, acquired beds, hangings and carpets. Charles had also been a numismatist and had formed a collection of 12,000 coins which were kept in the royal library. Of these 8,000 were looted before Charles II returned to the kingdom.

* * *

The death of Cromwell in 1658 altered the whole situation. The public were determined not to submit to his weak son, Richard

Cromwell. The military were also opposed to him and St James's Palace became their conspiratorial headquarters. Troops instructed by Richard Cromwell to march immediately to Whitehall went instead to St James's Palace. Another regiment (Colonel Whalley's) also deserted, followed by Richard Cromwell's own guard. He was only too pleased to abdicate and disappear into the country after a brief ten months of power. Shortly afterwards, General Monk entered London at the head of his army and planned the Restoration from St James's Palace.

Charles II landed at Dover on 25 May 1660 with his brother James and the Commonwealth was over.

5. His Majesty's mistresses

NOT surprisingly, the two royal brothers made Whitehall Palace their headquarters. St James's Palace had been a combination of prison and barracks for eighteen years and most of its treasures had been looted or sold. St James's Park, which was an integral part of the palace, had also been allowed to go to ruin.

Charles's first action was to renovate both the palace and its grounds and compensate his father's faithful retainers. He received endless petitions. John Walker asked for a patent to himself and his son William of the 'Keepership of the house and yards built for fowls at St James's'. Henry de Puy asked to be appointed 'Master of the Pall Mall' with an allowance to pay for its upkeep, and power to prevent members of the public playing there without his permission. John Rose petitioned for reinstatement as keeper and gardener of St James's Park.

Thomas Ross requested repayment of all the money which he had spent on recovering much of the royal library from people who had bought it during the Protectorate and then cataloguing it. For this, incidentally, he was given an annuity of £200. Isabella Lumsden pointed out that her late father had spent £425 in maintaining the game of Pall Mall and also asked for compensation. James Farr, the royal organ-maker, was granted £20 a year to 'keep up His Majesty's organs' at St James's Palace.

While enlargements and improvements were being made to the park, including the importation of the ancestors of the various rare wild-fowl still in St James's Park today, the redecoration of St James's Palace was going on apace. The only part of the palace then in use was the Queen's Chapel. A still greater improvement to its surroundings was the importation of the famous French landscape gardener, Le Nôtre, who had laid out the grounds of Versailles. In addition, Dr Robert Morrison was appointed Botanical Physician and Chief Herbalist while Andrew and Gabriel Mollett were given £240 as royal gardeners.

All this involved vast sums of money. True, Charles had been given 50,000 gold sovereigns to pay his debts incurred when in exile. But both he and the country were in very low financial straits. There was only one thing to do, to marry a rich wife. When in Breda he had proposed marriage to Princess Henrietta of Orange but her mother had refused the match on the grounds that she saw no likelihood of his being able to support her.

Marriage to Catharine of Braganza, a Portuguese princess, was now mooted. Both Louis XIV and the Earl of Clarendon were in favour of this, for different reasons. The usual negotiations were started and not only did Catharine's mother offer £500,000 sterling in ready cash as dowry, but also Tangier, Bombay, and trading rights in Brazil and the East Indies which were far more valuable than the cash.

Charles was naturally delighted and when some of his advisers suggested that he should marry a Protestant German princess, he exclaimed impatiently, 'Odds fish, they are all dull and foggy. I cannot like any one of them for a wife.'

Another suggestion was made by the Earl of Bristol—that he should marry one of the Infantas of Spain. The Earl was sent secretly to Parma to take a close look at both of them. A single glance was enough. One was so fat and the other so ugly that he did not dare take the risk of recommending either of them to such a connoisseur as Charles. Meanwhile, a special courier arrived with a message from Louis XIV, saying that the Infanta of Portugal was a lady 'of great beauty and admirable endowments'. He had, he said, once thought seriously of marrying her himself and ended up by offering a bribe of 300,000 pistoles if Charles did so.

Needless to say, the wily as well as merry Monarch had no intention of buying a pig in a poke. He asked for a portrait of her.

It duly arrived, showing her as a glowing brunette with beautiful dark eyes and chestnut hair. Charles, who always liked brunettes, came to the conclusion that however much the artist had flattered Catharine she was bound to be comparatively good-looking, decided to marry her and signed the treaty with Portugal which has made that country our oldest ally.

In handing over Bombay as part of Catharine of Braganza's dowry Portugal gave England her first footing in the East. Tangier was also an invaluable acquisition in view of its naval, military and commercial importance in the Mediterranean.

As soon as the marriage treaty was ratified in Lisbon, Catharine assumed the title of Queen of Great Britain. Scarcely had this taken place, however, when the Queen's mother told the Earl of Sandwich, Charles's Ambassador in Lisbon, that she had become so impoverished from the latest Spanish campaign that she could only pay half the money down, though promising to pay the rest within twelve months.

The Earl was placed in a very considerable dilemma. Tangier had already been taken over. What was far worse was that the Queen of Portugal paid fifty per cent of the dowry not in gold, but in sugar, spices and other merchandise. Sandwich vainly protested but succeeded in insisting that Diego Silvas, a rich Portuguese Jew, should come over with the goods and arrange for their sale in London.

The unfortunate Catharine, who was aged twenty-three, set sail for England. She had spent the whole of her life in a convent and was totally unprepared for the lax form of living at Charles's Court. Little did she know of his amorous adventures in exile with Hortense Mancini or that he was already keeping the notorious Barbara Villiers. Barbara Villiers at this time was Mrs Palmer, but her husband was rapidly elevated to the Earldom of Castlemaine and proved to be one of the most complaisant husbands of all time. Charles was actually sleeping with her the night before Catharine arrived in England, and waited five days after Catharine's arrival in Portsmouth before meeting her.

The Portuguese princess was still confined to her bed as a result of acute sea-sickness when he finally appeared. At first sight of her, according to the Earl of Dartmouth, Charles exclaimed that he thought, 'they had brought me a bat instead of a woman.' Another eye-witness, however, quotes Charles as saying, 'her face is not so exact as to be called a beauty, though her eyes are excellent good, and nothing in her face that in the least degree can disgust one. If I have any skill in physiognomy, which I think I have, she must be as good a woman as ever was born. She has a most agreeable voice. I think myself very happy, for I am confident our two humours will agree very well together.'

After the registration of their marriage in Portsmouth they spent one night at Windsor and arrived at Hampton Court to celebrate Charles's birthday and the anniversary of his Restoration.

John Evelyn, who was presented to the Queen at her first levee, wrote 'she was quite the best looking of all her Portuguese retinue and, though low of stature, prettily shaped, with languishing and excellent eyes, but her teeth wronging her mouth, by sticking a little too far out; for the rest, lovely enough'.

The new and brilliant scenes in which the convent-bred Queen was now required to play the leading part were first both frightening and fatiguing, and she paid many visits with her priests to the chapel in St James's Palace. Nevertheless, for the first six weeks of the marriage everything went well. Charles found her innocence and confiding fondness for him most attractive; her naïveté made him regard her as a new toy. During this period he arranged every possible entertainment for her, plays, music, balls, sailing on the Thames and walking in St James's Park.

Another reason for the successful start of the marriage was that Lady Castlemaine was *hors de combat*, having produced a son by Charles a few days after the marriage. The minute that she was out of bed, however, she burst in on the unfortunate Catharine who, though she heard before leaving Lisbon of Charles's previous infatuation with her, never supposed that the liaison would continue after marriage.

It would appear that Charles had not the slightest suspicion that she knew anything of this until he presented her with a list of the women he recommended for appointment to her Household. To her horror, Catharine saw Lady Castlemaine's name at the head of the list. She immediately scratched it out and told Charles that he must either grant her this privilege or send her back to Lisbon. After solemnly promising to have nothing more to do with Lady Castlemaine, Charles outraged all decency by leading her by the hand and presenting her before the assembled Court. To everyone's surprise, Catharine received her graciously and allowed her to kiss her hand. The fact was that, not yet being familiar with the sound of English names, she had no idea that this was indeed Lady Castlemaine. One of her Portuguese ladies-in-waiting whispered the truth. At once she flushed and burst into tears, struggled for a moment to repress her feelings, had a violent nose-bleed and was removed in a minor fit.

The quarrel was violently renewed when Catharine recovered. The Earl of Clarendon now acted as peacemaker, explaining to her that she could scarcely expect a man of Charles's age to be a virgin and asked whether Catharine really thought that the Court of Lisbon was as moral as all that. This had a mild effect for a few days, but not for long. Charles started to blame her personally for the failure to complete the original marriage settlement.

During the first few months of their marriage, incidentally, Charles and Catharine could only speak Spanish to one another. This could have caused some of their misunderstandings because it was of course a foreign language to both of them.

Fortunately Queen Henrietta, Charles's mother, arrived from abroad to congratulate them on their marriage and so there was once again a temporary reconciliation.

Meantime, Lady Castlemaine was received at Court willy-nilly by Catharine. She was also compelled to receive 'young Croft', as Charles first called his illegitimate son before making him Duke of Monmouth. One day Lady Castlemaine entered her bedchamber while the Queen was at her toilet and asked presumptuously, 'How can you have the patience to sit so long a-dressing?' 'Madame,' replied Catharine, 'I have so much reason to use patience that I can well bear such a trifle.' And indeed she had every reason to exert her patience. Officially she was entitled to an annual income of £30,000 a year. All that she actually received was £4,000 a year, with the result that she was permanently short of money and was not even able to go to Tunbridge Wells for the cure.

By this time Lady Castlemaine had been installed in St James's Palace. James had also taken up residence there. Catharine, not surprisingly, became ill and in her delirium thought that she had given birth to a son. Later she thought she had triplets, one of them a girl who looked very much like Charles. It was a long time before she recovered.

Then, to everybody's surprise, the King was seen one day riding hand-in-hand with her in St James's Park. According to Samuel Pepys, she looked 'mighty pretty in a white laced waistcoat, and a crimson short petticoat, with hair *à la negligence*'.

> Here also (he went on), was my Lady Castlemaine, riding among the rest of the ladies; but the king took, methought, no notice of her, nor when she alighted did anybody press (as she seemed to expect, and staid for it) to take her down, but was taken down by her own gentelman. She looked mighty out of humour, and had a yellow plume in her hat, (which all took notice of) and yet is very handsome, but very melancholy; nor did anybody speak to her, or she so much as smile or speak to anybody. I followed them up Whitehall, and into the Queen's presence, where all the ladies walked, talking and fiddling with their hats and feathers, and changing and trying them on each other's heads, and laughing. It was the finest sight to me, considering their great beauties and dress. But, above all, Mistress Stuart in this dress, with her hat cocked, and a red plume, with her sweet eyes, little Roman nose, and excellent taille, is now the greatest beauty I ever saw, I think, in all my life; and if ever woman can, does exceed my lady Castlemaine, at least in this dress, which I verily believe is the reason of his coldness to my lady Castlemaine.

'La Belle Stuart' was the daughter of Lord Blantyre. She was very young, very vain and very pretty indeed. At first Lady Castlemaine, who had turned Roman Catholic to please Charles, was livid about her rival. Charles raved about La Belle Stuart, said that her legs were the finest in England and openly took her in his arms and kissed her in public. He even wrote a poem about her:

I pass all my hours in a shady old grove,
But I live not the day when I see not my love;
I survey every walk now my Phillis is gone,
And sigh when I think we were there all alone:
 O then, 'tis O then, that I think there's no hell
 Like loving, like loving too well.

While alone to myself I repeat all her charms,
She I love may be locked in another man's arms,
She may laugh at my cares and so false she may be
To say all the kind things she before said to me:
 O then, 'tis O then, that I think there's no hell
 Like loving too well.

But when I consider the truth of her heart,
Such an innocent passion, so kind without art,
I fear I have wronged her, and hope she may be
So full of true love to be jealous of me:
 And then 'tis I think that no joys be above
 The pleasures of love.

Worse still, from Lady Castlemaine's point of view, the King
having been given a calash, a very smart French carriage, the
only one in England, La Belle Stuart asked Charles if she could
drive in it in Hyde Park. Lady Castlemaine threatened to bring
on a miscarriage if Charles agreed to this request. La Belle
Stuart said that if her request was refused she would never be
in a condition to have a miscarriage. She won the day. In consequence, Lady Castlemaine refused to allow her to come to
her apartments in St James's Palace. Whereupon Charles said
that he would not visit her unless La Belle Stuart were there.
So Lady Castlemaine made the best of a difficult situation by
becoming close friends with her. They soon were inseparable,
and once when Charles found them in bed together Lady
Castlemaine suggested that he should join them, a request which
he readily obeyed.

Not long afterwards Lady Castlemaine had her revenge. She
knew that the Duke of Richmond, an elderly, ugly man who
drank very heavily, had become infatuated with La Belle
Stuart. Learning that he was visiting her in her bedroom Lady
Castlemaine told Charles, who ordered the Duke to leave the

Court. La Belle Stuart escaped from St James's Palace with him and married him near Gravesend. Charles completely lost his temper and La Belle Stuart was banished from Court. The following year she caught smallpox and ceased to be La Belle. This, however, did not prevent Charles, in remorse, from rowing alone down the river to her residence, clambering over the garden wall so as not to disturb the doorkeeper, and making love to her.

While Charles was unable to get himself a son by Catharine, Lady Castlemaine was giving birth to his royal bastards almost every year. Her blue, almond-shaped eyes, auburn hair and seductive figure had been and were irresistible to him for years. When in debt she blackmailed him by threatening to publish all his letters to her. This was in spite of her £11,000 a year income from the Excise and Post Office and £5,000 a year for each of her bastard children. In addition she was created Countess of Southampton and Duchess of Cleveland.

The five bastards whom he recognized as his own (though Lady Castlemaine tried to make him believe that several others were also by him) were the Duke of Southampton, the Duke of Grafton, the Duke of Northumberland, the Countess of Sussex and the Countess of Lichfield, most of them being born in St James's Palace. Not that Charles remained faithful to her or she to him. One of her lovers was the future Duke of Marlborough who made a hurried departure through a window of St James's Palace when the King arrived unexpectedly in her suite. Charles leaned out of the window and shouted to the half-naked lover, 'I forgive you because you do it for your bread', and indeed John Churchill, as he then was, owed a great deal to Lady Castlemaine for his early army promotion.

As for Charles, his other mistresses included Moll Davis, Margaret Hughes, Jane Roberts, Mary Knight, Winifred Wells and Lady Falmouth, not to mention Nell Gwynne. The offspring of these various liaisons were so many that, having run out of such variations as Fitzroy and Fitzcharles, the College of Arms had to fall back on Beauclerk, Lennox and Tudor. The courtiers called Charles 'Old Rowley'—the name of a stallion in the Royal Mews. There was no need to have an annual honours list in those days; Charles was adding all the time to the peerage.

Among his other bastards were the Earl of Plymouth, the Countess of Yarmouth, the Countess of Derwentwater and the Duke of St Albans, the son of Nell Gwynne.

Nell Gwynne was born in an alley off Drury Lane and started to earn her living by acting as a barmaid to the clientele of a local brothel. Later, as is better known, she sold oranges in the pit of the King's Theatre where she kissed the men who took her fancy and often caused more gaiety in the audience than the actors on stage. Until the Restoration, all women's parts were played by men. It was now legal for girls to play feminine parts and indeed play men's parts. Nell Gwynne drove Pepys into ecstasies over her comedy parts and she soon became the mistress of Lord Buckhurst, later the Earl of Dorset. At this stage, King Charles, too, became infatuated with her and bought her from Buckhurst for a pension of £1,000 a year as a Groom of his Bedchamber.

Nell Gwynne undoubtedly had a great sense of humour and liked to call Charles 'My Charles III', her first two lovers having been Charles Hart and Charles Buckhurst. She was a bold, merry slut and never asked Charles for a sinecure or a title, but did want something done for her son, who was now six years old and still known merely as Charles Beauclerk. All Charles's other children by his mistresses had been ennobled at birth. So one day she called to him in his father's hearing, 'Come hither, you little bastard.' When Charles remonstrated she replied, 'I have no better name to call him by.' The lad was promptly made Earl of Burford and when thirteen was created Duke of St Albans and Master Falconer of England, with a very considerable revenue. To this day the Duke of St Albans is the only one of the monarch's subjects who is allowed to drive a carriage along Rotten Row (always excepting the driver of the official water-cart).

Charles had long ago given up all hope of having an heir by Catharine of Braganza. His next mistress was Louise de Kérouaille whom he had met during his exile in France. He appointed her a maid-of-honour and gave her apartments in St James's Palace. By all accounts she was a very pretty woman with a peaches and cream complexion. True, she had a slight cast in one eye and Nell Gwynne called her Squintabella. Nell was frequently witty at her expense and when Louise went into mourning for a French prince, she wore black for the Cham of Tartary who had recently died. When asked why she had done this, she replied that she was as closely related to the Cham as Louise de Kérouaille was to the French prince.

It is said, incidentally, that there was a mock ceremony of marriage between Charles and Louise in a Suffolk country-house near Newmarket where Charles, a first-class gentleman jockey, had just won the big race. John Evelyn wrote in his diary, 'It was universally reported that the fair Lady Whore was bedded one of these nights and the stocking flung, after the manner of a married bride.' Nine months later Louise gave birth to a son who was made Duke of Richmond while she herself was raised to the rank of Duchess of Portsmouth.

St James's Palace was indeed a doubly royal bordel. Not only did Charles install his mistresses there, but so too did his brother James.

His first mistress, whom he later married less than two months before the birth of their first offspring, was Ann Hyde, daughter of the Earl of Clarendon. His second mistress was Lady Ann Carnegie (later Lady Southesk). His next intended mistress was Lady Chesterfield but before he was able to seduce her, Lord Chesterfield packed her off to his country estate in Derbyshire. Similarly Lady Robartes was whisked away by her husband to Snowdonia, just in time.

Strangely enough, his wife Ann proceeded to choose only the prettiest women as her maids-of-honour and ladies-of-the-bedchamber. Miss Jennings was the first of these who James decided were his personal private property. Miss Jennings, however, refused his blandishments although James sent her a billet-doux almost every day, often slipping them into her muff or one of her pockets. Miss Jennings made sure that anyone who saw it should also observe them being dropped unopened by shaking her muff or pulling out her handkerchief. (Charles II was equally unsuccessful with her. Later she married Dick Talbot, James's chief ponce.) Elizabeth Hamilton was another who eluded him. Miss Goditha Price was, however, amenable, as too was Lady Denham, who had previously set her cap at Charles without success. Samuel Pepys records, 'The Duke of

ST JAMES'S CONDUIT ABOUT 1660

ABOVE: CHARLES I
BELOW : OLD GUARD CHAMBER, ST JAMES'S PALACE

HENRIETTA MARIA
AND THE DWARF JEFFREY HUDSON

York' (as James still was at that time) 'is wholly given up to his new mistress, my Lady Denham, going at noon-day with all his gentlemen with him to visit her, she declaring she will not be his mistress as Miss Price, to go up and down the privy stairs, but will be owned publicly, and so she is.'

Next came Arabella Churchill, sister of the future Duke of Marlborough. She was witty but plain. So much so that Charles once asked his brother whether his mistresses were imposed upon him by his priests as a penance. At first, indeed, it looked as if her lack of looks would prevent James from making her his mistress. Then an odd event took place. The Duke and Arabella were riding in the country when her horse ran away with her and finally threw her. The Duke jumped down to help and could not fail to see, because her skirts were over her head, that she had exquisite legs. From that moment she became his mistress.

In the meantime the Duchess of York died, having given birth to the future Queens Mary and Anne and other children, six of whom died in infancy.

* * *

During the Plague, James and his Court left St James's Palace, as did Charles and his Court Whitehall Palace, in favour of Oxford, where Prince Rupert joined them. Incidentally, the rooms which Prince Rupert occupied in St John's College have remained virtually unchanged and the King Charles Club and the Archery Club still survive, both being blessed with the most magnificent Jacobean silver.

The two royal brothers returned to London before the out-break of the Great Fire which destroyed nearly two-thirds of London but did not affect St James's Palace. It was thanks largely to James and Charles that the fire was not even more destructive. They gave instructions for the blowing up of a number of houses in the path of the flames without waiting for the permission of their owners.

A year later, when the Dutch sailed up the Medway, Pepys noted that Charles was supping at St James's Palace in the company of Lady Castlemaine, the entire party being engaged in chasing a moth.

St James's Fair, suspended during the Commonwealth, had

long since been revived. According to one of the Rugge manuscripts:

> This year the Fair called St James' Fair was kept the full appointed time, being a fortnight, but during that time many lewd and infamous persons were, by his Majesty's express command to the Lord Chamberlain, and his lordship's direction to Robert Nelson, Esq., Committed to the house of Correction; their names are these: Tory Rory, Mrs Winter, Jane Chapman, Rebecca Baker, Anne Browne, Elizabeth Wilkinson, Rachel Brinley, Mrs Munday, Alice Wiggins, Nell Yates, Betty Marshall. Some of these were very impudent in the Fair, and discovered their nakedness to several persons, when these whores were drunk, as that they often were.

The historian is, however, chiefly indebted to Pepys and Evelyn for what happened outside the palace walls; thus Pepys: '. . . Then met with Ned Pickering and walked with him into St James's Park (where I had not been a great while) and there found great and very noble alterations. And, in our discourse, he was very forward to complain and to speak loud of the lewdness and beggary of the Court, which I am sorry to hear, and which I am afeared will bring all to ruin again.'

Or again:

> Got up betimes and walked to St James', and there to Mr Coventry, and sat an hour with him—Thence to the Park—the Queen coming by in her coach, going to her chappell at St James' (the first time it hath been ready for her) I crowded after her, and I got up to the room where her closet is; and there stood and saw the fine altar, ornaments, and the fryers in their habits, and the priests come in with their fine copes and many other fine things. I heard their musique too: methinks it may be good, but it did not appear so to me, neither as to their manner of singing, nor was it good concord to my ears, whatever the matter was. The Queen very devout; but what pleased me best was to wait upon my dear Lady Castlemaine, who, tho' a Protestant, did wait upon the Queen to chappell. By and by, after mass was done, a fryer with his cowl did rise up and preach a sermon in Portuguese; which I not understanding, did go away, and to the King's chappell, but that was done, and so up to the Queen's presence-chamber, where she and the King were expected to dine: but she staying at St

James', they were forced to remove the things to the King's presence-chamber; and thence he dined alone.

Evelyn's description of a visit to St James's Park is as follows: 'I went to St James' Park, where I saw various animals. . . . The Park was at this time stored with numerous flocks of severall sorts of ordinary wild fowle, breeding about the Decoy, which for being neere so greate a Citty, and among such a concourse of souldiers and people, is a singular and diverting thing. There were also deere of severall countries—white; spotted like leopards; antelopes; an elk; red deere; roebucks; staggs; Guinea goates; Arabian sheepe, etc. There were withy-potts or nests for the wild fowle to lay their eggs in, a little above ye surface of ye water.' Evelyn also noted a wrestling match for £1,000 in St James's Park in front of the King and his Court between the Western and Northern champions, which was won by the man from the West. Vast sums changed hands on the result.

The Queen's Chapel at St James's Palace continued in the meantime to be thronged by Roman Catholics. So an Order of Council announced that only the Queen and members of the Royal Family were to be allowed to attend Mass on pain of prosecution.

At about this time there was some excitement over the loss of one of James's dogs in St James's Park. It was described as: 'a little Spaniel Dog of his Royal Highness; he will answer to the name Towser, he is liver colour'd and white spotted, his legs speckled with liver colour and white, with long hair growing upon his hind legs, long ears, and his under lip a little hanging; if any can give notice of him they shall have five pounds for their pains.'

James now decided to marry again and Mary d'Este of Modena was selected, much to her distress, as the future chatelaine of St James's Palace, out of a short list of four possibles. The others were the Duchess of Guise, Princess Mary of Wurtemburg, and an unnamed princess of the House of Reuss.

Each of them was scrutinized in advance by the Earl of Peterborough, who was sent out by Charles on his brother's behalf to secure first-hand evidence of their looks. Even before he saw

Mary of Modena, Peterborough fell in vicarious love with a portrait of her and sent back a message to say that if she was anything remotely as beautiful in real life she would be his choice for James. When Peterborough saw her, after having inspected the other three, he realized that she was indeed much the best looking, although the poor child was still only fourteen. He learned that she could write and read Latin and French, was passionately fond of music, but knew so little about history and geography that she had never heard of England, much less of the Duke of York. When her mother, the Duchess, told her that the Duke of York was forty, the poor little girl burst into tears and suggested that her aunt who was thirty would be far more suitable than herself. It took all Louis XIV's pressure on her and her mother to force the marriage between her and the Earl of Peterborough as proxy. When the news reached the Duke of York at St James's Palace that he was technically married, he sent word to his daughter that 'he had provided a play-fellow for her'.

Mary refused to leave the country unless her mother came too. Much though Charles and James objected to this, they had no alternative. In the meantime, rumours of the impending marriage had reached the House of Commons and Parliament implored Charles not to allow it to proceed. He told them, however, that it was too late.

On arrival at Dover, Mary was married all over again, this time to James according to the Protestant religion, having previously been married with Roman Catholic rites. After this, they made straight for St James's Palace where the ambassadors of France, Portugal, Sweden, Denmark and the Venetian Republic paid their respects.

In the marriage agreement it had been stipulated that Mary, as Duchess of York, would be allowed to use the Catholic chapel at St James's Palace. When this became known there was so much hysteria among the populace that Charles decided to withhold this permission, primarily for her sake.

After six weeks, the Duchess of Modena was compelled to return home because of the intrigues of her son against her. As for Mary, James was proud of her beauty and flattered by her jealousy when she learned about his various mistresses. He treated her with the greatest affection, but there was so little in age between her and his eldest daughter that he seems to have regarded her more as a plaything. Mary, being completely ignorant of the manners and customs of the English Court, had to submit for guidance to James's various mistresses, whom, according to the usual routine, he had made ladies of her bed-chamber.

Bassett (a version of Faro) and other gambling games were very fashionable. Mary disliked cards and was terrified at the idea of high stakes. She was told, however, that she must behave like everyone else or she would become unpopular and be laughed at. In the circumstances it is not surprising that she lost a great deal of money at the card table without deriving the slightest pleasure from it.

Young as she was, though, she gave birth to a baby within eighteen months of her marriage. It proved to be a girl whom she had baptized privately on her own bed according to the Roman Catholic rites. Unfortunately it died of convulsions at the age of ten months. A second daughter was born a year later, also at St James's Palace. She was christened Isabella but died at the age of five.

In the meantime James took a new mistress, Catharine Sedley. It was infatuation at first sight. 'It cannot be my beauty because he must see I have none,' she told her friends, 'and it cannot be my wit for he has not enough to know that I have any.' However, she had several bastards by him—one of whom, Catharine, married the Duke of Buckingham.

About this time smallpox broke out at St James's Palace. Princess Anne caught it and so did Lady Frances Villiers, the governess of the royal children. Mary had just given birth to her next child, who was a boy, and given the title of Duke of Cambridge. Very unwisely, she showed so little fear of infection that she allowed her step-daughter, Princess Anne, to visit her, as a result of which the infant died ten days later.

Not long afterwards she was terrified by a nightmare. She dreamt that Lady Frances Villiers appeared to her and said that she was damned and in the flames of Hell. When Mary replied, 'How can this be? I cannot believe it', Lady Frances reiterated, 'Madame, to convince you, feel my hand.' In her nightmare Mary did so and it was so hot that she woke up screaming. To recuperate, she went on a visit with Princess Anne to the Prince of Orange and his wife Mary. On her return she found that Charles had been forced to sign a declaration exiling James because of his Papist tendencies. Within a few days she had to leave the country once again for Holland, where she and her husband were compelled to live in exile for five months. But this did not prevent St James's Palace from being occupied by the various royal mistresses whose numbers had been increased by the arrival of Hortense Mancini, Duchess of Mazarin.

Hortense was the niece of Cardinal Mazarin who had rejected Charles II's offer of marriage to her while the King was a poverty-stricken exile. In those days Hortense had been only fourteen. She was now thirty. In the meantime she had married the rich son of a French marshal who went mad shortly after the wedding. In spite of his lunacy, however, she had several children by him before running away. Her husband promptly shut her up in a penitentiary convent and, while she brought an action against him to secure her personal property, officially accused her of misbehaviour with a eunuch, of incest with her brother, and of being a Lesbian. Hortense nevertheless won her case, and escaped from France with a woman, both of them dressed as men, which suggests there might have been something in the husband's last-named accusation.

After various affairs in different parts of Europe, Hortense decided to seduce Charles II which she immediately succeeded in doing. However, she did not remain faithful to him for long. The handsome Prince Louis of Monaco, whose mistress she had been, followed her to London. In a moment of jealousy Charles withdrew Hortense's pension of £4,000 a year, whereupon Prince Louis hastened to give her a similar sum. Later, cured of his passion and very nearly bankrupt, Prince Louis returned to Monaco and promulgated a complete new set of laws with excessive penalties for any form of immorality.

As for Hortense, a contemporary historian wrote of her as

one of those Roman beauties in which there is no doll-prettiness, and in whom unaided nature triumphs over all the arts of the coquette. Painters could not say what was the colour of her eyes.

They were neither blue nor grey, nor yet black nor brown nor hazel. Nor were they languishing nor passionate, as if either demanding to be loved or expressing love. They simply looked as if she had basked in love's sunshine. If her mouth were not large, it was not a small one, and was suitably the fit organ for intelligent speech and amiable words. All her motions were charming in their easy grace and dignity. Her complexion was softly toned and yet warm and fresh. It was so harmonious that though dark she seemed of beautiful fairness. Her jet-black hair rose in strong waves above her forehead as if proud to clothe and adorn her splendid head.

Almost from the start she intrigued against the Duchess of Portsmouth to displace her as chief mistress, but without success. Similarly the Duchess of Portsmouth tried to have her removed from St James's Palace.

Charles had promised James and Mary that they should be allowed to return to England. He was as good as his word and back they came to St James's Palace, where Mary stayed while her husband and the King went to the races at Newmarket. On his return, the levees at St James's Palace were once again well attended, but the Earl of Shaftesbury was powerful enough to compel Charles to banish James and Mary to Scotland, where they remained for two years.

Golf and tennis were the favourite amusements of the gentry in those days and James was frequently seen 'in a golfing party on the links of Leith'. One of his caddies was Andrew Dixon who recalled that, when a boy, he used to carry the Duke's golf clubs and then run ahead and announce where the balls fell: the original fore-caddy.

An anecdote of the day concerned James and the Duke of Lauderdale who played four-ball matches against each other. On one occasion, there was a very heavy wager. James's partner was John Paterson, a shoemaker. They won. When the Duke of Lauderdale paid up some hundreds of broad pieces James handed the gold to Paterson saying, 'through your skill I won this game and you are therefore entitled to the reward of the victory'.

At last Charles was strong enough to arrange for James and Mary to return to London. They went by sea in the well-named

Happy Return. Once again they established themselves at St James's Palace. Mary was only twenty-four and so beautiful that at her first appearance in the theatre with the Duke, the most riotous applause broke out. Once again she produced a baby, but it died of convulsions like her first.

* * *

During the events preceding the death of Charles II, John Evelyn noted, 'I can never forget the inexpressible luxury and profaneness, gaming and all dissoluteness, and as it were total forgetfulness of God (it being Sunday evening) which I was witness of, the King sitting and toying with his concubines, Portsmouth, Cleveland, and Mazarin etc., and a French boy singing love songs in that glorious gallery, whilst about 20 of the great courtiers and other dissolute persons were at basset round a large table, a bank of at least £2000 in gold before them upon which two gentlemen who were with me made reflections with astonishment'.

The King went to bed that night cheerfully enough, telling Lord Bruce that he would be very happy to have his house covered with lead during the coming week. He was referring to his new palace at Winchester. In fact, he was in a lead coffin on the following Saturday.

The association of St James's Palace with his death was indirect but important. He had been dining with the Duchess of Portsmouth. Next morning he had a violent fit of apoplexy. Catharine of Braganza hurried to his apartment, followed by Mary. Meanwhile James was urged by Catharine and also the Duchess of Portsmouth to arrange for the Last Offices prescribed by the Church of Rome. But according to the laws of England, the death sentence could be imposed on any priest who performed the Last Rites. What made it particularly difficult was that the royal bedroom was crowded by people day and night—bishops, peers, ambassadors, privy councillors and doctors. James, asking everybody to move back slightly, knelt down and whispered to Charles,

'Sir, will you receive the Sacrament of the Catholic Church?'

'Ah,' said Charles, 'I will give everything in the world to have a priest.'

'I will bring you one,' said the Duke.

'For God's sake, brother, do, but will you not expose yourself to danger by doing it?'

'Sir, though it costs me my life I will bring you one.'

Father Huddleston, who had saved Charles's life by hiding him after the Battle of Worcester and was consequently exempted from all the penalties attached to his function as a Catholic priest, was summoned, but in such a hurry that he had forgotten to bring the Host. Discovering how urgent it was he sent one of the Queen's Portuguese priests to fetch everything necessary for the Last Rites from St James's Chapel. Then, disguised in a wig and cassock, the usual costume of the clergy of the Church of England, he was brought by a secret staircase and entered the alcove in which King Charles's bed was standing. James presented him with the words, 'Sir, I bring you the man who once saved your life. He now comes to save your soul.' Charles replied faintly, 'He is welcome.'

Strangely enough, he rallied for an hour or two, but knowing that the end was near, made his famous apology, 'I have been a most unconscionable time a-dying and I hope you will excuse it.' Before he finally did so, he recommended the Duchess of Portsmouth over and over again to James, saying, 'I have always loved her and now love her to the last.' He further recommended the Duke of Richmond and all his other children, with the exception of the Duke of Monmouth. He also prayed God to send James a long and prosperous reign and asked him 'not to let poor Nellie starve'. He was only fifty-four when he died.

A few years previously he had asked the Earl of Rochester to write his epitaph. He obliged with the famous lines:

> Here lies our Sovereign Lord the King
> Whose word no man relies on.
> Who never said a foolish thing
> And never did a wise one.

Charles had retorted, 'The matter is easily accounted for; my discourse is my own, my actions are my ministers.'

6. The riddle of the royal birth

'THE King is dead. Long live the King.'

James was immediately recognized as the new monarch by the Privy Council without a dissentient voice. On the following Sunday he and Mary went publicly to Mass in the Queen's Chapel at St James's Palace. For the next few days they were chiefly occupied in receiving the compliments and condolences of the various foreign ambassadors.

Next, suddenly anxious to reform the Court, James persuaded his current mistress, Catharine Sedley, to go away, much to the delight of the public. He also persuaded Mary to wear rouge for the first time. Father Seraphin was surprised when he saw her make-up and when she said that it had been made necessary by her pallor, the friar reiterated, 'I would rather see Your Majesty yellow or even green than rouged.'

It was not long, however, before Catharine Sedley returned. Why James should prefer a coarse, ugly woman to his beautiful and affectionate wife is one of the riddles of history.

It was now time for the Coronation. On the Maundy Thursday previously, James washed the feet of fifty-two poor men, according to the number of his own years, to each of whom he gave a guinea which he had borrowed, and touched several for the King's Evil. The night before the Coronation Mary slept at St James's Palace, which she always preferred to Whitehall. Next morning, having performed her devotions, she was attired in purple velvet, furred with ermine, and looped with rubies and pearls. On her head was a cap of purple velvet embroidered with gems and a circlet of gold heavily adorned with large diamonds. She then went privately in her sedan chair to White-hall and from there to Westminster Hall.

James had taken a great deal of care about Mary's crown but none about his own. This had been made for Charles II who had a much broader forehead. When it was placed on James's head by the Archbishop of Canterbury it shook. Henry Sidney put out his hand and stopped it from falling as he said, 'This is not the first time, Your Majesty, that my family have supported the Crown.' Most of the spectators regarded this incident as a bad omen.

Once he became King, James ceased to live in St James's Palace but gave it to Mary together with 'the court yards, orchards, gardens and other appurtenances, to hold for her natural life'.

During the previous reign St James's Park had been increased by thirty-six acres. A canal was made from the Parade to Mulberry Gardens and towards the south-east was a decoy known as Duck Island. On the south-west side was Rosamond's Pond which rapidly became the local lovers' lane. 'There's a thousand cuckolds a year made by Rosamond's Pond,' wrote Thomas Otway.

The Mall lay on the north side with a vista of half a mile. Birdcage Walk was bordered by the aviary. Mulberry trees, of which there is still one survivor, were planted with a view to starting a silk industry but without success. As for the palace,

> though it is pleasantly situated along the north side of the Park, and has very convenient, and not inelegant apartments, it is an irregular brick building, without one single beauty on the outside to recommend it, being at once the contempt of foreign nations, and the disgrace of our own (wrote a visitor at the time). Indeed there is not much to be said in commendation of this palace. In the front next St James's Street there appears little more than an old gatehouse; and on passing through the gate we enter a little square court, with a piazza on the west side of it leading to the grand stair case; the buildings are low, plain and mean, and there are two other courts beyond, which have not much of the air of a palace. The windows however look into a pleasant garden, and command a view of St James's Park which seems to be the only advantage this edifice can boast . . . altogether the royal stables

have the air of a palace, and the royal palace has the air of a stable.

In the meantime, the rebellions of the Duke of Argyll in Scotland and the Duke of Monmouth in England strengthened the throne rather than shook it, because of the speed with which they were both suppressed.

Among the prisoners in the Duke of Monmouth's rebellion was the demagogue Story, who had tried to excite the indignation of the people against James by repeating all the libellous accusations made by the Duke of Monmouth. Edward Calamy, one of the courtiers, described what took place.

When Story was brought before the King and the Privy Council, he looked so miserable that everyone was astonished at his haggard and squalid appearance. James looked at him and asked, 'Is that a man or what is it?' He was told that it was Story. 'Oh, Story,' said the King. 'I remember him. That is a rare fellow indeed!' Then turning towards him, 'Pray, Story,' says he, 'you were in Monmouth's army in the west, were you not?' He, according to the advice given him, made answer presently, 'Yes, an't please your Majesty.' 'Pray,' said the King to him, 'you were a commissary there, were you not?' Again Story replied, 'Yes, an't please your Majesty.' 'And you,' said King James, 'made a speech before great crowds of people, did you not?' He again very readily answered, 'Yes, an't please your Majesty.' 'Pray,' said King James, 'if you have not forgot what you said, let us have some taste of your fine speech, let us have some specimen of some of the flowers of your rhetoric?' Whereupon Story readily made answer, 'I told them, an't please your Majesty, that it was you that fired the City of London.' 'A rare rogue, upon my word,' said the King, 'and pray, what else did you tell them?' 'I told them,' said he, 'an't please your Majesty, that you poisoned your brother.' 'Impudence in the utmost height of it,' said the King. 'Pray let us have something further, if your memory serves you?' 'I further told them,' said Mr Story, 'that your Majesty appeared to be fully determined to make the nation both Papists and slaves.' By this time the King seemed to have heard enough of the prisoner's speech, and therefore cried out, 'A rogue with a witness!' Then, cutting off short, the King rejoined, 'To all this, I doubt not, but a thousand villainous things were added. But what would you say, Story, if, after all this, I were to grant your life?' To which

74

he, without any demur, made answer, that he would pray for his Majesty as long as he lived. 'Why, then,' said the King, 'I freely pardon all that is past, and hope that you will not, for the future, represent your king as inexorable!'

The next mistress whom James acquired was the profligate young Duchess of Norfolk. In the meantime he made Catharine Sedley the Countess of Dorchester and built a fine house in St James's Square for her. Mary was further upset by the death of her mother who, just before she died, visited the shrine of Our Lady of Loretto with votive offerings and prayers that her daughter might have a son. By this time all Mary's four children were dead and she went to Bath to take the cure.

It was now that James received his first solemn warning that his son-in-law William of Orange was planning to dethrone him. The news came from Louis XIV but James refused to believe it.

It also became apparent that Mary was going to have a baby and her pregnancy was announced by royal proclamation. But her health was in a precarious state and she was frequently bled. One of the most famous dates in the history of St James's Palace was 10 June 1688, the day when the baby, the future James Francis Edward of York, later called 'the Old Pretender', was born, to survive for 77 years of exile and vain hopes of returning to England. For her services Mrs Wilkins, the midwife, received 500 guineas.

On the previous day the Queen had suddenly left Whitehall for St James's Palace where she gave birth shortly before 10 a.m. Alarming symptoms were observed the following night and the Court physicians were summoned at 3 a.m. After being treated for a fit, the infant Prince apparently recovered. That morning, however, according to the Earl of Clarendon, there was a strong rumour that the young Prince had died.

The Duchess of Modena, writing about this event many years later, quoted the Queen herself as saying: 'The physicians prescribed something for him which they say is good for babies. I don't remember now what it was, but this I know, that every one thought he was dying. As I was in Childbed, the King would not have me awakened with these tidings; but while every one was in a state of distraction he retired into his oratory to offer that child, who was so precious to him, to God. I awoke in the

75

meantime and asked for some broth, but saw no one near me, neither nurse nor attendant. I then called. The only person who remained to take care of me was a chamber-maid not more than one and twenty years old, and thus I learned that which they wished to conceal from me. The Countess of Sunderland was lady of the bed that night, and it was her duty to have watched beside me.'

The birth took place in the end room of the south front of St James's Palace overlooking the garden. The bed itself was close to the door leading on to a flight of stairs which descended to an inner court. Enemies of the King swore that the Prince had really died and a changeling was substituted. A contemporary pamphlet was published explaining how easily this could have been done, together with a map of the palace showing the place where the alleged mother of the changeling gave birth, and the doors and the passages through which it was conveyed to the Queen's bedchamber.

Bishop Burnet clearly believed this story. His account is as follows:

Now a resolution was taken for the Queen's lying-in at St James', and directions were given to have all things quickly ready. Either the Bath waters did not agree with the Princess, or the advices of her friends were so pressing (who thought her absence from the Court at that time of such consequence) that in compliance with them she gave it out that Bath did not indeed agree with her, and that therefore she would return in a few days.

The day after the Court had this notice, the Queen said she would go to St James' and look for the good hour. She was told that it was impossible upon so short a warning to have things ready. But she was so positive that she said she would lie there that night, though she should lie upon the boards. And at night, though the shorter and quicker way was to go from Whitehall to St James' through the Park, yet now, by a sort of affectation she would be carried thither by Charing Cross through Pall Mall. And it was given out by all her train that she was going to be delivered. Some said it would be next morning, and the Priests said very confidently it would be a boy.

The next morning about 9 o'clock she sent word to the King that she was in labour. The Queen Dowager was next sent to; the two ladies were sent for—so that no women were in the room, but two dressers and one under-dresser. The Queen lay all the while abed, and in order to the warming one side of it, a warming-pan was brought. But it was not opened, that it might be seen that there was fire, and nothing else in it. So here was matter for suspicion with which all people were filled.

A little before 10 the Queen cried out as in a strong pain, and immediately afterwards the midwife said aloud, 'that she was happily brought to bed'. Then the Lords all cried out, 'of what?' The midwife answered, 'The Queen must not be surprised,' only she gave a sign to the Countess of Sutherland, who upon that touched her forehead, by which it being the sign before agreed on, the King said, 'he knew it was a boy'. No cries were heard from the child; nor was it showed to those in the room. It was pretended more air was necessary. The under-dresser went out with the child, or somewhat else, in her arms to a dressing-room, to which there was a door near the Queen's bed. But there was another entry to it from other apartments.

The King continued with the Lords in the bed chamber for some minutes, which was either a sign of much phlegm upon such an occasion, for it was not known whether the child was alive or dead; or it looked like the giving time for some management. After a little while they went into the dressing-room, and then the news was published.

That night one Hemings, a very worthy man, an Apothecary by his trade, who lived in St Martin's Lane, the very next door to a family of an eminent Papist (Brown, brother to the Viscount Montacute, lived there), the wall between his parlour and theirs being so thin that he could easily hear anything that was said with a louder voice, he, (Hemings) was reading in his parlour late at night, when he heard one coming into the neighbouring parlour, and say with a doleful voice, The Prince of Wales is dead. Upon which a great many that lived in the house very quickly came down stairs. Upon this confusion he could not hear anything more—but it was plain they were in great consternation. He went the next morning with the News to the Bishops in the Tower.

The Countess of Clarendon came there soon after, and told them she had been at the young Prince's door, but was denied access. She was amazed at it, and asked if they knew her. They said they did, but that the Queen had ordered that no person whatsoever should be allowed to come in to him. This gave credit to Hemings' story, and looked as if all was ordered to be kept shut up close, till another child was found. One that saw the child two days after, said to me, 'that he looked strong and not like a child so newly born'. Windebank met Walgrave the day after this birth and reminded him of what he had told him eight weeks before. He acknowledged what he had said, but added 'that God wrought miracles', to which no reply could or durst be made by the other. It needed none. So healthy a child, being so little like any of those the Queen had borne, it was given out that he had fits and could not live. But those who saw him every day observed no such thing. On the contrary, the child was in a very prosperous state. None of those fits ever happened when the Princess was at Court, for she could not be denied admittance, though all others were. So this was believed to be given out, to make the matter more credible.

Thus I have related all such particulars as I could gather of his birth, to which some more shall be added, when I give an account of the proof that the King brought afterwards to put this matter out of doubt, but by which it became indeed more doubtful than ever. I took most of these from the informations that were sent over to the Prince and Princess of Orange as I had many from the vouchers themselves. The Queen seemed to be soon recovered, and was so little altered by her labour, either in her looks or voice that this helped not a little to increase jealousies . . .

So strong was the rumour about the switch that King James assembled the Privy Council and other nobles to whom he said: 'I have called you together upon a very extraordinary occasion, but extraordinary diseases must have extraordinary remedies. The malicious endeavours of my enemies have so poisoned the minds of some of my subjects that by the reports I have from all hands, I have reason to believe that many do think that this son whom God has pleased to bless me with, to be none of mine, but a supposed child. But I may say that by a particular Providence, scarce any Prince was born where there were so many persons present. I have taken this time to have the matter heard and examined here, expecting that the Prince of Orange with the first Easterly wind will invade the Kingdom; and therefore I thought it necessary to have it now done, in order to satisfy the minds of my subjects, and to prevent this Kingdom being engaged in blood and confusion after my decease.'

King James, besides writing a gory account of the birth, still preserved in Windsor Castle, then called forty witnesses, all of whom swore that it was not a changeling. Among them was the Countess of Sunderland, who said that she went to St James's Chapel at 8 a.m. but before she could take Holy Communion was summoned to the Queen. As soon as the Queen saw her she told her that she believed her hour was come, by which time the bed had been warmed and the Queen got into it. This is strong testimony to the time when the warming-pan was used.

The royal family was so unpopular at this moment that the public found it easy to believe that the Queen had never been pregnant, or that if she had been, the child was indeed a changeling.

One pamphleteer claimed that the real mother was a Mrs Mary Grey who lived in two small rooms attached to the suite of the Marchioness of Powis in the narrow gallery which led to the Roman Catholic chapel.

An alleged eye-witness claimed that as he was standing in the gallery he saw a woman come from Mrs Grey's bedroom and go with a warming-pan into the Queen's bedroom. Fuller, the pamphleteer, asked why the Queen was left alone not long before she gave birth and why was the bed not aired but standing in the next room, which enabled the warming-pan to be brought in? Fuller later admitted that his story was a fabrication. But it was the final straw, and when news came of the arrival of William of Orange at Torbay not long afterwards, the King was deserted by most of his troops as well as by his daughter Anne, then living at St James's Palace. Anne had been put in the awkward predicament of taking sides against either her father, James II, or her sister, Mary, and brother-in-law, William. She chose to support the latter and sent a secret message to him to say that she was intending to escape. To facilitate this she had a private staircase specially constructed to take her from her bedroom into St James's Park. Lord Dorset and the Bishop of London agreed to wait for her there with a hackney coach at 1 a.m. if she could keep the rendezvous. Not trusting her lady-in-waiting, Mrs Danvers, Anne went to bed in the antechamber and waited for Lady Fitzharding, whose sister was the mistress of William of Orange. She and Lady Churchill came up the secret staircase, collected her, and as the clock struck one, stole out into the black November night.

It was pouring with rain and St James's Park was so muddy that the Princess lost one of her high-heeled shoes. By this time Lord Dorset had appeared in the darkness and while she tried to hop forward on one foot he pulled off his leather gauntlet glove and begged her to let him put it on her foot as some protection against the mud. This was done and they made good their escape.

William of Orange now marched into London. King James sent a message offering St James's Palace as his headquarters so that the two of them could discuss state affairs. He received no official answer, but the hint was dropped to him that it would be advisable for him to leave the country. This he did by frigate to France. On the day he left, Dutch guards were sent to take charge of all the sentry duties at St James's Palace. Lord Craven, the commanding officer, refused to take orders from William of Orange and hand over. Finally, with sullen dignity he marched off with the small body of Household Troops still under his command.

Within the hour the Peers of the Realm assembled in the palace and thanked William of Orange for intervening in the affairs of the country.

Now came the question of his status. The original idea was to offer Mary the throne but she refused to allow him to be merely Prince Consort. He, too, said he was not prepared to be her gentleman usher, with the result that it was suggested that he alone should be crowned King. This plan was also shelved and it was at last arranged to crown them as joint sovereigns.

In Mary's retinue was Elizabeth Villiers, a cousin of the notorious Barbara. Mary did not seem to mind that she was already William's mistress. Not that she had any looks; Jonathan Swift, indeed, swore that she squinted like a dragon. The public, however, was so used to royal mistresses that no outward resentment was shown.

William himself never achieved popularity. It was said that he was so ill-tempered that he never showed the manners of a gentleman. What is more, when he dined at the palace, no one was allowed to sit at table with him except Marshal Schomberg and some of his Dutch officers. If any English peers entered the Presence during dinner, as was the tradition of the day, they had to stand behind his chair without a word being addressed to them by the surly King, who only broke his taciturnity at night when drinking heavily with his foreign officers.

After James, who had gone to Ireland from France, was defeated at the Battle of the Boyne, Mary herself ordered the Colours which had been captured from him to be carried in triumphant procession and then hung in the Queen's Chapel of St James's Palace. The Jacobites were highly indignant. One of them, Sir Robert Strange, wrote the following:

ON SEEING THE COLOURS HUNG IN ST JAMES'S CHAPEL

> Walking the Park, I, to my horror, there
> Saw what from kindest hearts might force a tear,
> The trophies of a monarch openly
> Displayed in scorn before each vulgar eye
> A crime which Absalom did never do.
> Did even he to every cobbler show
> The relics of his father's overthrow?

This chapel, which until then had been used purely for Roman Catholic worship, was now lent to French Protestants. In the meantime, Princess Anne and her husband, Prince George of Denmark, took up residence in St James's Palace, William and Mary having moved across to Whitehall Palace. Other occupants of St James's Palace included Lord Peterborough, the Earl of Scarbrough, the Duke of Leeds and half a dozen other members of the nobility.

Not long afterwards, the first of two major fires broke out in Whitehall Palace. Mary, who was a very heavy sleeper, nearly lost her life. She was dragged, semi-conscious, in her nightdress into St James's Park where, incidentally, Colonel Oglethorpe and Sir John Fenwick, who had been devoted to her father, followed her all the way to St James's Palace, cursing her by the lurid light of the flames and telling her that the sins against her father would come home to roost. (Sure enough, she died three years later of smallpox.)

The year 1697 marked a milestone in the history of St James's Palace. Whitehall Palace was completely burned down, twelve people dying in the flames and all the pictures and other treasures being destroyed. It was thus necessary to appoint a new

Court. From that time onwards St James's Palace became known as the Court of St James, to which all foreign ambassadors were and still are accredited, and the rambling palace was enlarged for Princess Anne and her husband.

Among the guests in 1698 was Peter the Great. One evening, dining at the palace with King William, he was asked what he thought of Greenwich Hospital, which he had just visited. 'Extremely well, Sir,' he replied. 'Indeed, if I were permitted to advise your Majesty I should recommend you to remove your Court there and convert your palace into a hospital.'

There are many anecdotes about Peter's stay in England. For example, he received King William in his shirt-sleeves in the house in Buckingham Street, Strand, where he had asked to stay for the first few days of his visit, and the air was so foul that notwithstanding the bitter weather it was necessary to open a window. From this house he called on Princess Anne and Prince George at St James's Palace. Princess Anne made a deep impression on him. Next he visited the Tower, the Mint and the Observatory in the company of Lord Carmarthen, who bought the monopoly of the tobacco trade in Russia from him.

Smoking had been a capital crime in Russia for the previous fifty years. In spite of this, the use of tobacco became so prevalent that Peter the Great made smoking legal. Lord Carmarthen paid twenty thousand gold sovereigns for the monopoly. For this he was allowed to export a million and a half pounds of tobacco every year.

Peter and William III had become close friends, and William persuaded him to have his portrait painted at the palace by Sir Godfrey Kneller. Soon after his arrival in London, however, he moved to Deptford where he occupied Sayes Court, the house of John Evelyn, so that he could be as close to the ship-building yards as possible. Apparently he was a thoroughly bad tenant. Evelyn's man-servant wrote, 'the house is full of people and right nasty. The Czar lies next to your library and dines in the parlour next to your study. He dines at 10 o'clock and sups at 6 at night.' Later Evelyn persuaded Sir Christopher Wren, the King's Surveyor as he then was, to estimate the damage done. He was given a grant of £350, a very considerable sum of money in those days.

Apart from a week at Portsmouth where he was present at the Naval Review at Spithead, Peter the Great spent most of his time at Deptford. He dressed as an ordinary seaman and frequently rose at 4 a.m. During his stay he signed contracts with sixty technical experts, including a hydraulic engineer, to return with him to Russia. Before his departure he attended a session of the House of Commons but was so anxious to remain incognito that he looked down from a hole in the ceiling. He also revisited the Mint to obtain ideas about altering the Russian coinage. His last action before leaving in the yacht *Transport Royal*, given him by King William, was to present him at St James's Palace with an enormous uncut diamond.

* * *

Any building over four hundred years old cannot fail to have at least one documented ghost story connected with it. St James's Palace is no exception. The Duchess of Mazarin became a close friend of Madame de Beauclair, one of the mistresses of James II. At first they lived in the lap of luxury in St James's Palace but as time went on, both were dropped by their protectors, and in lieu of more engaging company, became mutual friends. Their discussions turned on the immortality of the soul and the possibility of reappearing on this earth. They made a compact that the one who died first should come back and tell the other all that she had learned about the future life. The Duchess was the first to go. Time passed on. One day Madame de Beauclair began talking to a friend about the Life Everlasting, then suddenly said, with great fervour, that she could not believe there was any such thing, explaining that her compact with the late Duchess was responsible for her agnosticism. A few weeks later, so the narrator of the story says:

> I happened to be at the house of a person of condition, who since the death of the Duchess, had the greatest intimacy with any of her acquaintance. We were just sitting down to cards, about 9 o'clock in the evening, as near as I can remember, when a servant came into the room with all speed, and told the lady with whom I was engaged in conversation that Madame de Beauclair had sent to entreat her to come at once, and not on any account to delay if she wished to see her again alive. The lady was considerably

83

surprised to receive this message, and at once made inquiries of the bearer of the note, who turned out to be no less than Madame de Beauclair's groom of the chambers, as to his mistress's state of health; and upon his assuring her that he had not heard of anything amiss, she manifested her vexation and replied, 'I desire you'll make my excuse, as I have really a great cold, and am fearful the night air may increase it; but tomorrow I will not fail to call upon her very early in the morning.' The messenger left, but before very long came back, not alone this time, but accompanied by a Mrs Ward (Madame de Beauclair's maid), and both, on arrival, seemed breathless and agitated. 'Oh, Madame,' cried Mrs Ward, 'my lady expresses an infinite concern that you refuse this request, which, she says, will be her last. She says that she is convinced of not being in a condition to receive your visit tomorrow, but as a token of friendship she sends you a casket containing her watch, chain, necklace and other trinkets.'

The lady, upon hearing this message, was naturally anxious to elicit information from Mrs Ward, who seemed equally desirous of avoiding conversation, assuring her that she had left only an under-maid with her mistress, and that consequently she must return as soon as possible. Upon this, the lady said that she would at once accompany Mrs Ward, for she felt sure within herself that something must be wrong. As soon as Madame de Beauclair was told that her friend was in the house, she begged that she might be asked to come upstairs at once with the gentleman who accompanied her.

Upon entering the room, the lady found Madame sitting in an armchair close to the bedside, and, to all appearances, in the most robust health. Inquiries were at once made by the friend whether Madame de Beauclair could in any way account for the strange feelings and presentiments which possessed her; upon which the latter replied in the negative, yet adding with considerable emotion, 'You will soon behold me pass from this world into that eternity which I once doubted but am now assured of.' Madame's friends did what they could to cheer her, and tried to impress upon her the importance of not giving way to such gloomy thoughts, when suddenly she said, 'Talk no more of that; my time is short, and I would not have the small space allowed me to be with you wasted in vain delusion. Know (she continued) I have seen my dear Duchess of Mazarin. I perceived not how she entered; but, turning my eyes towards yonder corner of the room,

I saw her stand in the same form and habit she was accustomed to appear in when living. Fain would I have spoken to her, but I had not the power of utterance. She took a little circuit round the chamber, seeming rather to swim than walk, then stopped by the side of that Indian chest', pointing with her hand to a piece of furniture in one corner of the room, 'looking at me, she said, "Remember, between the hours of 12 and 1 this night you will be with me." The surprise I was in at first being a little abated, I began to ask some questions concerning that future world I was soon to visit; but on the opening of my lips for that purpose, the duchess vanished from my sight—I know not how!'

Time passed on. The clock was now close upon the stroke of twelve. Yet Madame de Beauclair's companions did not perceive the slightest symptoms to alarm them, and so they again tried to allay her apprehensions as best they could; but they had scarcely spoken when they noticed that her countenance had changed, and they heard her cry, 'Oh, I am sick at heart.' Mrs Ward and those in the room did what they could to restore animation, but all to no purpose. In about half an hour the action of the heart ceased, and Madame de Beauclair passed into that world whither her friend had preceded her, and at the precise time foretold by the apparition.

7. *Corruption in the Court*

DURING this phase in the history of St James's Palace Anne's husband, Prince George, took to the bottle and persuaded her to follow his example, in spite of the remonstrances of Bishop Burnet. Burnet was a great moralist and soon realized that the ladies of the Court were not looking at him while he was preaching 'his thunderous long sermons', as Queen Mary had called them, but instead turned their attention to and ogled the courtiers. With some difficulty he persuaded Anne to raise all the pews in the chapel so high that only he could be seen in the pulpit. His action was imitated by clergymen all over the country but he found no favour with the ladies of the Court, who said that it was bad enough to have to listen to him without having to look at him at the same time. One of the gentlemen of the Court, probably Lord Peterborough, composed the following ballad:

> When Burnet perceived that the beautiful dames
> Who flocked to the Chapel of holy St James,
> On their lovers alone their kind looks did bestow,
> And smiled not at him when he bellowed below,
>   To the Princess he went,
>   With a pious intent.
> This dangerous ill in the Church to prevent.
> 'Oh Madam!' he said, 'our religion is lost
> If the ladies thus ogle the knights of the toast.
>
> Your Highness observes how I labour and sweat
> Their affections to raise and attention to get:
> And sure when I preach all the world will agree
> That their eyes and their ears should be pointed to me:

But now I can find
No beauty so kind
My parts to regard or my person to mind;
Nay I scarce have the sight of one feminine face,
But those of old Oxford or ugly Arglass.

Those sorrowful matrons, with hearts full of ruth,
Repent for the manifold sins of their youth.
The rest with their tattle my harmony spoil,
And Burlington, Anglesey, Kingston and Boyle
Their minds entertain
With fancies profane,
That not even at Church their tongues will restrain
E'en Henningham's shape their glances entice,
And rather than me they will ogle the vice!

These practices, Madame, my preaching disgrace
Shall laymen enjoy the just rights of my place?
Then all may lament my condition so hard,
Who thrash in the pulpit without a reward.
Therefore, pray condescend
Such disorders to end,
And to the ripe vineyard the labourers send
To build up the seats that the beauties may see
The face of no brawling pretender but me.'

The Princess, by the man's importunity prest,
Though she laughed at his reasons, allowed his request:
And now Britain's nymphs, in a Protestant reign,
Are locked up at prayers like the virgins in Spain.

Not so long afterwards, William III fell off his horse, broke
a collar-bone and died from the resulting illness; so the Crown
passed to Anne. As her ultimate epitaph said very truly, 'I am
Queen Anne of whom 'tis said, I am chiefly known for being
dead.' She was a very dull woman. Her three claims to personal
fame are that she gave birth to fifteen children, not one of whom
reached the age of maturity, that she inaugurated Ascot as a
race-course and gave her name to a brand of Scotch Whisky.

One of the first acts of her reign was to pass the following
Royal Orders on 15 January 1703.

The following regulations shall be observed in St James's
Park and the keeper and his servants, gate keepers, etc., shall
take care that they are duly obeyed.

1. No groom, coachman or other person shall ride on the grass.
2. No coaches or carts shall go on the grass.
3. No public passage shall be suffered through the park with carts.
4. No rude, disorderly people or beggars or rude boys shall be admitted into the park.
5. No person shall be permitted to sell anything there.
6. No persons shall be suffered to walk on the grass but only on the gravelled path or in the Mall, except only such as are employed in the park about planting and pruning the trees and other work.
7. The park-keepers and others above mentioned are to take care to keep hogs and dogs out of the park.

These were supplemented on the following 20 May by regulations which 'shall be observed in St James's Park under pain of the Queen's displeasure'.

1. Sentinels or gatekeepers to be placed at every public gate leading into the park, and directions given them by the Deputy Ranger not to admit any ordinary or mean people, beggars or dogs into the park, nor any persons who carry any sort of burthens.
2. No coaches whatever to be admitted to the park except those bearing the Queen's livery or that of the Prince Consort, 'except the Duke of Buckingham, and only from his house through St James's Mews passage into St James's Street and no otherwise, and except also the Earl of Bradford'.
3. No public carting to be made through the park, but only employees engaged in repairing the park to be allowed to cart.
4. Nobody to ride through or about St James's Park on horseback, except only Henry Wise.
5. No person to walk on the grass, but on the Mall or gravelled foot-path, and in all wet weather to walk only on the gravelled foot-paths and not on the Mall; and that no person be admitted to walk in the park with pattens.
6. No person to go into the wilderness or plantation where the deer lie, nor to disturb them or any of the wild fowls, nor to disturb the colts or fillies.
7. No person to make any doors, passages or encroachments

into the park or throw down or demolish any of the park walls.

8. No person to presume to sell anything whatsoever in the park or dry any linen therein.

9. The officer on guard to send a corporal and soldiers when necessary to assist the keepers in enforcing these regulations and bringing offenders before a justice of the Peace.

10. Nor shall any person by any grant or pretence receive any money or gratuity for any doors to passages open to the park, the same being at pleasure and permitted gratis.

A splendidly vivid account of St James's Palace, gardens and Fair at this time is provided by Ned Ward in his *London Spy*. Thus:

'Now,' says my friend, 'I believe we are both tired with the labours of the day, let us therefore dedicate the latter part purely to our pleasure, take a coach, and go see May Fair.'

So we took leave of the Temple, turned up without Temple-Bar, and there took coach for the general rendezvous aforementioned.

By the help of a great many slashes and Hey-ups, and after as many jolts and jumbles, we were dragged to the fair, where the harsh sound of untunable trumpets, the catterwauling scrapes of thrashing fidlers, the grumbling of beaten calves-skin, and the discording toots of broken organs set my teeth on edge, like the filing of a handsaw, and made my hair stand as bolt upright as the quills of an angry porcupine.

We ordered the coach to drive through the body of the fair that we might have the better view of the tinsery heroes, and the gazing multitude, expecting to have seen several corporations of strolling vagabonds; but there proved but one company, amongst whome Merry Andrew was very busie in coaxing the attentive crowd into a good opinion of his fraternities and his own performances, and when, with abundance of labour, sweat and nonsense, he had drawn a great cluster of the mob on his parade, and was just beginning to encourage them to walk in and take their places, his unlucky opposite, whose boarded theatre entertained the publick with the wonderful activity of Indian Rope Dancers, brings out a couple of chattering homunculusses, drest up in scaramouch habit; and everything that Merry Andrew and his second did on the other side, was mimicked by the little flat-nos'd comedians. On the other side the two diminutive buffoons, by their comical gestures had so prevailed upon the gaping throng that though Merry Andrew had taken pains with all the wit he had to collect the straggling rabble into very proper order, yet like unmannerly audience, they turn'd their backs upon the players, and devoted themselves wholly to the monkeys, to the vexation of Tom-fool, and all the strutting train of imaginary lords and ladies. At last out comes in a country jacket, and under her arm a kitten for a nursling, and in her contrary hand a piece of cheese, a little matron with a very motherly countenance, and when her youngster mew'd, she dangled him, and rock'd him in her arms, with as great signs of affection as a loving mother could well shew to a disorder'd infant, then bites a piece of cheese and after she had mumbled it about in her mouth, then thrust it in with her tongue into the kitten's, just as I have seen nasty old slats feed their own grandchildren.

Beyond these were a parcel of scandalous boosing-Kens, where soldiers and their trulls were skipping and dancing about to most lamentable musick, performed upon a crack'd crowd by a blind fidler. In another hut, a parcel of Scotch pedlars and their moggies, dancing a Highlanders jig to a Horn-pipe. Over against 'em the Cheshire Booth, where a gentleman's man was playing more tricks with his heels in a Cheshire rind than ever were shown by the mad coffee-man at Sedlers Musickhouse. Those intermixt with here and there a Poppet-Show, where a senseless dialogue between Punchenello and the devil, was convey'd to the ears of the listening rabble thro' a tin-squeaker, which was thought by some of 'em as great a piece of conjuration as ever was performed by Dr Faustus.

We now began to look about us and take a view of the spectators, but could not, amongst the many thousands, find one man that appear'd about the degree of a gentleman's valet, nor one whore that could have the impudence to ask above six-pence wet and six-pence dry, for an hour of her cursed company. In all the multitudes that ever I beheld, I never, in my life, saw such a number of lazy, lousie-look'd rascals, and so hateful a throng of beggarly, sluttish strumpets, who were a scandal to the Creation, meer antidotes against leachery and enemies to cleanliness.

There being nothing further that occur'd, or any thing to be seen, worth notice, only a Turkey-Ram, with as much wooll upon his tail as would load a wheel-barrow, and a couple of Tygers, grown now so common they are scarce worth mentioning. For want of glasses to our coach, having drawn up our tin-sashes, pink'd like the bottom of a cullender, that the air might pass thro' the holes, and defend us from the stiffling, we were convey'd from the fair thro' a suffocating cloud of dusty atoms, to St James's Palace, in reverence to which we alighted and discharg'd our grumbling Essedartus, who stuck there close to our backsides, and mutter'd heavily, according to their old custom, for t'other Six-pence; till at last, moving us a little beyond our patience, we gave an angry positive denial to his unreasonable importunities, and so parted with our unconscionable carrion-scourger, who we found, like the rest of his fraternity, had taken up the miserly immoral rule, viz. never to be satisfied.

We passed thro' a lofty porch into the first court, where a parcel of Hob-Nail'd Loobies were gazing at the Whale's rib with great amazement; being busily consulting what creature it could be that could produce a bone of such unusual magnitude. Who should come by, in this interim, but a Fingalian conjuror, posting to (as my friend supposed) Duke Humphrey's Walk in the park to pick his teeth, and loiter away his supper-time. But seeing the country hobbies stand gaping at this puzzling rarity, he put himself amongst the rest, to deliver his judgment of this amazing object. 'I pray you, sir,' says one of the countrymen to him, 'what sort of bone do you take this to be?' To which the dear boy, after taking a little snuff, most judiciously reply'd, 'By my shoul, Egra, I believe it is the Jaw bone of the Ash, wid which Shampson killed the Philischines: and it ish nail'd up here dat no body shou'd do any mischief wid it'. 'I wonder,' said another of the plough-jobbers, 'how he could use it, 'tis such a huge unwieldy weapon?' 'By shoul', reply'd Teague, 'Let Shampson look to dat his own shelf for it ish none of my business.'

From thence we went thro' the palace into the park, about the time when the Court ladies raise their extended limbs from their downy couches, and walk into the Mall to refresh their charming bodies with the cooling and salubrious breezes of the gilded evening. We could not possibly have chose a luckier minute, to have seen the delightful park in its greatest glory and perfection; for, the brightest stars of the creation sure (that ever shone by no other power than Humane Excellence) were moving here, with such an awful state and majesty that their graceful deportment bespoke 'em goddesses. Such merciful looks were thrown from their engaging eyes upon every admiring mortal, so free from pride, envy, or contempt, that they seem'd, contrary to experience, to be sent into the world to compleat its happiness. The wonderful works of Heaven were here to be read in beauties' characters. Such elegant compositions might be observed among the female quality, that it's impossible to conceive otherwise than that such heavenly forms were perfected after the unerring image of Divine Excellence.

Having thus seen what the Mall afforded, we stept over its boarded bonds into Duke Humphrey's Walk as my friend inform'd me, where he showed me abundance of our neighbouring billfactors, distinguish'd by their flat noses and broad faces, who were walking away their leisure hours beneath the umbrage of the lime trees, etc.

From there we took a walk upon the Parade which my friend told me, us'd in a morning, to be cover'd with the bones of redherrings; and smelt as strong about breakfast time, as a wetsalters shop at Midsummer.

*　　*　　*

Once again St James's Palace had become the scene of brilliant courts and ceremonial processions, including those commemorating the Duke of Marlborough's four major victories against the French—Blenheim, Ramillies, Oudenarde and Malplaquet. It is scarcely surprising that the Duke of Marlborough's wife, the famous Sarah Churchill, became close friends with the Queen and very soon dominated her completely. According to Swift, Sarah was the victim of 'three furies which reigned in her breast. Sordid avarice, disdainful pride, ungovernable rage.'

The Duke and his wife had made a fortune out of the sale of commissions and the enormous bribes and percentages which they insisted on taking from the army contractors. Some of the returning troops, in protest, threw their wretched army jackets and clothing over the wall of the Queen's garden at St James's Palace. It is said that Anne wept at seeing 'the flimsy rags which the avarice of the generalissimo and the Jew contractors had provided for the common men to abide the damp and agueish seasons of the Low Countries'.

This behaviour, combined with the Duchess's rudeness to the Queen, proved her downfall. The finishing touch was the Duchess of Marlborough's insistence on a grant of the land on which the present Marlborough House stands. The building cost nearly £50,000.

St James's Fair, in the meantime, continued its degenerate career. According to Stype,

> between St James's and Hyde Park is kept May Fair, yearly, where young people did use to resort, and by the temptation they met with, did commit much sin and disorder. Here they spent their time and money in drunkenness, fornication, gaming, and lewdness, whereby were occasioned oftentimes quarrels, tumults, and shedding of blood. Whereupon, in the month of November 1708, the grand jury of Westminster, for the body of the county of Middlesex, make a presentment to this import, 'That being sensible of their duty, to make presentment of such matters and things as were public enormities and inconveniences, and being encouraged by the example of the worthy magistracy of the City of London in their late proceedings against Bartholomew Fair, did present, as a public nuisance and inconvenience, the yearly riotous and tumultuous assembly in a place called Brookfield, in the parish of St Martin-in-the-Fields, where persons did rendezvous, draw, and allure young persons, servants and others, to meet there to game and commit lewdness, etc.'

The Court was seldom more corrupt than during this period. Among other things, the elderly retainers played a series of confidence tricks on members of the public, promising to sell them Court appointments. One rich country bumpkin was deceived into thinking that he might become Vice-Chamberlain. He was told that Queen Anne was tired of her existing Vice-Chamberlain but £7,000 was the lowest sum required and that he must be able to talk French. Further, he must walk up and down in one of the courtyards of St James's Palace so that the Queen's foster-sister could decide whether or not he looked sufficiently distinguished for the appointment. The candidate walked up and down for a considerable time 'on view'.

One day the courtier brought his victim to see the Queen walking to St James's Chapel. As the Vice-Chamberlain led the Queen by her hand, the victim said loudly, 'Ah! sir, what happiness! I wish all our friends were here now, to see the Vice-Chamberlain handing the Queen, i'faith the place is worth t'other thousand!' Thomas Coke, the Vice-Chamberlain, overhearing this, made suitable inquiries. His would-be successor, thinking everything was above-board, told the whole story and the courtier was duly examined. It was found that he had already pocketed several dozen guineas for services to be rendered. He had also drunk two or three hampers of wine provided by his victim. The inquiry lasted a week, during which the Court was convulsed with laughter. Vice-Chamberlain Coke, finding that the Queen had every intention of keeping him in his post, decided that on the whole he had benefited from the swindle and allowed the confidence trickster to keep his small apartment in St James's Palace with no punishment except the universal ridicule to which he was subjected for the rest of his life.

Court etiquette, nevertheless, was strictly maintained throughout Queen Anne's reign. When Prince Eugène was presented to the Queen by Lord Bolingbroke minus the usual Court wig, she was with difficulty persuaded to receive him, saying, finally, that she was doing so only because of the 'particular celebrity of his character which should not be drawn into precedent'. On another occasion, an army captain who arrived with despatches from abroad arrived post-haste wearing a major wig. The Queen immediately noticed this breach of etiquette and asked how he dared to appear before her in undress? After he had apologized, he was told that if she permitted this indignity she might expect to see all her officers come into Court in boots and spurs. The captain hurried home, put on a Court wig, and was then graciously received.

The protocol of the royal toilet was indeed rigid. According to Mrs Masham, who succeeded the Duchess of Marlborough as the Queen's confidante,

> The bedchamber woman came in to waiting before the Queen's Prayers, which was before Her Majesty was dressed. The Queen often shifted in a morning; if Her Majesty shifted at noon, the bedchamber lady being by, the bedchamber woman gave the shift to the lady without any ceremony, and the lady put it on. Sometimes, likewise, the bedchamber woman gave the fan to the lady in the same manner, and this was all that the bedchamber lady did about the Queen at her dressing.
>
> When the Queen washed her hands, the page of the backstairs brought and set down upon a side table the basin and ewer; then the bedchamber woman set it before the Queen, and knelt on the other side of the table over against the Queen, the bedchamber

DUCHESS OF
PORTSMOUTH

LADY CASTLEMAINE

MARY OF MODENA

JAMES II

QUEEN ANNE

THE CROWN BEING OFFERED TO WILLIAM AND MARY

lady only looking on. The bedchamber woman poured the water out of the ewer upon the Queen's hands.

The bedchamber woman pulled on the Queen's gloves when she could not do it herself.

The page of the backstairs was called in to put on the Queen's shoes.

When the Queen dined in public the page reached the glass to the bedchamber woman, and she to the lady in waiting.

The bedchamber woman brought the chocolate, and gave it without kneeling.

In general, the bedchamber woman had no dependence on the lady of the bedchamber.

Among the occupants of the palace at this time was Henry Purcell, the composer of 'Lillibulero', the song which had laughed King James out of Ireland:

> There once was a prophecy found in a bog
> That Ireland would be ruled by an ass and a dog.
> Now the prophecy's come to pass,
> Tyrconnell's the dog and King James is the ass.

Purcell lived in a suite of rooms reached by a winding staircase in the Clock Tower. When Dryden, the poet, was being pestered by his creditors, he used to stay with Purcell for weeks at a time.

Swift was another regular visitor to the palace.

During the last few years of her reign Queen Anne was exceedingly popular. On Guy Fawkes Day the Queen's Guards made an enormous bonfire outside the gates of the palace into which they put the effigy of the Pretender. This they shot at and shouted that they only wished that they could do the same thing to the Pretender himself, who was then living in France.

Anne finally died on 1 August 1714 of an attack of apoplexy after witnessing a violent quarrel in the Council Chamber between Bolingbroke and Oxford.

8. Germans at St James's

THE next occupant of St James's Palace was King George I, and a very reluctant occupant at that. When Lord Clarendon arrived at Herrenhausen at 2 a.m. to inform him that he had been proclaimed King, although there were at least thirty or forty other people with a stronger title to the throne than he, he listened patiently, yawned, expressed a keen dislike of the whole thing, turned over, and went promptly to sleep again. So little anxious was he to take over his new dominions that he did not arrive in England for another six weeks, landing at Greenwich, from where he went direct to St James's Palace, surrounded by a large German retinue.

His first experience of English life was peculiar, as he himself remarked (in German): 'The morning after my arrival at St James's, I looked out of the window and saw a park with walks, and a canal, which, they told me, were mine. The next day Lord Chetwynd, the Ranger of my Park, sent me a fine brace of carp, out of my canal, and I was told I must give five guineas to Lord Chetwynd's servant for bringing me my own carp out of my own canal in my own Park.'

At his first official Court, a Colonel Chudleigh took exception to some jocular remark by Mr Aldworth, the M.P. for New Windsor, and in the ensuing argument called him the rudest thing he could think of, namely, a Jacobite—this within a few feet of the throne. Aldworth called him out. They left the throne room and drove together to Marylebone Fields. Within a matter of minutes the gallant Colonel stretched Aldworth dead on the ground and returned alone to the palace.

The first Drawing-Room—the royal occasions when notables

were presented to the King and Queen—also produced an intriguing situation. By some strange coincidence, the Duchess of Portsmouth, who had had several bastards by Charles II, the Countess of Dorchester, who had done the same thing for King James, and the Countess of Orkney, who had been William III's mistress, found themselves side by side in front of the King. Lady Dorchester, famous for her coarse witticisms, exclaimed, 'Good God, who would have thought that we three whores should have met here?'

George himself had, at the age of twenty-one, married his sixteen-year-old cousin Sophia of Zelle, a delightful girl who, ten years after her marriage, was involved in a passionate love affair with Count Königsmarck. The Count was murdered and the following year George divorced her and imprisoned her for life in the Castle of Ahlden. Their two small children were taken from her and she was never permitted to see them again. It is possible that the King's doubt about the parentage of his only son had much to do with his ultimate hatred of him.

Lord Chesterfield, writing of George I, said:

> George the First was an honest, dull, German gentleman as unfit as unwilling to act the part of a King (which is to shine and to oppress), lazy and inactive even in his pleasures, which were therefore lowly sensual. He was coolly intrepid and indolently benevolent. He was diffident of his own parts which made him speak little in public, and prefer in his social, which were his favourite hours, the company of wags and buffoons. Even his mistress, the Duchess of Kendal, with whom he passed most of his time, and who had all influence over him, was very little above an idiot. Importunity alone could make him act, and then only to get rid of it. His views and affections were singly confined to the narrow compass of his Electorate; England was too big for him . . . The King loved pleasure and was not delicate in his choice of it. No women came amiss to him if they were very willing and very fat. . . . The standard of his Majesty's taste made all those ladies who aspired to his favour, and who were near the suitable size, strain and swell themselves like the frogs in the fable to rival the bulk and dignity of the ox. Some succeeded and others burst.

Although George I had brought his son and heir (the future George II) with him to St James's Palace, he had instructed his daughter-in-law, the former Caroline of Ansbach, to stay behind for a few weeks. When she arrived, her duties as Princess of Wales began almost immediately. The Court lacked a Queen and all that the presence of a Queen implied. Caroline did her best but it was not easy, in view of the King's jealousy. Nevertheless she was unquestionably the first lady of the land and her earlier training at the Court of Berlin stood her in good stead at St James's Palace. She and her husband were at least able to speak English, unlike George I, though when she became excited she would utter a mixture of French, English and German.

From the start she claimed to be a great Anglophile, saying that she would as soon live on a dung-hill as return to Hanover. Every day she and her husband became more popular and appointments in her Household were greatly sought. Among the first to be taken on were the Duchess of Bolton, the illegitimate daughter of the Duke of Monmouth, the Duchess of St Albans, wife of the illegitimate son of Charles II by Nell Gwynne, and Mrs Howard, in spite of the fact that she was the Prince of Wales's mistress.

The Court was indeed far less exclusive than it had been during the reign of Queen Anne. The wife of the Venetian ambassador was so hustled one night that she cried aloud, 'Don't touch my face.' Whereupon the King turned to a courtier and said, 'Don't you hear the ambassadress? She offers you all the rest of her body provided you don't touch her face.'

The Duchess of Bolton often recommended plays to George I. At one of the parties in St James's Palace she told him how much she had enjoyed Colley Cibber's *Love's Last Shift*. The King, not understanding the title, asked her to translate it into French. 'La Dernière Chemise de l'Amour', she answered gravely.

George was in no way majestic. He disliked uniforms and usually appeared in a shabby brown suit, liberally sprinkled with snuff. He ate too much and he drank too much and was too old to change his habits. He disliked ceremonial occasions and after the first year of his reign left almost everything to the Princess of Wales, while he spent his evenings with one of his mistresses, smoking a pipe, drinking German beer or playing ombre. To these parties few of his English subjects were ever invited. A notable exception was Lady Mary Wortley Montagu, daughter of the profligate Duke of Kingston. As a girl she had been allowed to run wild among the stables and kennels of her father's country place. Nevertheless she taught herself Latin, Greek and French. Having eloped with Wortley Montagu, who became a Lord of the Treasury, she immediately created a sensation at Court and the Prince of Wales soon began to pay her marked attention. This soon wore off, however, when he discovered that she had so many favours shown to her by his father.

Lady Mary Wortley Montagu gives a real close-up of the King's character.

In private life he would have been called an honest blockhead, and Fortune, that made him a king, added nothing to his happiness, only prejudiced his honesty and shortened his days. No man was ever more free from ambition; he loved money, but loved to keep his own, without being rapacious of other men's. He would have grown rich by saving, but was incapable of laying schemes for getting more; he was more properly dull than lazy, and would have been so well contented to have remained in his little town of Hanover, that if the ambition of those about him had not been greater than his own, we should never have seen him in England; and the natural honesty of his temper, joined with the narrow notions of a low education, made him look upon his acceptance of the Crown as an act of usurpation, which was always uneasy to him. But he was carried by the stream of the people about him, in that, as in every action of his life.

He could speak no English and was past the age of learning it. Our customs and laws were all mysteries to him, which he neither tried to understand, nor was capable of understanding if he had endeavoured it. He was passively good-natured, and wished all mankind enjoyed quiet, if they would let him do so. The mistress that followed him hither, (the Countess of Schulenberg), was so much of his own temper, that I do not wonder at the engagement between them. She was duller than himself, and consequently did not find out that he was so; and had lived in Hanover almost forty year, (for she came hither at threescore), without meddling in any affairs of the Electorate; content with the small pension he allowed her, and the honour of his visits when he had nothing else to do, which happened very often. She even refused coming hither at first, fearing that the people of England, who, she thought, were accustomed to use their kings barbarously, might

chop off his head in the first fortnight; and had not love or gratitude enough to venture being involved in his ruin. So the poor
man was in peril of coming hither without knowing where to pass
his evenings; which he was accustomed to do in the apartments
of women, free from business. But Madame Kilmansegg saved him
from his misfortune. She was told that Madame Schulenberg
scrupled the terrible journey, and took the opportunity of offering
her service to his Majesty, who willingly accepted of it, though he
did not offer to facilitate it to her by the payment of her debts,
which made it very difficult for her to leave Hanover without the
permission of her creditors. But she was a woman of wit and
spirit, and knew very well of what importance this step was to
her fortune. She got out of the town in disguise, and made the
best of her way in a post-chaise to Holland, from whence she embarked with the King, and arrived at the same time with him in
England, which was enough to make her called his mistress, or
at least so great a favourite that the whole Court began to pay her
uncommon respect.

This lady deserved I should be a little particular in her
character, there being something in it worth speaking of. She was
past forty; she had never been a beauty, but certainly very agreeable in her person when adorned by youth, and had once appeared
so charming to the King, that it was said the divorce and ruin of
his beautiful Princess, the Duke of Zelle's daughter, was owing
to the hopes of her mother (who was declared mistress to the
King's father in her place) and that the project did not succeed,
by the passion which Madame Kilmansegg took for M. Kilmansegg, who was son of a merchant of Hamburgh, and, after having
a child by him, there was nothing left for her but to marry him.
Her ambitious mother ran mad with the disappointment, and died
in that deplorable manner, leaving 40,000 pounds which she had
heaped by the favour of the Elector, to this daughter, which was
very easily squandered by one of her temper. She was both
luxurious and generous, devoted to her pleasures, and seemed to
have taken Lord Rochester's resolution of avoiding all sorts of
self-denial. She had a greater vivacity in conversation than ever
I knew in a German of either sex. She loved reading, and had a
taste of all polite learning. Her humour was easy and sociable.
Her constitution inclined her to gallantry. She was well-bred and
amusing in company. She knew both how to please and be pleased
and had experience enough to know it was hard to do either without money. Her unlimited expenses had left her with very little

remaining, and she made what haste she could to make advantage
of the opinion the English had of her power with the King, by
receiving the presents that were made her from all quarters, and
which she knew very well must cease when it was known that the
King's idleness carried him to her lodgings without either regard
for her advice, or affection for her person, which time and very
bad paint had left without any of the clearness which had once
attracted him.

Altogether, George I brought a hundred Germans, both men
and women, with him from Hanover. In addition, he was accompanied by Mustapha and Mahomet, a couple of Turks. They
were appointed pages of the backstairs and ponced for him. In
addition to his ministers, he brought doctors, trumpeters, a
chaplain, even a washerwoman. There was also, of course,
Madame von Schulenberg, already described by Lady Mary,
whom he lodged in St James's Palace and who acted as his
hostess. Like all royal mistresses she was very mercenary and
made a fortune handing over State offices when appointed
Master of the Horse.

Not surprisingly, the general public thoroughly disliked these
foreign mistresses. (At least Charles and James had usually
picked English girls for their seraglios.) One day, when Madame
von Schulenberg and another of the royal harem were on their
way back to St James's Palace, a hooting mob surrounded their
coach. Von Schulenberg put her head out of the window and in
broken English cried, 'Goot people, vy you abuse us? We only
come for your goots.'

'Ay, damn ye, and for our chattels too,' some wit retorted
smartly.

Von Schulenberg could at least speak some kind of English,
which is more than King George ever did. Too idle to learn the
language of the country he ruled, he was forced to speak in
French or even Latin to those who did not know German,
which meant practically everybody.

This refusal to speak English was the direct origin of the
system of the Government ruling by Cabinet in the absence of the
monarch. At his first meeting with the Privy Council he told his
Ministers that he knew nothing about the English Constitution
and therefore placed himself entirely in their hands and would

govern through them. 'Then,' he added, 'you will become completely answerable for everything I do.' Thereafter he never again presided over the meetings, as all previous English monarchs had done, and ever since then government meetings have been held without the presence of the Sovereign.

Another of his early actions was to call in Sir Christopher Wren and Sir John Vanbrugh to renovate St James's Palace. The Minute Book of the Board of Works shows that estimates had to be made for a new backstairs for the young Princesses and a parquet floor for the Countess of Schulenberg. In addition, the music gallery was refitted. Extensions which included the building of an entirely new room for the Princess of Wales at a cost of £400 were approved, an engine room was put in hand and the mews renovated. The stables were given an arcade of brick and a turret and staircase were built at the end of the coachhouses. In the following year, the kitchens and larders were extended, the wainscotting of the royal apartments was cleaned, painted and whitewashed—also the ceiling of Mahomet's bedroom under the King's apartment. Sir Christopher Wren was further responsible for two new rooms being built in Pheasant Court for the women of the bedchamber. The Duchess of Munster's bedroom was given a parquet floor and larger squares of glass were put into some of the windows.

Sir Christopher Wren was responsible for all these improvements over a period of three years. After his departure, Grinling Gibbons joined the Commissioners of H.M. Works. Once again, Mahomet benefited. A pair of small deal doors was made at the head of the staircase leading to his room and a small closet for his own use was added.

An odd entry occurs in January 1722: 'Ordered, that the removing of the windows in the King's Kitchen of St James's to prevent the young Princesses being annoyed by the steaming and stinks thereof, to be respited until the Lady Portland's pleasure be known thereon.'

A special door to enable the Duchess of Kendal to escape from the old building in case of fire was the next improvement. It may be noted that the cost of alterations to Mahomet's room amounted to £259 19s 4½d. Another £212 6s 9d was the price of decorating Mustapha's rooms. The building of the engine house cost £210 15s 9d. Fitting up the kitchen for the Board of Green Cloth was another expensive item. A new confectionery was also added to the kitchens.

Two years later the King announced his intention of revisiting his beloved Hanover, greatly to the distress of the Government. He told them, however, that he was going whether or not they liked it. This meant that a Regent or a Council of Regency had to be appointed. It was naturally assumed that the Prince of Wales would be appointed as Regent, but the King objected. Finally, he yielded to the extent of naming his son 'Guardian of the Realm and Lieutenant', an office unknown since the days of the Black Prince.

Nobody regretted his departure, least of all the Prince of Wales (the future George II) and his wife Caroline. They kept open house at St James's Palace until the end of July 1716 when they moved temporarily to Hampton Court. George I returned at the end of November to open Parliament.

The relations between him and the Prince of Wales now became increasingly strained. They rarely spoke to one another in public, seldom met in private, and the Prince's friends were regarded by the King as his enemies. The situation had been aggravated by the fact that both the Prince and the King lived in St James's Palace. The final rupture occurred at St James's Palace in the bedchamber of the Princess of Wales.

It seems [says Walpole], that the Princess had but a few weeks previously been delivered of a child, and the Prince proposed to the King that he and the Bishop of Osnaburg should stand godfathers to the infant. The King, however, took exception to the name of the Bishop of Osnaburg, and wished Thomas, Duke of Newcastle, to be godfather in his stead, though His Majesty knew that the Prince had a peculiar dislike to this nobleman . . . On one side of the bed stood the godfathers and godmother, on the other the Prince and Princess's ladies. No sooner had the Bishop closed the ceremony than the Prince crossing the foot of the bed in a rage, stepped up to the Duke of Newcastle, and holding up his hand and forefinger in a menacing attitude, said 'You are a rascal, but I shall find you', meaning, no doubt, that he would find a way to be avenged.

The wretched Princess tried to get out of bed. The Archbishop protested. The Prince strutted up and down like a turkey-cock,

cursing and swearing, while the Duke of Newcastle hurried off
to tell the King.

The King too was greatly enraged, regarding the attack upon
the duke as an insult offered to himself, and Schulenberg and Kilmansegg were greatly shocked by this filial disrespect. The Duke
believed, or pretended to believe, that the Prince had said: 'I
will fight you!' and so had practically challenged him to a duel.

The long-smouldering resentment of the King burst into flame;
he had more self-control than his son. He did not stamp about
and make scenes, but his anger was more deadly. When he had
relieved his feelings by a few round oaths, he gave orders that the
Prince be put under arrest. The Princess declared that if her
husband were arrested she would be arrested too, and so he
remained the night in his wife's chamber under guard.

As soon as he heard this, Walpole told the King that the
heir to the throne could really not be shut up in his room as if
he were an eighteenth-century juvenile delinquent. While the
King seriously wanted to put both the Prince and Princess in the
Tower, Walpole persuaded him against this and he merely
ordered them to leave St James's Palace, which they were only
too pleased to do. Next, he sent a formal announcement to all
the foreign ambassadors, peers and Privy Councillors, to say that
if any of them received the Prince they would be *persona non
grata* at St James's Palace. More cruelly still, the King ordered
the baby, which had been temporarily allowed to stay at the
palace, to be moved to Kensington. It did not survive the journey. The lampoonists of the day were quick on the job. Here
is a typical comment:

> God prosper long our noble King
>   His Turks and Germans all,
> A woeful christ'ning late there did
>   In James's house befal.

> To name a child with might and main
>   Newcastle took his way,
> We all may rue the child was born,
>   Who christ'ned was that day.

> His sturdy sire, the Prince of Wales,
>   A vow to God did make,
> That if he dared his child to name
>   His heart full sore should ache.

But on the day straight to the Court
　This Duke came with a staff;
Oh, how the Prince did stamp and stare,
　At which the Duke did laugh.

Hereat the Prince did wax full wroth
　Ev'n in his father's hall;
'I'll be revenged on thee,' he said,
　'Thou rogue and eke rascal.'

The Duke ran straightway to the King,
　Complaining of his son;
And the King sent three Dukes more
　To know what he had done.

The King then took his grey goose-quill
　And dipt it o'er in gall,
And by Master Vice-Chamberlain
　He sent to him this scrawl:

'Take hence yourself, and eke your spouse,
　Your maidens, and your men,
Your trunks, and all your trumpery,
　Except your children.'

Then up the street they took their way,
　And knocked up good Lord Grantham,
Higledy-pigledy they lay,
　And all went rantum scantum.

Now sire and son had played their part;
　What could befal beside?
Why, the babe took this to heart,
　Kick'd up his heels, and died.

God grant the land may profit reap,
　From all this silly pother,
And send these fools may ne'er agree
　Till they are at Han-o-ver.

George I continued to live mostly at St James's, his next mistress being Sophia Charlotte, sister of the Countess of Platen. As time passed on she grew immensely fat and the younger Walpole recalls as a boy being frightened by her enormous figure and 'the fierce black eyes, large and rolling beneath two lofty arched eyebrows, two acres of cheeks, spread with crimson, an ocean of neck that overflowed, and was not distinguished from the lower part of her body, and no part restrained by stays'.

* * *

Daniel Defoe recorded his impressions when he visited St James's Palace in 1724:

> Though the winter receptacle of all the pomp and glory of this kingdom, it is really mean in comparison with the glorious Court of Great Britain. The splendour of the nobility, the wealth and greatness of the attendants, the economy of the house, and the real grandeur of the whole royal family, outdo all the courts of Europe; and yet this palace comes beneath those of the most petty princes in it: although there cannot be in the world a nobler situation for a royal palace than Whitehall. And it is with some concern, that we see so fine a spot become a sacrifice to private sport, so much of it being given away to particular families, as makes more remote, than we might otherwise expect, the hope of seeing a palace built there, worthy of the glory of our monarchs.
>
> Many plans have been drawn for the rebuilding of this palace; but the most celebrated draughts are those of Inigo Jones, and may be seen in Mr Campbell's Vitruvius Britannicus, and Mr Kent's edition of Jones's works. The last of these, if executed, would, for magnificence and beauty, transcend even the temple of Solomon, if we are to form a judgment from the plans given of that famous edifice. But it is a question whether the expense would not exceed that of St Peter's at Rome, which cost forty-millions of Roman crowns.

Meanwhile, the King was unable to take away the Prince's allowance of £100,000 without the permission of Parliament. Nor could he prevent him from being the official heir to the throne, but he did everything possible to humiliate him and his daughter-in-law. They were deprived of all official marks of distinction. Worse still, he deprived them of their children. The three young princesses, Anne, Amelia and Caroline, were kept at St James's Palace, while the Prince and Princess established themselves at Leicester House; Leicester Square being the fashionable part of the town in those days.

Once again, George I returned to Hanover, accompanied by the Duchess of Kendal. On his return, through the mediation of Walpole, a temporary reconciliation was effected between father and son at St James's Palace and Caroline was allowed to visit her children there. After the reconciliation, the Princess of Wales was restored to her position and precedence and regularly attended the Drawing-rooms in St James's Palace. George I even asked her to play Ombre and Quadrille with him, but he still maintained his resentment against the Prince of Wales. During the next few years, the Princess gave birth to three more children, one of them the notorious Duke of Cumberland.

Now came the collapse of the South Sea Bubble, the company which had been established in 1711 to relieve taxation. The public had been promised dividends of fifty per cent. Nor was it the only company which defrauded the public. Some of them were quite preposterous, such as companies to 'make salt water fresh' (not so preposterous now), 'to build hospitals for bastard children', 'for making oil from sunflower seeds' (again not so preposterous today), 'for extracting silver from lead', 'for importing a number of large jackasses from Spain', and, strangest of all, 'for an undertaking which shall in due time be revealed'. For this last scheme the trusting subscribers were invited to pay two guineas 'and hereafter receive a share of one hundred, with the disclosure of the object'. So gullible was the public that a thousand subscriptions were paid in the course of the morning. That night the promoter left the country and the object of the undertaking was disclosed. As for the South Sea Bubble, the general public felt that someone ought to be hanged and George's mistresses were suspected of having received bribes to publicize the venture.

* * *

It was George I who finally discontinued the ancient custom of touching for the King's Evil, first performed by Edward the Confessor in 1058. Dr Wiseman, Court Physician to Charles II, published a book in 1676 in which he claimed that the power of healing the King's Evil was due to the secret rays of divinity which attend kings.

The King's Evil was another name for scrofula and the number of scrofulous people in those insanitary days was very considerable. There was, of course, no guarantee that the cure would be successful and no patient was ever allowed a second chance if the touch of the royal hand failed on the first occasion. Nevertheless, crowds of people were always anxious to be healed and, according to Evelyn, several people in the reign of Charles II were trampled to death when applying for tickets to present their children to the King. During his reign nearly a hundred thousand people were touched for the Evil, and according to Dr Wiseman, they were nearly all cured.

William III was the first King to refuse to take part in the ceremony but Queen Anne revived the practice. Samuel Johnson, as a child, was brought all the way from Lichfield to be touched by Queen Anne on the advice of the celebrated Sir John Floyer, a leading physician. This is how Dr Johnson, years later, described his experience: 'I was taken to London to be touched for the evil by Queen Anne. I remember a boy crying when I went to the Palace to be touched. I shall always retain some memory of this journey although I was then but thirty months old.' When Boswell asked him if he could recall Queen Anne, he replied he had a confused but solemn recollection of a lady in diamonds and a long black hood.

The ceremony of touching took place either in the Chapel Royal or in Queen Anne's drawing-room in St James's Palace where she sat in full state. The chaplain carried a number of white ribbons on his arm, according to the number of recipients (sometimes two hundred or so) each strung with a piece of 24-carat gold. The Queen then stroked the sufferers and either placed the charms round their necks or tied them to their arms.

The service of healing was formerly part of the Book of Common Prayer. After the Collect, the Gospel (always from Saint Mark) and the Lord's Prayer, the Rubric directed that 'the infirm persons, one by one be presented to the Queen upon their knees . . . and while the Queen is laying her hands upon them and putting gold about their necks, the chaplain turning himself to her Majesty shall say these words following: God give a blessing to this work and grant that these sick persons upon whom the Queen lays her hands may recover. Through Jesus Christ Our Lord, Amen.' Further versicles and Collects followed, ending with the general benediction.

The gold medallions were regarded as talismans.

As for the morals of the Court of George I, they are made abundantly clear by Lady Mary Wortley Montagu in her letters to the Countess of Mar, among others, thus:

As for news, the last wedding is that of Peg Pelham, and I think I have never seen so comfortable a prospect of happiness; according to all appearance she cannot fail of being a widow in six weeks at farthest, and accordingly she has been so good a housewife as to line her wedding-clothes with black. Assemblies rage in this part of the world; there is not a street in two free from them, and some spirited ladies go to seven in a night. You need not question but love and play flourish under these encouragements: I now and then peep upon these things with the same coolness as I would do on a moving picture. . . .

I was told by a very good authority, who is deep in the secret, that at this very minute there is a Bill cooking-up at a hunting-seat in Norfolk, to have *not* taken out of the Commandments and clapped into the Creed, at the ensuing session of Parliament. This bold attempt for the liberty of the subject is wholly projected by Mr Walpole, who proposed it to the secret committee in his parlour. William Young seconded it, and answered for all his acquaintance voting right to a man: Doddington very gravely objected, that the obstinacy of human nature was such, that he feared when they had positive commandments to do so, perhaps people would not commit adultery and bear false witness against their neighbours with the readiness and cheerfulness they do at present. This objection seemed to sink deep into the minds of the greatest politicians at the board, and I don't know whether the bill won't be dropped, though it is certain it might be carried on with great ease, the world being entirely 'revenue de bagatelle', and honour, virtue, reputation, &c. which we used to hear of in our nursery, are as much laid aside and forgotten as crumpled ribands.

To speak plainly, I am very sorry for the forlorn state of matrimony, which is as much ridiculed by our young ladies as it used to be by young fellows: in short, both sexes have found the inconveniences of it, and the appellation of 'rake' is as genteel in a woman as in a man of quality; it is no scandal to say Miss . . ., the maid of honour, looks very well now she is up again, and poor Biddy Noel has never been quite well since her last confinement. You may imagine we married women look very silly; we have nothing to excuse ourselves, but that it was done a great while ago, and we were very young when we did it. . . .

I cannot deny, but that I was very well diverted on the Coronation day. I saw the procession much at my ease, in a house which I filled with my own company, and then got into Westminster-hall without trouble, where it was very entertaining to observe the variety of airs that all meant the same thing. The business of every walker there was to conceal vanity and gain admiration. For these purposes some languished and others strutted; but a visible satisfaction was diffused over every countenance, as soon as the coronet was clapped on the head. But she that drew the greatest number of eyes, was indisputably Lady Orkney. She exposed behind, a mixture of fat and wrinkles; and before, a very considerable protuberance which preceded her. Add to this, the inimitable roll of her eyes, and her grey hairs, which by good fortune stood directly upright, and 'tis impossible to imagine a more delightful spectacle. She had embellished all this with considerable magnificence, which made her look as big again as usual; and I should have thought her one of the largest things of God's making if my Lady St John had not displayed all her charms in honour of the day. The poor Duchess of Montrose crept along with a dozen of black snakes playing round her face; and my Lady Portland (who is fallen away since her dismission from court) represented very finely an Egyptian mummy embroidered over with hieroglyphics. In general, I could not perceive but that the old were as well pleased as the young; and I, who dread growing wise more than any thing in the world, was overjoyed to find that one can never outlive one's vanity. . . .

The sequel to Lady Mary Wortley Montagu's death was as cynical as any of her voluminous letters. Her husband, who had been the English Ambassador in Constantinople, put an advertisement in the *Public Advertiser*, through the good office of his friend Romney, the painter, which read: 'A good gentleman who has filled two successive seats in Parliament, is nearly sixty years of age, lives in great splendour and hospitality, and from whom a considerable estate must pass if he dies without issue, hath no objection to marrying a widow or single lady provided she be of genteel birth, like manners, and is five or six months gone in her pregnancy. Letters addressed to Brecknock at Will's coffee House will be honoured with due attention, secrecy, and every mark of respect.'

This advertisement was successful up to a point. A woman

having the necessary qualifications actually went to Paris to meet Wortley, who reached Lyons on his way from Venice to the French capital. There, however, while he was eating an ortolan, a bone stuck in his throat and cost him his life, thus putting an end to his remarkable scheme.

* * *

In spite of his reconciliation with the Princess of Wales King George was almost invariably mean to his daughter-in-law. All his gold and jewellery went to his mistresses. The only sign of generosity to her was when returning from one of his last visits to Hanover he brought with him 'the wild boy', the original Tarzan, by all accounts. We read:

> The wild boy, whom the King hath presented to the Princess of Wales, taken last winter in the forest of Hamlin, walking on all fours, running up trees like a squirrel, feeding on twigs and moss, was last night carried into the drawing-room at St James's into the presence of the King, the Royal Family and many of the nobility. He is supposed to be about twelve or thirteen, some think fifteen, years old, and appears to have but little idea of things. 'Twas observed that he took most notice of his Majesty, whom he had seen before, and the Princess giving him her glove, he tried to put it on his own hand, and seemed much pleased with a watch which was held to strike at his ear. They have put on him blue clothes lined with red, and red stockings, but the wearing of them seems extremely uneasy to him. He cannot be got to lie on a bed but sits and sleeps in a corner of the room. The hair of his head grows lower on the forehead than is common. He is committed to the care of Dr Arbuthnot, in order to try whether he can be brought to the use of speech and made a sociable creature. He hath begun to sit for his picture.

In 1726, George's divorced wife died after thirty-three years of imprisonment in the Castle of Ahlden. Whereupon he forbade the Prince of Wales to wear mourning for his mother or to make any allusion to her death. He himself, having received the news, left ostentatiously for the theatre, attended by his mistresses. At the same time, being superstitious, he remembered the prophecy made many years before that he would not survive his wife by a twelve-month. And so it turned out.

On his way to Hanover by way of Holland, he had an enormous dinner, including several water-melons, and then drove off at full speed in the small hours of the morning. At one of the post-stations, a letter written years ago by his ill-fated wife, reminding him of the prophecy, was thrown into his carriage. The combination of the letter and the meal caused him to have a fit. When he partly recovered, his courtiers again urged him to rest, but he refused. The King himself urged on the postillions, shouting: 'To Osnabruck, to Osnabruck!' Here he was borne into the castle but never recovered consciousness.

9. Queen Caroline in charge

THE news of George I's death reached Walpole four days later. Saddling a horse, he rode at full speed to Richmond to pay homage to the new King. On arrival at 3 p.m. he was told that he could not see him because he had gone to bed after luncheon. Nevertheless, George II, as he now was, was persuaded to get up and go into the ante-chamber in such a hurry that he was carrying his breeches in his hand. Walpole went on one knee and told His Majesty that he was now King of England. 'Dat is von big lie,' shouted George II, then snatched the despatch from Walpole's hand and read it. 'Go back to Chiswick and take your directions from Sir Spencer Compton,' he said brusquely and turned his back. Walpole did as instructed, while George II and Queen Caroline drove up to Leicester House. The glad news had already spread and it was there that he held his Accession Council.

The aged Duchess of Kendal was the only person who really regretted the death of George I. Within a week he was as completely forgotten as though he had never been born and Court mourning came to an end as soon as he had been buried at Herrenhausen. On the day of the Coronation the royal couple left St James's Palace for Westminster Hall. Its magnificence was the talk of the town for a long time.

From the moment that Caroline became Queen she governed with Walpole until her death. George II loved pageantry but he had neither wit nor good taste and as soon as he became King decided to assume a stiff pomposity. He was exceedingly precise, resented the most trifling breach of etiquette as a reflection on his royal dignity and knew exactly the number of buttons required for the vest of a page of the back stairs. The Queen was highly in favour of this as it left her free to arrange the policy of the nation with Walpole.

One of the first acts of the new Sovereign was to tour the royal palaces which had been practically closed to him for many years. George did not care for Windsor any more than his father. On the other hand, he liked Kensington Palace, though St James's Palace remained his favourite.

In the meantime, his son Frederick remained at Hanover, where he had lived since birth. Possibly because he realized what a nuisance he himself had been to his father, the King was afraid that he might be equally irritating to him—so much so that the Queen agreed that Frederick should be kept away from England as long as possible, with the idea of making her younger son, the Duke of Cumberland, the next King.

No doubt Frederick would have been left still longer in Hanover if he had not been prevented at the last minute from marrying Princess Wilhelmina of Prussia. When George II heard of the plan, he sent for him immediately. On arrival he was smuggled up the back stairs of St James's Palace as if he had been a criminal rather than the heir-apparent. He was only twenty-two and very frightened of his father and everyone else. Until now he had been known as the Duke of Gloucester, but George II was compelled to make him Prince of Wales.

Both George II and Caroline continued to show an unnatural dislike for him and it became a major scandal in an age of scandals. 'My dear first-born is the greatest beast in the whole world,' the King said on one occasion, 'and I most heartily wish he were out of it.' Caroline's comment was, 'Fred is a nauseous beast and he cares for nobody but his nauseous little self.' So it was scarcely surprising that the new Prince of Wales made a habit of taking opposite sides from his parents on every possible occasion. Thus, because they liked the music of Handel he supported his rival, Giovanni Buononcini. A contemporary lampoonist promptly wrote:

'Some say compared to Buononcini
That Mynher Handel's but a ninny;
Others aver that he to Handel

Is scarcely fit to hold a candle.
Strange all this difference should be
'Twixt Tweedledum and Tweedledee.

Caroline's personal hatred of her eldest son became quite
remarkable. On one occasion when the Inner Temple looked as if
it were going to be burnt down, the Prince of Wales bravely
led the fire-fighters and became very popular in doing so. This
heroism in no way placated Caroline. 'My God!' she exclaimed,
'popularity always makes me sick, but Fred's makes me vomit.'

The unfortunate son and heir had by now married Princess
Augusta of Saxe-Gotha. She had finally been selected by George
II in preference to other German princesses who had hereditary
insanity owing to in-breeding, on the grounds that, 'I don't think
that ingrafting my half-witted coxcomb upon a mad woman
would improve the breed.'

When Prince Frederick's wife arrived in England [says
Smucker], her reception at St James's Palace was cheerful and even
magnificent. On her arrival at the palace, the bridegroom took
her hand and conducted her into the presence chamber of the monarch, where the whole court had been assembled. As she approached her father-in-law, she prostrated herself before him.
She had been informed that the haughty and punctilious little
king would be grateful by such a profound act of homage. He
courteously raised her from the floor, kissed her on each cheek,
and handed her over to the embraces of the Queen. The princess,
who was unaccompanied by a single friend, behaved on this somewhat trying occasion with extraordinary self-possession and grace
and won the admiration of all observers.

On the evening of the day of the arrival of the princess, the marriage was celebrated at St James's by the Bishop of London,
dean of the Chapel Royal. When the hour arrived for the obser-
vance of that most ridiculous of ceremonies, the 'bedding' of the
youthful pair, the bride was conducted to her sleeping apartment
by her attendant ladies, where she was disrobed and arrayed in
her nightdress. While this was going forward, Prince Frederick
was undergoing the same process in another room, where the
King did him the honour to hand him his shirt and even aid him
in putting it on. The princess having been placed in her bed, her
husband was conducted thither by several noblemen. He was
arrayed in a nightgown of silver stuff, and a cap of finest lace.

The attire of the princess consisted of a nightdress of equal elegance. The Prince took his place in bed beside his wife, and both sat upright to give the courtiers an opportunity to behold this rare and edifying spectacle. After the royal family and all the court had sufficiently satisfied their curiosity, they gradually withdrew, the lights were put out, the doors were locked, and the young couple were left to themselves.

Caroline had previously spread the rumour that her son and heir was impotent, realizing that if he were to produce a son of his own, her plans to alter the succession would be thwarted. As events proved, Augusta soon became pregnant, though the young parents did their best to conceal the fact from Caroline, who was furious when she finally learned that the baby was due in a month.

'At her labour I will positively be,' she is quoted as saying, 'for she cannot be brought to bed as one can blow one's nose— but I will be sure it is her child.' Augusta and her husband did their best to foil her. At the first sign of labour pains he bundled her into a carriage and drove at full gallop to St James's Palace, which they reached at 10 p.m. No preparation had been made for the emergency. Nevertheless, a girl baby was born at 10.45 p.m. and was promptly wrapped in a table napkin. News of the birth reached George II at Hampton Court some three hours later. Half an hour afterwards Queen Caroline set out for London.

She felt much better after her first look at the baby. 'Well, upon my honour,' she said to one of the courtiers, 'I no longer doubt this poor little bit of a thing is the Princess's child . . . . if there had been a brave jolly boy instead of this poor, ugly, little she-mouse, I should not have been cured of my suspicions.'

The Prince of Wales did his best to calm his parents by saying that the obstetric specialist had diagnosed his wife's labour pains as colic, but of no avail. Just as George II had been banished from St James's Palace by his father, so he now banished his son and daughter-in-law and grand-daughter. Further, notice was given to all peers, peeresses and Privy Councillors, that anyone who paid court to the Prince and Princess of Wales would not be admitted to Their Majesties' presence. Thus history repeated itself in succeeding generations.

The Princess of Wales was a tall, long-nosed, awkward, unattractive woman. When she had married she was still an adolescent, played with dolls in public and was so homesick that her German governess had to be imported. Whatever her husband did was right in her eyes and she felt compelled to obey him as a wifely duty. As Queen Caroline commented, 'Poor creature, if she were to spit in my face I should only pity her for being under such a fool's direction and wipe it off.'

Even when they went to church, the Princess and her husband managed to insult the Queen. They always came late so that the Princess had to push past her in the royal pew, a difficult operation because the Queen was very fat and the pew was very narrow. Caroline therefore ordered the verger to stand at the main entrance of the Royal Chapel after she had gone in, and forbid anyone through until the service was over. This meant that the Princess would have to go round to another door or stay out of the chapel altogether. The Prince of Wales solved this problem by telling his wife that if she was not ready to go into the chapel with the Queen she was not to go at all.

The general public was now becoming increasingly dissatisfied with the Court. It became further irritated when the Gin Act received the Royal Assent. Its object was to decrease drunkenness originally caused by the importation of Dutch gin. So bath-tub gin soon made its appearance. In Southwark, an inn specializing in hard liquor put up the sign:

> Drunk for one penny
> Dead drunk for twopence
> Clean straw for nothing.

The Act had no effect. Gin was sold as before but under fictitious titles such as 'Cuckold's Comfort', 'Make Shift', 'Lady's Delight', and 'Colic and Gripe Water'. The Prince of Wales, to infuriate his parents, drank gin publicly in one of the taverns on the day the Act came into force.

'The character of the Prince is this,' said the Earl of Egmont, 'he has no reigning passion; if it be, it is to pass the evening with six or seven others over a glass of wine and hear them talk of a variety of things, but he does not drink. He loves play and plays

117

to win, that he may supply his pleasures and generosities which last are great, but so ill-placed that he often wants wherewith to do a well-placed kindness, by giving to unworthy objects. He has had several mistresses, and now keeps one, an apothecary's daughter of Kingston; but is not nice in his choice and talks more of his feats this way than he acts. He can talk gravely according to his company, but is sometimes more childish than becomes his age.'

As for George II, he was an even greater gambler than his father. In 1729 a ball took place at the palace, but there were several gaming tables for people who did not want to dance. The King and Queen between them lost 500 guineas at Ombre. (This was a Spanish card game, the pack being reduced from fifty-two to forty by discarding all 10's, 9's, and 8's. In a desiccated form it survives today as Solo.) The Earl of Sunderland lost 1,000 guineas and Lord Finch 250 guineas. The winners were Lord William Manners (1,200 guineas), the Duchess of Dorset (900 guineas), and the Earl of Chesterfield (550 guineas). To rationalize these sums today it would be necessary to multiply by ten. Another popular gambling game during the reigns of George I and George II was Commerce. This was a kind of abbreviated draw-poker but with only three cards, and three of a kind ranking above a straight flush.

Apart from his gaming propensities, George II was a great stickler for etiquette and revived the custom of dining in public on Sundays to the sounds of an orchestra. A special State room was set aside for it. Selected members of the public who were so lucky as to obtain the necessary admission tickets were allowed to stand behind the railings and watch royalty enjoying their meal rather like friends and members of the Royal Zoological Society watching the lions and tigers being fed on Sundays.

As chief concubine, George II had long previously selected Mrs Howard (née Maynard) and later Countess of Suffolk. Unlike other mistresses she was not rapacious and held a literary salon which included Pope, Gay and Swift. At St James's Palace she took over the suite of the Duchess of Kendal. Her husband, Charles Howard, pretended not to be a *mari complaisant* and one day entered the quadrangle at St James's Palace and loudly demanded the return of his wife. He was quickly removed but was granted a pension of £1,200 a year for the loss of conjugal rights. With this he was completely satisfied.

Oddly enough, by modern standards, the Queen was exceedingly amiable to the concubine. Indeed, when one night Lord Chesterfield, having won a considerable sum of money at cards in the rooms below, asked Mrs Howard to look after his money until the next morning, he was recognized by the Queen, who took for granted that his visit was anything but innocent. From that moment onwards Chesterfield was *persona non grata* at Court and in desperation joined the Opposition.

There was no doubt that Queen Caroline 'wore the trousers'. Of this George II seemed quite unaware. He once said to some of his courtiers, 'Charles I was governed by his wife; Charles II by his mistresses; James II by his priests; William III by his men; Queen Anne by her women favourites,' and then, with a smug expression, asked, 'And who do they say governs now?' His courtiers naturally said, 'You, sire,' but one of the lampoonists of the day was quick off the mark with:

You may strut, dapper George, but 'twill all be in vain;
We know 'tis Queen Caroline, not you, that reign—
You govern no more than Don Philip of Spain,
Then if you would have us fall down and adore you,
Lock up your fat spouse, as your dad did before you.

One day, Queen Caroline decided to exclude the public from St James's Park although it had been open to them since the days of Charles II. She asked Walpole what it would cost. 'Only three Crowns,' he replied drily.

* * *

One of the most fantastic characters ever to become an habitué of St James's Palace was that epicene nobleman, Lord Hervey, whose memoirs, truncated though they be, are an invaluable reference book for much of the reign of George II.

The man was completely bisexual. He had eight children by his lawful wedded wife and yet could address Stephen Fox, later Lord Ilchester, as 'Mon bien aimé' and 'mea vera et sola voluptas', adding with truth that if any stranger were to read his letters, 'they would certainly presume that they came from a mistress rather than from a friend.' Thus he wrote: 'At dinner at Lord Harrington's, Sir William Irby sat next me, and the Lord Chancellor, designing to drink his health and taking him for you, called to him by your name. When, without the least affectation, I assure you I coloured and felt just as I imagine your favourite and fondest mistress would have done.'

No wonder that William Pulteney called him 'Pretty little Master-miss'. But one must give him his due—that he fought a duel with Pulteney as a result of a pamphlet called 'Sedition and Defamation Displayed' thought to be written by Hervey, and another definitely written by Pulteney in which references were made to 'Pretty Mr Fainlove who was of such a nice composition of the two sexes that it is difficult to distinguish which is the more predominant'. Pulteney could easily have killed Hervey, but let him off with a slight flesh wound.

At first, Hervey believed himself to be the favourite of Frederick, Prince of Wales; then found that he was no longer. He wrote to Fox, 'That fool (the Prince) plagues my heart out. He is as false as he is silly and appears everything he is not, but wise.' Incredibly enough, he was keeping a Miss Vane as his mistress and when later on Frederick took her away from him, his chief annoyance was that Miss Vane had supplanted him in Frederick's favours.

Now Alexander Pope took up his vitriolic pen again. In those days, there were no laws of libel. 'The Epistle to Arbuthnot' was perhaps the most vicious attack on any human-being in history. The chief character is Sporus. The original Sporus was a boy whom Nero had arranged to be castrated because he resembled Sabina and used him in every way as a wife, finally 'marrying' him.

Some of the lines read:

> What, that thing of silk?
> Sporus! that mere white curd of asses' milk,
> Satire or sense alas! Can Sporus feel?
> Who breaks a butterfly upon a wheel?
> Yet let me flap this bug with gilded wings,
> This painted child of dirt that stinks and stings. . . .
> Whether in florid impotence he speaks
> And as the prompter breathes, the puppet squeaks,

Or, at the ear of Eve, familiar toad,
Half froth, half venom, spits himself abroad
In puns, or politics, or tales, or lies,
Or spite, or smut, or rhymes, or blasphemies,
Now high, now low, now master up, now miss,
And he himself one vile antithesis.

Hervey never challenged Pope to a duel. Maybe he enjoyed the revolting publicity he was receiving. He had now moved from Leicester House to St James's Palace where, as the gigolo of Queen Caroline and as a Member of Parliament, he was able to provide her and King George with all the latest political gossip. So long as Queen Caroline lived, he was, metaphorically, Chief Eunuch of the Palace, with a reasonable possibility of becoming Grand Vizier.

Without him, it would have been impossible to appreciate the fantastic state of the Court at St James's Palace. There was, for instance, the case of the marriage of the Princess Royal to the Prince of Orange.

The Prince was lodged at Somerset House. Next day he came to St James's Palace through crowded streets and tremendous applause although the King had only sent him one miserable coach and a couple of footmen. Apparently the King had decided to make it clear that the Prince of Orange was a nobody until he had married his daughter and that becoming her husband would make him everything. So the Tower guns were not allowed to salute him nor the Guard to turn out.

With the utmost reluctance, the King allowed Hervey to call on the Prince officially. On his return to St James's Palace the Queen sent for him at once to let her know 'without disguise what sort of hideous animal she was to prepare herself to see'.

Lord Hervey assured her that he was nothing like as bad as she had imagined. Quite true, he was no Adonis; his figure was appalling, but his face was not entirely disagreeable and he seemed quite unselfconscious of his appearance. (The Princess Royal herself was marked a good deal with smallpox. 'The faults of her person were that of being very ill-made, though not crooked, and a great propensity to fat.' To make up for this she spoke English, French, German and Italian, could sing anything at sight, and was a first-class needlewoman.)

'For my part,' said the Queen, 'I never said the least word to encourage her to this marriage or to discourage her from it.' The King, too, left her absolutely at liberty to accept or reject it. But as she thought the King looked upon it as a proper match, the Princess said she was resolved, even if it was a monkey, she would marry him. Whereupon the Prince of Orange fell ill and no member of the royal family was allowed to see him.

The wedding nevertheless took place in 1734. During the ceremony, the Prince of Orange behaved most correctly but the Queen and the Princess Royal's two sisters were clearly so upset that the wedding looked more like 'the mournful pomp of sacrifice than the joyful celebrations of marriage'.

In fact, the Prince of Orange was a less shocking, less ridiculous figure than could have been expected of such a fabled monster, for the long wig which flowed all over his back hid his humpiness. But when, according to the astonishing rigid etiquette of the day, he was undressed and came in his nightgown and nightcap into the Princess Royal's room to go to bed with her in front of all the courtiers, his appearance was indescribable. 'From the shape of his gown and that of his back, he looked behind as if he had no head and before as if he had no neck and no legs', recalls one spectator.

The Queen, speaking in private the next morning with Lord Hervey, said in French, 'My God, when I saw this monster come to sleep with my daughter, I thought I would die. Tell me, Lord Hervey, did you observe this monster and have you no pity for my poor Anne? Good God, it is very silly of me but I am still weeping about it.'

The sisters who had all been present took much the same view as the Queen. Princess Emily said that nothing on earth would have induced her to marry the monster. Princess Caroline said she had to admit it was a very bad business but, considering everything, if she had been her sister she thought she would have married him. The extraordinary sequel, according to Lord Hervey, was that the Princess Royal treated her husband just as if he had been an Adonis. He in turn hardly ever took any notice at all of her, nor gave one look by which anyone could have guessed they had ever slept in the same bed.

When it was finally time for the pair of them to go to Holland, there was a melancholy parting between the Princess Royal and her family except for her brother, the Prince of Wales, who never said goodbye at all. Her father, the King, gave her a thousand kisses and a shoal of tears but not one guinea. Her mother never stopped crying for three days. Yet three weeks later the Princess was as forgotten as if she had been buried three years.

The modern historian is indebted to Lord Hervey for many other close-ups of the Court of St James. There was the time when the Duchess of Queensberry was determined to publicize *Polly*, John Gay's sequel to *The Beggar's Opera*, which the Lord Chamberlain had refused to allow to be played in public because of its attack on Sir Robert Walpole. The Duchess decided to have it printed and sold to subscribers. Few people refused the guinea subscription and the Duchess went so far as to enter the Queen's apartment at St James's Palace and persuaded even the King's courtiers to contribute to the printing of this play which the King himself forbade to be done in public. Here the King caught her red-handed, asked what she had been doing and, when informed, promptly expelled her from Court. Being a high-spirited character, she retorted with the following letter:

The Duchess of Queensberry is surprised and well pleased that the King hath given her so agreeable a command as to stay from Court, where she never came for diversion, but to bestow a great civility on the King and Queen; she hopes by such an unprecedented order as this is, that the King will see as few as he wishes at his Court, particularly such as dare to think or speak truth. I dare not do otherwise, and ought not, nor could have, imagined that it would not have been the very highest compliment that I could possibly pay the King to endeavour to support truth and innocence in his house, particularly when the King and Queen both told me that they had not read Mr Gay's play. I have certainly done right, then, to stand by my own words rather than his Grace of Grafton's, who hath neither made use of truth, judgment, nor honour, through this whole affair, either for himself or his friends.

C. Queensberry.

In May 1729 George II decided to go to Hanover and left Queen Caroline behind as Regent, which she was delighted to become, although she managed to produce some tears of regret when he announced his departure.

It was during this visit that George II challenged the King of Prussia to a duel at any place he would name, leaving him the choice of weapons, all because the Prussians had kidnapped some of his tall Hanoverians for the Potsdam Guards. It would of course have been splendid for everybody if the two kings had killed each other. Unfortunately, the notorious cousins had the matter patched up by Lord Townshend.

Lord Hervey is once again invaluable with his account of George II's insistence on going to Hanover in 1735. His ministers were afraid that this might lead to war but the Queen was on his side and finally prevailed. What she did not foresee was that on his arrival in Hanover he would fall madly in love with Madame Walmoden, a young married woman of good family. The fantastic part about this intrigue was that from the very start the King let the Queen know by letter of every step he took, of the growth of his infatuation, how he went about it, how he succeeded, indeed, down to the minutest details. He added that he was proud of the fact that he had bought her for a mere thousand ducats—greater proof of his economy than of his infatuation.

On his return, nobody could recommend anything English without his retorting that it could be done better in Germany. No English, or even French chef could 'dress a dinner'; no English pastry-cook could make good pastry; no English actor could act; no English coachman could drive nor were any English horses fit to be driven or ridden; no Englishman knew how to come into a room correctly nor any English woman how to dress herself; nor were there any entertainments in England, public or private, or any man or woman whose conversation was to be tolerated—the one talking of nothing but dull politics and the other of nothing but her clothes. Whereas at Hanover all these things were quite perfect. The men were patterns of politeness, bravery and gallantry; the women of beauty, wit and entertainment; his troops there were the bravest in the world; his counsellors the wisest; his manufacturers the most ingenious; his subjects the happiest. At Hanover, in short, plenty reigned, magnificence resided, diversions abounded, riches flowed, and everything was of the utmost perfection that contributes to make a prince great or a people blessed.

Never had the Court of St James been so unhappy. Everyone who came near the King had some proof of his bilious temper, and everyone talked about it.

In the meantime, the three princesses, Caroline, Mary and Louisa, led singularly purposeless lives at the palace, spending most of their time playing cards and dancing. Peter Wentworth, in a letter to his brother Lord Strafford, wrote:

> The quadrille table is well known, and there is a large table surrounded by my master (the Prince of Wales), the Princesses, the Duke of Cumberland, the bedchamber ladies, Lord Lumley, and all the belle-assemblee, at a most stupid game, to my mind, lottery ticket. £100 is sometimes lost at this past-time. The Maids play below with the King in Mrs Howard's apartment, and the moment they come, the Queen starts up and goes into her apartment. . . . T'other night Lord Grantham and the Queen had a dispute about going to a room without passing by the back-stairs; she bade him go and see; he did, and came back as positive as before. 'Well,' says she, 'will you go along with me if I show you the way?' 'Yes, madame,' says he. Up she starts, and trots away with one candle, and came back triumphant over my Lord Grantham. The belle-assemblee was in an uproar, thinking the King was ill, when I told them 'twas a wager between the Queen and my Lord Grantham.

The Queen was fond of these little jokes. On another occasion we find Peter Wentworth noting:

> Sunday, in the evening the Queen commanded me to order her a chaise and one horse, and a coach and six to follow, for Monday, at six o'clock in the morn, and six Life Guards and two Grenadiers, and your humble servant a-horseback, which was to be kept a great secret. When I had put her Majesty into her chaise with Princess Mary, she bid me ride and tell the Colonel of the Guard not to beat the drum as she passed out (of St James's). We drove to the foot ferry at Kew, where there was a barge of four oars which carried her Majesty, Princess Mary, Mrs Purcell and I to the Queen's house at Kew. The whole joke of keeping this a secret was upon Lord Lifford, who had said 'twas impossible

for her Majesty to go out at any time but he should know it. When we came there, therefore, the Queen sent for the other Princesses, Lord Hervey and Lord Lifford to breakfast with her. Lord Hervey, Princess Caroline and Princess Louisa came before ten; the Queen, Mrs Purcell and I walked twice round the garden before they came. *We* had a fine breakfast, with the addition of cherries and strawberries we plucked from the garden, some of which the Queen gave me with her own hand; and said to Lord Hervey, *C'est un très bon enfant*, and repeated it several times, Lord Hervey assenting. I never suspected she spoke of me, which she, perceiving, said in English: 'We are speaking of you; you know I love you, and you shall know I love, I do really love you'. I made low bows, but had not the impromptu wit nor assurance to make any other answer.

And again:

On Saturday when the Queen was at Kew, the Blue Horse Guards in stocks stood sentry there. As she goes up the court she says to Lord Lifford and me: 'I'll lay you what you will, he of the right is a Scotsman, and he of the left an Englishman and a Yorkshireman.' When she came up to them, she asked him of the right, who was a handsome young fellow and a gentleman volunteer: 'What countryman are you?' 'A Scotsman, your Majesty.' 'What's your name?' 'Hamilton.' 'Of what family?' 'The Dukes of that name.' 'How long have you been in the regiment?' 'Ever since it has been the Duke of Argyll's.' Then she turns to t'other man, and asks what countryman he was? 'An Englishman, your Majesty.' 'Your name?' 'Hill.' 'What county?' 'Yorkshire.' The Queen was pleased (and so was I, for I would always have her pleased) and turned about to my lord and me, and said: '*N'est-ce pas que j'ay dit vray? Je connais bien la physiognomie.*'

As time marched on, the quarrel between Walpole and Townshend reached a crisis. They were dining with Colonel Selwyn and his wife in Cleveland Row opposite St James's Palace. Walpole, as usual, became drunk and shouted at Townshend, 'My Lord, for once there is no man's sincerity whose I so much doubt as your Lordship's.' Townshend sprang on Walpole and seized him by the throat. The Prime Minister retaliated. Both men clapped hands on their swords, Mrs Selwyn ran out shrieking to summon the guard of St James's Palace. . . .

Queen Caroline took a genuine interest in literature. Among

those who received her patronage at St James's Palace was Voltaire, who had been exiled after some months in the Bastille. She persuaded the King to give him a present of £500 to which she added a further £200 from her private purse.

Once again George II went to Hanover, whereupon some wag put up a notice actually on the gates of St James's Palace announcing:

> Lost or strayed out of this house, a man who has left a wife and six children on the Parish. Whoever will give any tidings of him to the Churchwardens of St James's Parish, so as he may be got again, shall receive 4s. 6d. reward.

> N.B.—This reward will not be increased, nobody judging him to deserve a crown.

As before, Caroline was made Regent and Walpole introduced his Excise Bill; but there was so much opposition that, after a furious debate in the House, he had to go to St James's Palace and have a conference with the Queen to discuss the dropping of the Bill. George II, who had now returned, put on the hat he wore at Malplaquet and was running his finger along the edge of a sword he had worn at Oudenarde, quite ready to put himself at the head of his troops and march on the House of Commons.

The scenes in London that night were fantastic. Bonfires were lit in the streets, and, at Charing Cross, a fat woman representing the Queen was burnt in effigy amid the shrieks and howls of the populace.

During this period, the Prince of Wales was becoming more of an embarrassment than ever to the King. Not that it was entirely the Prince's fault. Although Parliament had given his father £100,000 for his living expenses, he received only a small proportion of this, at irregular intervals. It was no wonder that he ran up debts. His chief friend, Bubb Doddington, was quite happy to become the butt of his not very intelligent practical jokes. On one occasion, according to Walpole, he was rolled in a blanket and trundled downstairs. In spite of this he lent the Prince of Wales £5,000 which he knew he would never see again.

The Prince now followed royal protocol by setting up with an accredited mistress. His first, as has been described, was Vanilla Vane, daughter of Lord Barnard, one of the Queen's maids-of-honour, who, it was neatly said, 'was willing to cease to be one on the first opportunity' and gave birth to a son in her apartments in St James's Palace. The child was baptized in the Chapel Royal and received the name of Fitz-Frederick-Vane, an open confession that the Prince of Wales was the father. Miss Vane was immediately dismissed by Queen Caroline and the Prince was told that in the future he must carry on his intrigues outside the circle of her household. So he quickly took Lady Archibald Hamilton as his next mistress, although she was the mother of ten children.

The Prince, it is true, offered Miss Vane £1,600 a year for life if she left the country, but added 'that if she would not live abroad, she might starve for him in England'. When Miss Vane allowed this news to become known, everybody sympathized with her and blamed the Prince. Ballads and pamphlets circulated everywhere with such titles as 'Vanilla on the Straw', 'Vanilla or the Amours of the Court' and 'Vanessa or the Humours of the Court of Modern Gallantry'. Soon afterwards Miss Vane died at Bath of a broken heart.

Meanwhile, the private life of the Court was increasingly dull. The former Mrs Howard, now Countess of Suffolk, gave fewer and fewer parties, and finally retired after having been insulted by George II. Immediately afterwards, she jotted down her last interview with the Queen at St James's Palace. It is a perfect example of the complaisance of royalty at open adultery. Thus:

Lady Suffolk: 'Madam, I believe your Majesty will think that I have more assurance than ever anybody had to stay so long in your family, after the public manner His Majesty has given me of his displeasure. But I hope, when I tell you that it occasioned my not waiting sooner upon your Majesty, you will not think it was owing to assurance. I have always had, and I hope I have always shown, the greatest duty and attention for everything that relates to your Majesty, and I could not think it was proper, whilst you were so indisposed, to trouble you with anything relating to me, but I come now, madam, to beg your leave to retire.'

The Queen: 'You surprise me. What do you mean? I do not believe the King is angry. When had he shown his displeasure? Did I receive you as if you were under mine?'

Lady Suffolk: 'No, madam. If your Majesty had treated me in the same manner as his Majesty did, I never could have had the assurance to appear again in your presence.'

The Queen: 'Child, you dream. I saw the King speak to you; I remember now.'

Lady Suffolk: 'Yes, madam, and his words marked more strongly his displeasure, than his silence, before and since.'

The Queen: 'Tell me, has the King really never been down with you since your return?'

Lady Suffolk: 'No, madam. Will your Majesty give me leave to tell what has passed?. . . .'

The Queen: 'Upon my word, I did not know it.'

Lady Suffolk: 'I hope you take nothing ill of me . . .'

The Queen: 'Come, my dear Lady Suffolk, you are very warm, but believe me I am your friend, your best friend. You do not know a Court. It is not proper of me to say this, but indeed you do not know a Court.'

Lady Suffolk: 'I am very sensible that I do not, and feel I do not; I have had a most convincing proof that I am ignorant. But I am afraid, madam, if I have not got knowledge in twenty years I never shall now.'

The Queen: 'Why don't you talk to your friends? I always do so. Indeed you cannot judge this for yourself.'

Lady Suffolk: 'Madam, if twenty years' service has not been able to prevent me from falling a sacrifice to my enemies, would your Majesty have me, by calling in my friends, make them answerable for the measure I shall take, and involve them in my ruin?'

The Queen: 'Child, your enemies want to get you out, and they will be the first to drop you. Oh! my dear Lady Suffolk, you do not know, when you are out, how different people will behave . . . You cannot judge for yourself. Let me prevail. Put yourself in somebody's hands and let them act for you. Indeed you are so warm you are not fit to act for yourself. Nor indeed very respectful. But you will repent it. I cannot give you leave to go.'

Lady Suffolk: 'If anybody could feel as I feel, and could be so entirely innocent as to let me be the only sufferer for the advice they give, I might follow the method your Majesty proposes, but as that is impossible, I must beg leave to act for myself. I wish I might know what I am accused of. In my absence I have been ruined in his Majesty's favour. At Bath I have a thousand witnesses of my behaviour. I know my own innocence. Nobody dare tell me that to my knowledge I have ever failed in my duty in any manner.'

The Queen: 'Lady Suffolk, pray consider, be calm.'

Lady Suffolk: 'Madam, I beg your Majesty will give me permission to retire. Indeed I have not slept since I came back to your house, and believe I never shall under this suspicion of guilt. Madam, will you give me leave to speak?'

The Queen: 'Do.'

Lady Suffolk: 'I am here by your Majesty's command. Your Majesty should look upon me when I assert my innocence. Your Majesty knows what I am accused of.'

The Queen: 'Oh! oh! Lady Suffolk, you want to get it out of me.'

Lady Suffolk: 'Madam, I do want to face the accusation; I am not afraid; I know it would be to the confusion of my accusers.'

The Queen: 'I will not give you leave to go, I tell you plainly. If you go today, you go without my consent.'

Lady Suffolk: 'Madam, I beg you to think of my unhappy situation. I own after what passed, that the next time I saw his Majesty, I should have dropped down if I had not gone out.'

The Queen: 'Well, Lady Suffolk, will you refuse me this? Stay a week longer, won't you; stay this week at my request.'

Lady Suffolk: 'Yes, madam, I will obey you, but as I am under his Majesty's displeasure, your Majesty will not expect my attendance, or that I come again to receive your commands.'

The Queen: 'Yes, I do, and I will see you again, because you will come again.'

Lady Suffolk: 'I will obey your Majesty.'

The Queen: 'Harkee, Lady Suffolk, you will come up as you used to do.'

Lady Suffolk stayed her week, and then, in spite of the protestations of Queen Caroline, resigned her appointment as Mistress of the Robes and left the Court for ever. The following year she married George Berkeley.

We are again indebted to Lord Hervey for his report on the last days of Queen Caroline, showing how little medicine had advanced since the tragic death of Prince Henry:

130

On Wednesday, 9th November 1737, the Queen was taken ill in the morning at her new Library in St James's Park. She called her complaint the Cholic. She came home, took Daffy's Elixir by Dr Tesier, the German and House Physician's advice, but was in such pain and so uneasy with frequent reaching to vomit, that she went into bed. However, when the Clock struck two and the King proposed sending Lord Grantham to dismiss the Company, and declare there would be no Drawing-Room she, according to the custom of the family, not caring to own how ill she was, told the King she was much better—that she would get up and see the Company as usual. As soon as she came into the Drawing-Room she came up to Lord Hervey and said, 'Is it not intolerable at my age to be plagued with a new distemper? Here is this nasty Cholic that I had at Hampton Court come again!' Lord Hervey asked her what she had taken, and when she told him, he replied, 'For God's sake, madam, go to your own room; what have you to do here?' She then went and talked a little to the rest of the company, and coming back again to Lord Hervey said, 'I am not able to entertain people.' 'Would to God,' replied Lord Hervey, 'the King would have done talking of the Dragon of Wantley, and release you.' (This was a new silly farce, which everyone at this time went to see.) The Queen soon retired, got immediately into bed, where she grew worse every moment. . . .

Early in the morning of Thursday, the 10th, the Queen was blooded . . . upon which her high fever abated.

However on this amendment, the King resolved to have a Levee, and that the Princess Emily should see the company at the usual hour of the Queen's going into her Drawing-Room and the King, in the midst of all his real and great concern for the Queen, sent to his pages to bid them be sure to have his last new ruffle sewed on upon the shirt he was to put on that day at his public dressing.

This same evening while Princess Caroline and Lord Hervey were with the Queen alone, she complaining and they comforting, she often said 'I have an ill which nobody knows of'. Princess Caroline's extreme concern and continual weeping gave her a return of her rheumatism, which settled in her back, and added to this, she had from this violent and perpetual weeping, a frequent bleeding at her nose and in great quantities. The King and Queen both persuaded her to go to bed, and insisted on her doing so, about midnight; Lord Hervey promising her to sit up, and giving his word he would frequently come and inform her how the Queen was exactly and without the least disguise. Lord Hervey went once or twice in the night as he had promised to Princess Caroline: the King sat up in the Queen's room.

At 6 o'clock on Friday morning, the 11th, the Queen was again blooded, upon which her fever went almost entirely off.

On Friday Lord Hervey hearing the Prince was in London, suspected he had done so in order to come to St James's to inquire for the Queen and perhaps to ask to see her. Lord Hervey told the King his conjecture, and asked his Majesty in case it should prove a true one, what he would have done. The King said 'If the puppy should in one of his impertinent affected airs of duty and affection dare to come to St James's, I order you to go to the scoundrel and tell him I wonder at his impudence for daring to come here—that he has my orders already and knows my pleasure, and bid him go about his business, for his poor mother is not in a condition to see him act his false whining tricks now, nor am I in a humour to bear his impertinence.'

About an hour or two afterwards while Lord Hervey was sitting with the Duke of Cumberland, drinking tea in the Queen's outer apartments, a message came from Lord North to say that the Prince was in the utmost affliction to hear of the Queen's illness, and was come to London in order to hear more frequently how she did, and that the only thing that could alleviate his great concern at this time was to be admitted to the honour of seeing her, upon which the King flew into a great rage and refused to allow an interview.

In the afternoon, the Queen said to the King, she wondered the Prince had not sent to ask to see her yet, and by the way in which she expressed herself evidently feared that he would wish to see her.

The King then bid her not to be under any apprehensions of this kind, for that he had already taken care to prevent it.

During the whole of Friday, the Queen grew worse.

The next day Saturday, the 12th, the King insisted upon telling Ranby in spite of the Queen's request to the contrary, that she was suffering from an umbilical rupture and bid him examine her. Upon Dr Ranby examining the Queen she called out with great eagerness 'I am sure now, you blockhead, you are telling the King I have a rupture.' 'I am so,' said Ranby, 'and there is no more time to be lost. Your Majesty has concealed it too long already, and I beg another surgeon may be called in immediately.' The Queen gave no answer. Another Physician however was summoned, and after they together had examined the Queen, they told the King she was in utmost danger.

About 6 o'clock this Saturday evening the surgeons performed a very painful operation for strangulation of the bowel, but without giving any great hope of her recovery.

The Earl of Egmont recalls the way in which Caroline reacted: 'Rangle, the surgeon, cut the Queen, who to show her contempt for the pain' (this was, of course, before the days of anæsthetic) 'asked what he would give to be using his wife in the same manner. . . . At the same time old Bussiere who is near the age of 90 and stood by Rangle happened to set fire to his wig with the candle in his hand, at which the Queen bid Rangle stop for a while for he must let her laugh.'

George II had previously blamed Caroline for eating too much and growing stout. 'Why do you stare like that?' he asked as she looked at him in pain and despair. 'Your eyes are like those of a cow whose throat has just been cut.' Apologetically, Caroline, who knew she was dying, replied that she was very silly and very whimsical.

Lord Hervey's report continued:

On Sunday, the 13th, the Queen's case was declared hopeless.

Nobody remained in her room with the Queen but the King, the Duke of Cumberland (now sixteen years of age), and her four daughters of whom she took leave in form, desiring they would not leave her till she expired.

She then took off a ruby ring from her finger, which the King had given her at her Coronation, and putting it upon his hand, said 'This is the last thing I have to give you . . . naked I came to you, and naked I go from you! . . . I had everything I ever possessed from you, and to you, whatever I have, I return. My will you will find a very short one. I give all I have to you!' She then asked for her keys and gave them to him.

The Queen had wished, in case she died, that the King should marry again, and she gave it now, as her advice, while she was dying: upon which his sobs began to rise, and his tears to fall with double vehemence. Whilst in the midst of this passion, wiping his eyes and sobbing, he got out this answer, *'Non, j'aurai des maîtresses'*. To which the Queen made no other reply than, *'Ah, mon Dieu, cela n'empêche pas.'*

Monday and Tuesday, the 14th and 15th, the Queen was better, and when the King used to tell her how much better the Doctors and surgeons said she was, the moment his back was turned, she used to look at the Princesses, shake her head and bid them not flatter themselves, and often in the day, used to tell them 'Believe me, my dear children, it won't do; at twenty-five I might have struggled through it, but at fifty-five I cannot resist.'

During this time the Prince's family had, little by little, under pretence first of enquiring of the Queen's health, as from the Prince and Princess and afterwards for themselves, [had succeeded in] coming every day and all day to St James's, till there was no part of the day in which there were not three or four of them dangling in that part of the Queen's State Apartments where the lady-of-the-bedchamber sat to receive all those who came to enquire about the Queen.

This evasion of the Queen's orders made the King extremely angry and he sent Lord Hervey to Sir Robert Walpole to know what way he should take to prevent these scoundrels (as he called them) coming every day to St James's in defiance of his order, to insult him and the Queen in their present distress. Walpole in reply said that they had not transgressed the literal sense of the order, which only forbade them the King's presence, and as the King might very well be supposed to know nothing of their coming, he thought it would be better for the King just at this time not to mix any marks of resentment against his son with those of affection for his wife.

Lord Hervey conveyed this advice to the King, who accepted it with much reluctance.

Hour by hour the Queen grew so perceptibly weaker that every one she lived was more than was expected. On Sunday evening, November 20th (1737) she asked Dr Tesier how long he thought it was possible for this pain which she was suffering to last, to which he answered: '*Je crois que votre Majesté sera bientôt soulagée*', to which she calmly replied, '*Tant mieux.*'

About 10 on Sunday night, the Queen began to rattle in the throat. All she said before she died was 'I have now got an asthma, open the window.' Then she said 'Pray.' Upon which Princess Emily began to read some prayers, of which she scarce repeated ten words, before the Queen expired. The Princess Caroline held a looking-glass to her lips, and finding there was not the least damp upon it, cried 'Tis over' and said not one word more.

The King kissed the face and hands several times, but in a few minutes left the Queen's apartments and went to that of his daugh-

ters, accompanied only by them. Then advising them to go to bed
and take care of themselves, he went to his own side, and as soon
as he was in bed, sent for Lord Hervey to come and sit by him,
where, after talking some time and calmly also of the Queen's
death, he dismissed him and sent for one of his pages, to sit up
in his room all night, which orders he repeated for several days
afterwards.

The King bitterly felt and bewailed the Queen's death. According to an eyewitness, his grief was displayed on one occasion
in a very characteristic manner. He was playing cards, when some
queens happened accidentally to be dealt to him. 'This renewed
his troubles so much, and put him into so great a disorder that
the Princess Amelia immediately ordered all the queens to be
taken out of the pack.'

Some time after the Queen's death the King observed to Baron
Brinkman, one of his German attendants, 'I hear you have a picture of my wife, which she gave you and which is a better likeness
than any in my possession; bring it to me.' On its arrival, he appeared extremely affected and after remarking that it was very
like, 'Put it,' he said, 'upon the chair at the foot of my bed, and leave
it till I ring the bell.' It was not till after a space of two hours
that he summoned his attendant, and when the Baron re-entered
the apartment, said 'Take this picture away. I never yet saw the
woman worthy to buckle her shoe.'

* * *

Immediately after the death of Caroline, George, true to his
word, imported Madame Walmoden and, having created her
Countess of Yarmouth, gave her a suite of rooms in the Palace
where she ran the Court as the Duchess of Kendal had done
before her.

Lord Chesterfield, who knew George II intimately for forty
years, wrote of him:

He had not better parts than his father, but much stronger
animal spirits, which made him produce and communicate himself more. Everything in his composition was little, and he had
himself all the weaknesses of a little mind, without any of the
virtues, or even the vices of a great one. He loved to act the King
but mistook the part . . . Avarice, meanest of passions, was his
ruling one; and I never knew him deviate into any generous
action. Little things, as he has often told me himself, affected

him more than great ones. Within certain bounds, but they were narrow ones, his understanding was clear, and his conceptions quick; and I have generally observed, that he pronounced sensibly and justly upon single propositions; but to analyse, separate, combine, and reduce to a point, complicated ones, was above his faculties . . . He well knew that he was governed by the Queen, while she lived; and that she was governed by Sir Robert Walpole; but he kept that secret inviolably, and flattered himself that nobody had discovered it . . . He had no favourites, and indeed no friend, having none of the expansion of heart, none of those amiable connecting talents which are necessary for both. This together with the sterility of his conversation, made him prefer the company of women, with whom he rather sauntered away than engaged his leisure hours. He was addicted to women, but chiefly to such as required little attention and less pay . . . he was extremely regular and methodical in his hours, in his papers, and above all in his private accounts, and would be very peevish if any accident, or negligence in his Ministers broke in upon that regular allotment of his time. He had a very small degree of acquired knowledge; he sometimes read history, and, as he had a very good memory, was exceedingly correct in facts and dates.

Lord Chesterfield went on to say that his normal ungraciousness became almost intolerable when he lost his temper. On those occasions his hat and sometimes his wig were thrown across the room. Once, when his quack, Dr 'Spot' Ward, manipulated his dislocated thumb, George cursed him and kicked his shins.

At least he was a brave little man, as is proved by his offer of a duel with the King of Prussia. And he was the last King of England to be present at a battle—that of Dettingen in 1742. He is quoted as saying, 'De haus of Bronsvig may have produced as many fools as any von sovereign haus in Europe, but Sturm und Wetter it never was known to produce von coward or poltroon.'

Nevertheless, his ill-temper and impatience were legendary. One day when the St James's Palace kitchens were deserted at the moment when he wanted a particular dish, he screamed, 'Vot! Shall I be King of England and not have a pudding in a hurry for my supper! Gott damn!' On another occasion, by contrast, a stranger paying a visit to the palace slipped down a flight of stairs and burst open the door of a room where, as a result of his fall, he lay stunned on the floor. When he recovered consciousness, he found a square little old gentleman with white eyebrows and a scarlet face carefully washing his bald head and applying bands of sticking plaster to the cuts. The man then picked up his wig and put it on his head. The visitor rose to express gratitude but the little man frowned and pointed to the door. It was the King and the room so abruptly entered was the royal closet.

Another anecdote also shows him in a better light than usual. The beautiful Miss Gunning, who became Duchess of Hamilton, was talking to him at one of the Drawing-Rooms at St James's Palace. The subject was public ceremonies. The Duchess said, quite forgetful of the underlying meaning of the remark, 'I have seen so much, your Majesty, that there is only one sight in the world which I would wish to behold and that is a Coronation.' George II, overlooking the gaffe, replied, 'I think you have not long to wait. You will soon have your desire.'

He remained a stickler for etiquette and when the Duchess of Bridgewater appeared in white gloves in the chapel of St James's Palace while the Court was still in mourning for Queen Caroline, he had her promptly evicted.

10. *Attempt on the King's life*

Six months after the death of Queen Caroline, the skinny baby who was to become George III was born. The infant Prince had a bad start with a family pedigree of semi-insanity and, though he was heir-apparent after his father, his parents were held in the deepest contempt by George II.

The Prince of Wales himself was an ignominious little man, extremely excitable and a great womanizer. In 1751 he died of pneumonia after a fortnight's illness. The church service was performed without either anthem or organ. Not a single English peer or bishop attended. Today he is remembered only by his epitaph:

> Here lies Fred,
> Who was alive and is dead;
> Had it been his father
> I had much rather.
> Had it been his brother
> Still better than another.
> Had it been his sister,
> No one would have missed her,
> Had it been the whole generation,
> Still better for the nation,
> But since 'tis only Fred,
> Who was alive and is dead—
> There's no more to be said.

Now that Frederick was out of the way, George II took an active hand in educating his grandson at St James's Palace. When he was fourteen his mother was asked by Bubb Doddington how his education was going. Said she, 'I wish that he was a little more forward and less childish at his age.' When he was eighteen the Princess of Wales told Doddington that he was still shy and backward. The boy was terrified of his fiery grandfather. One day he was summoned to the private chamber of George II, who wanted to find out what he knew of the government of England and Hanover. The boy was quite unprepared and answered in scarcely audible monosyllables. Whereupon the King slapped his face. 'You are only fit for reading the Bible to your mother,' he shouted.

By the time he was twenty the Prince was still a sullen child, sulking in corners and frequently sucking his thumb, one of the signs of manic-depressive insanity. Then one day he met the Earl of Bute. He was at the Egham Races when it started to rain and someone had to be found to make a fourth at whist. This happened to be Lord Bute and the future George III immediately took a liking for him, although it was soon said that Bute and the Dowager Princess of Wales became lovers.

Within a year the future George III was writing to Lord Bute about sex. 'You have often accused me of growing grave and thoughtful, it is entirely owing to a daily increasing admiration of the fair sex, which I am attempting with all the philosophy and resolution I am capable of to keep under; I should be ashamed after having so long resisted the charms of these divine creatures now to become their prey; Princes when once in their hands make miserable figures. The annals of France and the present situation of Government in the Kingdom I most love, are convincing proofs of this. When I have said this you will plainly feel how strong a struggle there is between the boiling youth of twenty-one years and prudence; the last I hope will ever keep the upper hand; indeed if I can weather it but a few years marriage will put a stop of this combat in my breast.'

This letter was largely attributable to the fact that he had fallen in love with Lady Elizabeth Spencer who shortly afterwards married the tenth Earl of Pembroke.

* * *

An interesting sidelight on Court favours at this period is supplied by Captain Dudley Bradstreet in his *Uncommon Adventures*. According to his story, he had acted as a military spy for the Duke of Newcastle during the '45 rebellion but received no reward for his dangerous and successful mission. He decided to make his case known to the King at St James's Palace. He actually succeeded in delivering a 'memorial' into the hand of George II, who promptly passed it over to a gentleman-in-waiting. Altogether, Captain Dudley Bradstreet presented four 'memorials' without success. Finally a friend at St James's Palace told him that the King never read 'memorials' given to him unless someone very important solicited him. Bradstreet soon discovered that the pages-of-the-backstairs were the only people who could oblige him. So he wrote yet another letter to the King. Now let him tell the story himself:

My greatest difficulty was how to convey this letter to his Majesty having no acquaintance with any of the Pages of the Backstairs; however, being so advised, I went to them; my surprize was pretty great to find them mostly old gentlemen, instead of young, which I expected; their apartment is very near the King's and by what I could hear afterwards, they were forbid to deliver him any letters; I had mine in my hand and addressed myself to one of them (you must excuse me for his name because it may still injure him) to tell me how to forward it; he, with great indifference, desired me to throw it on a table, which I did and asked when I should call for an answer; with an air of more indifference he told me, 'Tomorrow, a month, a year hence.' With this shocking answer I withdrew and though I despaired of success, called next day and saw my letter with some others on the table. 'Alas,' said I to the same Gentleman I spoke to before, 'little did I imagine when I served his Majesty at Derby at the hazard of my life, I should be thus shov'd about, and my letter to the King confounded among other frivolous papers.' 'Pray, sir,' says he, 'what service were you to his Majesty there?' I told him it was too long to relate but that the Duke gave me a horse at Litchfield with which I was with the rebels in less than four hours afterwards and that my intelligence to them that night was the cause of their retreat. 'I have heard of you, sir,' says he. 'Are you that man?' I told him I was. 'Well, sir, on that account I will give your letter this minute.' He took it to his Majesty and accordingly he brought me an answer to call next morning by ten o'clock. As I was going from the Pages apartment I heard the King's bell ring. The same gentleman who brought my letter to him waited upon him directly and immediately after called to me, desiring me to come at three o'clock in the afternoon. This answer from my King gave me new Spirit and Hopes. No amusements could divert me from my expectations till the appointed time came when I was with the page to know my doom, who with pleasure, told me, he heard his Royal Master read my letter to the Duke of Newcastle and that he seemed greatly affected at my being neglected so long, and his resentment of it (the particulars of which I do not think proper to relate) and that His Majesty had ordered me an hundred and twenty pounds, a present for himself, which I must go to the Duke of Newcastle for, to support me until the Duke of Cumberland's return from Scotland which was expected to be in two months and then I should be provided for.

It was, incidentally, after this revolution that finger-bowls were banned from royal banquets because Jacobites held their glasses of wine 'over the water' when drinking the loyal toast and it was not until 1905 that Edward VII restored finger-bowls to their place on the royal table. But to this day the Scots Guards' messes are still without them.

* * *

On the morning of 25 October 1760, the future George III was riding near Kew when a courier arrived with the news of the death of his grandfather.

From the start he behaved very well. He added 2,000 guineas from his own pocket to the 6,000 guineas he found in a package in his father's desk addressed to Lady Yarmouth.

One of his earlier acts was to allow Parliament control of his personal expenditure in return for a civil list of £800,000 a year. He also arranged for an Act to be passed granting judges a life tenure of office at the then huge salary of £5,000 a year. In the spring following his accession he became infatuated with Lady Sarah Lennox, great-granddaughter of Charles II through his mistress, Louise de Kérouaille. He met her at a Twelfth Night ball given at St James's Palace and asked her if she did not believe that children should be governed by their parents. 'Yes, sometimes,' she replied. 'But a German woman is not the person to govern a King of England.'

Overawed by his mother, he could only summon up enough

courage to deliver a half-hearted proposal of marriage by way of Lady Sarah's cousin. The next time he saw her at Court he asked what she thought of his message. 'Nothing, sir,' was the reply. The King turned away and murmured, 'Nothing comes of nothing.'

This invitation to become Queen of England had arrived at an unfortunate moment for Lady Sarah—at the moment when she was breaking up a romance between Lady Caroline Russell and Lord Newbattle. She then fractured her leg while hunting and Lord Newbattle sent her a crude message saying that she should not worry, because her legs weren't very pretty anyhow. The King, however, was still in love with her and asked her to reconsider his proposal of marriage. This time she accepted. Whereupon he became terrified at his own boldness because he had not consulted the Earl of Bute, to whom he wrote:

What I now lay before you I never intend to communicate to anyone; the truth is the D. of Richmond's sister arriv'd from Ireland towards the middle of Novr., I was struck with her first appearance at St James's, my passion has been encreas'd every time I have since beheld her; her voice is sweet, she seems sensible, has a thorough sense of her obligations to her sister Lady Kildare, in short she is every thing I can form to myself lovely.

I am daily grown unhappy, sleep has left me, which never was before interrupted by any reverse of fortune; I protest before God I never have had any improper thought with regard to her; I don't deny having flatter'd myself with hopes that one day or other you would consent to my raising her to a Throne; thus I mince nothing to you; the other day I heard it suggested as if the D. of Marlborough made up to her. I shift'd my grief till retired to my chamber where I remained for several hours in the depth of despair, I believe this was said without foundation. At least I will flatter myself so.

Having now laid the whole before you I submit my happiness to you who are the best of friends, whose friendship I value if possible above my love for the most charming of her sex; if you can give me no hopes how to be happy I surrender my fortune into your hands, and will keep my thoughts even from the dear object of my love, grieve in silence, and never trouble you more with this unhappy tale; for if I must either lose my friend or my love, I will give up the latter, for I esteme your friendship above

RECEPTION OF
KING GEORGE I
AT ST JAMES'S
PALACE

QUEEN CAROLINE, WIFE OF GEORGE II

GEORGE II

GEORGE III

ST JAMES'S PALACE IN GEORGIAN TIMES

THE QUEEN'S CHAPEL, ST JAMES'S PALACE

FREDERICK, PRINCE OF WALES

every earthly joy; if on the contrary you can devise any method
for my keeping my love without forfeiting your friendship, I shall
be more bound to you than ever, and shall thank Heaven for the
thought of writing to you on this subject.

On the whole let me preserve your friendship, and tho' my heart
should break, I shall have the happy reflexion in dying that I have
not been altogether unworthy of the best of friends tho' unfortunate in other things.

Pray let me have a line from you to night.

The fat was at once in the fire, for Lady Sarah's sister was the
wife of Henry Fox, a bitter enemy of the Earl of Bute.

The Dowager Princess of Wales's secretary, David Graeme,
was immediately sent off to the various courts of Europe shopping for a likely young Protestant princess, while George sat
beside his mother poring over the catalogues of them. The
field was finally narrowed down to the Princess of Darmstadt
and the Princess Charlotte of Mecklenburg-Strelitz. The
trouble with the Princess of Darmstadt was that she was
enormously fat and both her father and grandfather were
lunatics.

George finally decided to marry Princess Charlotte, after
reading the letter she had written at the age of fifteen to
Frederick the Great on behalf of her distressed country. The
betrothal ceremony, a symbolic marriage, was held at the
bride's home. Drummond, the British envoy, bared his leg
to the knee and inserted it under the covers of the sofa on which
Princess Charlotte lay. The Princess was greatly upset but her
brother said gruffly in French, 'Come on, don't be a baby. You
are going to be Queen of England.'

After a fortnight's voyage on which her ship was blown as far
as Norway, Princess Charlotte reached London. She was now
seventeen, and by no means a beauty. All that could be said for
her was that 'the bloom of her ugliness wore off with age'.
Indeed she had a yellow complexion, small dark eyes and an
ugly nose and arms.

On the night she arrived she was married, but George III
broke all Hanoverian traditions by refusing to allow the courtiers to view him and the Queen in bed on their bridal night.
Next morning, seeing Lord Hardwicke at the levee in St James's

Palace, he said it was a fine day, to which Lord Hardwicke retorted with a snigger, 'Yes, Sire, and it was also a very fine night.'

As for Lady Sarah, she married Sir Charles Bunbury a year later, was divorced and then married George Napier by whom she had two very distinguished sons, Sir Charles, who captured Scinde, and Sir William, the historian. Years later, she wrote, 'I like my sons better than I like royal sons, thinking them better animals, and more likely to give me comfort in my old age; and I like better to be a subject, than subject to the terrors of royalty in these days of trouble.'

Of all the English kings who reigned between Queen Anne and Queen Victoria, George III was the only one who kept the seventh Commandment. Indeed, he was frequently ridiculed for being faithful and having no mistresses. As a young man, he was much better looking than his grandfather or great-grandfather. Though he had the rather prominent eyes, the tremendous nose and full lips of his Hanoverian predecessors, he was tall, burly, fair-skinned and with white teeth.

'The young king has all the appearance of being amiable,' Horace Walpole reported a week after the accession. 'There is great grace to temper much dignity and extreme good nature which breaks out on all occasions. He has shown neither inveteracy nor malice—in short we have much gained—he cannot be so unfeeling, so avaricious, or so German as his grandfather.' A little later he wrote, 'I saw him yesterday, and was surprised to find the Levee Room had lost so entirely the air of the lion's den. The sovereign does not stand in one spot with his eyes fixed royally on the ground and dropping bits of German news. He walks about and speaks freely to everybody. I saw him afterwards on the Throne, where he is graceful and genteel and sits with dignity and reads his answers to addresses well.'

'The King seems resolved to bring all things back to their original principle and to stop the torrent of corruption and laziness,' wrote Laurence Sterne at Christmas. 'He rises every morning at six to do business—rides out at eight to a minute, returns at nine to give himself up to his people. . . . The King gives everything himself, knows everything and weighs everything maturely, and then is inflexible. This puts old stagers off their game. How it will end, we are all in the dark.'

George III had ascended the throne with the highest possible resolutions, after reading Bolingbroke's *Ideas of a Patriot King* from end to end. He was horrified to learn that Parliament could not be safely elected without recourse to huge bribes. He was most anxious to end the bloody but successful Seven Years' War in which England was engaged on many fronts, while driving the French out of Canada, India and the Ohio Valley. Pitt, however, was adamant and the war continued. In the meantime, through the Earl of Bute, he bought Buckingham House, which he renamed the Queen's House, although George IV was soon to be born in St James's Palace.

Fate seemed determined to punish George III throughout his life. He was, for instance, continuously plagued by John Wilkes, the squint-eyed pamphleteer, and it grieved him very considerably when Sir Francis Dashwood was made Chancellor of the Exchequer. Dashwood had become infamous as the founder of the Hellfire Club, a group of twelve degenerate young men of good family who held orgies which lasted a week at a time in Medmenham Abbey in Buckinghamshire. It was said that a figure of five digits was an incomprehensible mystery to him and that he put a tax on cider and perry because he could not understand the scheme of putting a tax on linen which was the original suggestion of his advisers.

The Hellfire Club, known originally as the Brotherhood, included at least one future Prime Minister, one Chancellor of the Exchequer, one First Lord of the Admiralty and various Cabinet ministers, all of whom, therefore, were regular visitors to St James's Palace. Later, it blasphemously converted itself into the Order of St Francis of Wykeham. According to Charles Johnston, 'Each member contributed equally towards the cost. All was regulated by the strictest economies, the slaves of their lusts being sent back to the brothels from whence they were brought and the servants of their luxury being discharged at the end of their meetings.'

Known as nuns, the prostitutes came partly from Mother Stanhope's Bagnio, a venture in which Sir Francis Dashwood was said to have shares; partly from Moll King's, Mrs Goadby's

'Nunnery' and Charlotte Hayes's Bagnio which was grandi-
loquently known as the 'Abbey of Santa Carlotta'. Each morning, according to the author of *Satan's Harvest Home*, she made
her rounds to all the inns to see what the country had sent to
London. When she found a pretty rural lass she tricked her up
with patch and paint and called the creatures 'milliners' or
'parson's daughters'. Santa Carlotta always had a stock of
virgins in store at King Street, and supplied the Stock Exchange
with a regular ration of immaculate maidenheads.

John Wilkes was a member and an entry in the wine books
shows that he shared with Sir Thomas Stapleton six bottles of
claret, one bottle of port and one of Lisbon in a single night.

According to Walpole, the twelve founder-members who
styled themselves Apostles elected an Abbot each year and the
Abbot had first choice of the women. Black magic, every kind
of sexual perversity and religious sacrilege were rampant.
Nevertheless, the Earl of Oxford, Lord Holland, the Earl of
Westmorland, the Duke of Kingston and the Marquis of Granby
were all members. Others were so-called poets who merely
wrote smut.

At least John Wilkes had a sense of humour. One night he
dressed up a baboon in a black robe with horns on its head and
hid it in a chest in the chapel in the Caves where all the rites
were performed. During one of the Chapters when the Brothers
were intoning their profane prayers, Wilkes opened the chest
and unleashed the baboon which went berserk, chattering away
in what must have sounded like satanic gibberish, its horns
shaking on its head. The Brothers panicked. Many of them
shrieked. Most of them fell on the ground to avoid seeing the
Devil himself. The baboon, however, was now thoroughly
enjoying itself and jumped on to the back of the Earl of Sandwich
and clung there screaming. Again, according to Johnston, the
noble earl who gave his name to the snack because he was so
keen on gambling that he could not be bothered to leave the
card table for a proper meal, fell to his knees and cried, 'Spare
me, gracious devil, I am still but half a sinner, I have never been
half so wicked as I pretend.'

When it was later discovered that John Wilkes had played
this practical joke on them, the Brotherhood agreed on solemn

oath that none of them should ever play similar tricks again, but too late. The 'monastery' had to be closed because some of the servants had seen the black-robed baboon, horns and all, and spread the rumour that the Devil himself had visited Medmenham. In spite of this, Sir Francis Dashwood was later made Lord Despencer and still later became Postmaster-General.

In March 1764, with Grenville (whom George III always called Greenville for some reason known only to himself), he submitted the notorious Stamp Act to the Colonial Agents in London. By this Act, all newspapers, lawyers' documents and the like had to bear stamps to make them legal. A number of ordinary objects also had to bear stamps: the tax on a pack of cards was 1s., a pair of dice 10s., a pamphlet 1s., while ½d. or 1d. was put on the copy of a newspaper according to its size. The idea was to raise £100,000 a year to pay for part of the standing army of 10,000 regular troops in the American colonies, and was at once rejected by all of them except Pennsylvania.

Ignorance of America and American affairs in England was colossal simply because the various ministerial posts concerned with America were straightforward sinecures. One Minister for the Colonies actually sent his despatches to 'The Governor of the Island of New England'. The senior revenue officers appointed by the Crown never went near America and one Treasury official declared that Grenville ultimately lost America because he read the despatches—which none of his predecessors had ever done. It has been well said that if the English aristocrats had included America in their Grand Tour, the American War of Independence might never have occurred.

It was Pitt who observed to Grenville, 'Remember the lines:

> Be to her faults a little blind,
> Be to her virtues very kind.'

George III could not understand this attitude. He genuinely believed that he was in the right and that the American colonies should pay something towards their defence from foreign powers such as France. And of course he was as right as he was unwise. This preyed on him so much that early the following year, while he was still in his late twenties, he had his first attack of mental illness. Everything was done by those close to him to conceal

147

the truth of the matter. Sir William Duncan, the physician in charge, said that his royal patient had a feverish cold. In fact, it was the first instance of the manic-depressive condition which ultimately ended in his going completely mad.

This attack was punctuated by days of dejection followed by bursts of tremendous over-activity. The sole treatment seemed to be to bleed him. The Queen was naturally upset and urged Grenville to prevent the King's seeing his ministers at St James's Palace. Walpole wrote, 'The King has been extremely ill with a fever and violent cough and a humour fallen on his breast. He was bled four times, recovered enough to take the air, caught another cold and was cupped last Friday.' It seems odd that he was allowed to go riding the day after the relapse and it seems still more odd that the King was really suffering from some kind of respiratory illness which permitted him to go out riding, but prevented him from signing State Papers, as was the case.

So dejected did the King become that he thought he was going to die and tried to draw up a political will naming his widowed mother as Regent, but the Cabinet refused to let him do so.

He was further agitated by a series of riots among the silk weavers in Spitalfields. The changes in the Cabinet also distracted him. He wrote to the Earl of Bute, 'Indeed I can neither eat nor sleep; nothing pleases me but musing on my cruel situation. If I am to continue in the life of agitation I have these three years, the next year there will be a Council of Regency to assist in that undertaking.' Undoubtedly he had been attacked by an affliction of the brain as a result of intense anxiety caused by the political feuds surrounding him.

In March 1769, the mob made its way to St James's Palace, attacking a number of city merchants who were going to address the King. A few were able to reach their destination but one of them who was carrying the actual address was compelled to hide in a coffee house for several hours before he could reach the palace. All this time the crowd was behaving in a most rowdy fashion at the royal gates and a squadron of cavalry at the Horse Guards was compelled to go to the palace, where the Riot Act was read twice. Later, as George III drove to the House of Lords from St James's Palace, there were shouts of

'Give us Bread'—'No famine, no war.' There were even cries of 'Down with George' or words to that effect; and there was worse to follow. When the King alighted on his return to the Palace, the mob almost entirely destroyed the state coach on its way to the Royal Mews.

Six months later, he had largely recovered and was able to remain calm when the news arrived that nine American provinces had formed a Congress in New York and passed resolutions against the Stamp Act. It cannot be said that his insanity was responsible for the loss of the American colonies. On the other hand, Pitt, who had been elevated to the Earldom of Chatham, had shown definite signs of insanity and thus was indeed partly responsible for the disaster. (Chatham had always been a neurotic and had many eccentricities. One was to have a chicken kept cooking day and night so that he could eat it immediately. He constantly changed houses and on one occasion insisted that all his servants who were travelling with him should have a fourteen-course meal.)

John Wilkes and Junius added to the King's mental discomfort. The most brutal slanders were printed about his mother, the Dowager Princess Augusta of Wales, who was continually baited right up to her death, when, according to a contemporary, the population 'huzzaed with joy and treated her memory with much disrespect'. His immediate family also behaved in a manner calculated to upset him. The Duke of Cumberland was cited by Earl Grosvenor, thus becoming the first royal prince to be brought into the divorce courts. Lord Grosvenor was awarded damages of £10,000 and £3,000 costs which George III had to pay.

The Duke next upset the King by marrying Anne Horton, of whom Walpole said, 'The new Princess of the Blood is a young widow of twenty-four, extremely pretty, very well made, with the most amorous eyes in the world and eye-lashes a yard long; coquette beyond measure, artful as Cleopatra and completely mistress of her passions and projects. Indeed eyelashes three-quarters of a yard shorter would have served to conquer such a head as she had turned.'

King George was greatly upset when he learned of the marriage. He told the Duke that he refused to see him again unless

Mrs Horton was known as such and not as the Duchess of Cumberland. Also, through the Lord Chamberlain, he notified the peers that anyone visiting Cumberland House would not be received at St James's Palace. Shortly after this, the unfortunate King was shocked by the liaison of his sister Caroline. At the age of fifteen she had been married to Christian VII of Denmark, a profligate, stupid homosexual. Soon afterwards she fell in love with John Frederick Struensee. Struensee was put to death and the Queen imprisoned in the Castle of Zelle, where George I's wife had also been incarcerated. But at least Caroline survived only six months instead of the thirty-three years of the previous occupant.

Earlier King Christian had visited London. George III had spent £3,000 on furnishing a royal suite for him at St James's Palace. Count Hokke, King Christian's favourite, exclaimed as soon as he saw it, 'This will never do. It is not fit to lodge a Christian.' As a result the Danish King at first refused to stay there, but at George III's insistence did so. As Lady Mary Coke wrote at the time, it was true that nothing much could be said in favour of the tarnished tapestry at St James's Palace or the wainscotted ballroom which was only fit for the market house of a country town and lit with tallow candles. . . .

Another current historian, Sir John Fielding, noted however that it was very pleasantly situated and contained many comfortable apartments:

> though in fact it is no better than an irregular brick building, devoid of any exterior beauty to attract and fix a beholder's eye. It reflects no honour on the Kingdom and is the jest of foreigners. Its entrance, even with the last alterations made, is at best but mean. Having passed through the gate which is no way conspicuous for either workmanship or taste, the curious enter a narrow square court, with a tinted piazza on the west side, that leads to what is called the Grand Staircase. The buildings that compose this merely nominal palace (for by all the rules of architecture it has no claim to the title) are low, plain and ignoble. There are two other courts beyond, which have not the least pretence to belong to a sovereign. The windows, however, that look into the garden on the south side and command a full view of St James's Park are the chief advantage belonging to the Palace as

to situation. It contains several articles of rich and curious furniture. But the decorations of the Queen's House which, indeed, promise magnificence, seem now to be the darling object.

The next family blow for George III was the discovery that the Duke of Gloucester, his favourite brother, had secretly married Maria, the illegitimate daughter of Sir Edward Walpole. When an heir was born to them, the King ignored the event, whereupon Wilkes moved an Address in the Common Council to congratulate His Majesty on the latest addition to the Royal Family.

As a result of all this, George III introduced the Royal Marriage Act which still holds good today. It laid down that the unmarried children of George III and future monarchs could not marry under the age of twenty-five without the King's consent. If the King refused, those over the age of twenty-five could apply to the Privy Council and if within one year neither the House of Commons nor the House of Lords objected, the proposed marriage would be permitted. The Opposition had objected to it as an insult 'giving leave to Princes of the Blood to lie with our wives and forbidding them to marry our daughters', but without success.

One compensation at this time was that Lord North became Prime Minister, for the King regarded him as an ideal choice. They had known each other since they were children. But the King never altered his attitude to what he called the American Colonists' 'unnatural rebellion'. The war had now started and dragged slowly on with the King as self-appointed Chief of Staff. He gave various instructions to Lord North about individual regiments being sent to America. He personally sampled the rations, including sauerkraut. He was said to have known the name of every officer in the Navy and the ship to which he was assigned; he knew the senior officers of each of the regiments, but there was not much he could do at such a distance and, looking at a list of the British commanders in America, he remarked that whatever the enemy might feel about a list of such names, they personally made him tremble.

Only a modern dictator equalled George III's activities during the American War of Independence; yet he never flinched from what he regarded as his duty. Even when General Burgoyne, followed by Lord Cornwallis, surrendered, he refused to be dismayed. When finally it became clear that American independence would have to be recognized he read the speech in Parliament announcing the fact in a firm voice. The ordeal over, he asked the Earl of Oxford what he thought of it, inquiring whether he had unconsciously lowered his voice during the actual pronouncement—and smiled faintly when told he had done so.

In spite of his rigid obstinacy, the King was able, on occasion, to change his attitude. The following two years showed that England's trade with America had not in any way suffered from the parting of the ways and the predictions that the British Empire would collapse were not fulfilled. Whereupon Pitt persuaded him to receive John Adams, first American Minister to the Court of St James. Fortunately, Adams left a verbatim account of their conversation, thus:

> *John Adams:* 'Sir, the United States of America have appointed me their Minister Plenipotentiary to your Majesty, and have directed me to deliver to your Majesty this letter that contains evidence of it. It is in obedience to their express command that I have the honour to assure your Majesty of their unanimous disposition and desire to cultivate the most liberal and friendly intercourse between your Majesty's subjects and their citizens, and for their best wishes for your Majesty's health and happiness, and for your Royal Family. The appointment of a Minister from the United States to your Majesty's Court will form an epoch in the history of England and America. I think myself more fortunate than all my fellow citizens in having the distinguished honour to be the first to stand in your Majesty's Royal presence in a diplomatic character; and I shall esteem myself the happiest man if I can be instrumental in recommending my country more and more to your Majesty's royal benevolence and in restoring an entire esteem, confidence and affection or in better words the old good nature and the old good humour between people who, though separated by an Ocean and under different Governments have the same language, a similar religion and kindred blood. . . .'
>
> *The King:* 'Sir, the circumstances of this audience are so extraordinary; the language you have now held is so extremely

proper and the feelings you have discovered so justly adapted for the occasion that I must say that I not only receive with pleasure the assurance of the friendly disposition of the United States, but I am very glad that the choice had fallen upon you to be their Minister. I wish you, Sir, to believe that it may be understood in America that I have done nothing in the late contest but what I thought myself indispensably bound to do, by the duty which I owed my people. I will be very frank with you. I was the last to consent to the Separation; but the Separation having been made and been inevitable, I have always said as I say now, that I would be the first to meet the friendship of the United States as an independent power. The moment I see such sentiments and language as yours prevail, and a disposition to give this country the preference, that moment shall I say, let the circumstances of language, religion and blood have their natural full effect.'

It was now Edmund Burke's turn to frustrate the unfortunate monarch. He had clearly done considerable research into the royal economy, or rather the lack of it, before he introduced his Plan for Economic Reform in the House of Commons. The primary object was to overhaul the Royal Household, abolish a number of sinecures and if possible to reduce the secret pensions given to Members of Parliament so that they should vote the way the King wanted them to do. 'Our Palaces,' he said in his speech, 'are vast inhospitable halls. There the bleak winds, howling through the vacant lobbies and clattering the doors of deserted guard-rooms, appal the imagination and conjure up grim spectres of departed tyrants . . . who stalk from desolation to desolation through the dreary vacuity and melancholy succession of chill and comfortless corridors. In former days when the Household was vast and the supply scanty and precarious, the Royal Purveyors sallying forth from under the Gothic portcullis to purchase provision with power and prerogative instead of money, brought home the plunder of an hundred markets and all that could be seized from a flying and hiding country and deposited their spoil in an hundred caverns with each its keeper. There every commodity received in its rawest condition went through all the processes which fitted it for use. Yet still the King retains Buttery, Pantry and all that rabble of places which, though profitable to the holders and expensive to the State are almost too mean to mention.'

Burke then proceeded to enumerate a number of other un-necessary offices. There was no reason, he said, why the Lord Chamberlain should not take over the Great Wardrobe which had cost the Crown £150,000 in quite a short time for 'naked walls or walls hung with cobwebs'. The truth was, he pointed out, the money spent was not to furnish the walls with tapes-tries and pictures, but to furnish Parliament with venal Mem-bers. He next raised the question of the Jewel Office, which existed solely for the purpose of taxing the King's gifts of plate. Why, too, have an office of the Robes and three useless Treas-urers?

'The King's domestic servants were all undone,' he thundered on, 'his tradesmen remained unpaid and became bankrupt—because the turnspit of the King's Kitchen was a Member of Parliament. His Majesty's slumbers were interrupted, his pil-low was stuffed with thorns and his peace of mind entirely broken down—because the turnspit of the King's Kitchen was a Member of Parliament. The judges were unpaid; the justice of the kingdom bent and gave way; the foreign ministers remained inactive and unprofited; the system of Europe was dissolved; the chain of our alliances was broken; all the wheels of Govern-ment at home and abroad were stopped; because the turnspit of the King's Kitchen was a Member of Parliament.' His final jibe was that a revolution of thirteen lords-of-the-bedchamber would be far more frightening than a revolt of thirteen colonies.

Two years passed before the repercussions of this speech had their effect. Then, according to Sir Nathaniel Wraxall, 'Many persons of high rank reluctantly disappeared from about the King's person and Court in consequence of Burke's Bill. The Earl of Darlington quitted the Jewel House and Lord Pelham the Great Wardrobe; the first of which offices owed its insti-tution to Elizabeth while the latter went back to the times of the Plantagenets. The Earl of Essex laid down the Stag Hounds as did Lord Denbigh the Harriers; while the disasters of Saratoga and Yorktown were thus felt by rebound through every avenue of St James's.'

No relief for George III was provided by Lord George Gor-don when his 60,000 followers marched on Parliament with a petition to repeal the Catholic Reform Bill. Troops had to be strengthened round St James's Palace following the riots. Convicts were released from various prisons. There was an attack on the Bank of England and on Black Wednesday 3,000 fires were started in London. George III assumed full responsibility and insisted on the Riot Act being read. Throughout the whole affair, Lord George appears as a very unbalanced character. During his trial he kept a Bible in front of him and showed fury when he was refused permission to read aloud four chapters of Zechariah. Defended by Lord Erskine, one of the most brilliant criminal lawyers in English history, he was however acquitted on the grounds that he had taken no part in the actual rioting and had indeed tried to assist the Government in suppressing it.

He was certainly a crackpot. He wore a long red beard, was converted to Judaism and underwent circumcision, a very painful matter indeed for a grown man before the days of anæsthetics.

Later he was accused of libelling Marie Antoinette, fled to Amsterdam, was arrested and brought back to England, where he was sentenced to five years' imprisonment. When his time was up he was asked to give security that he would be of good behaviour in the future. He was unable to do this and in consequence was sent back to Newgate Prison where he died of jail fever.

Lord George, however, was by no means the only deranged character in the latter part of the eighteenth century. For many years St James's Palace was plagued by lunatics of one kind or another. In 1778 as the King was stepping down from his sedan chair close to Friary Court, a middle-aged woman planted herself in front of him and refused to go away. When asked what she wanted she told him her name was Queen Beck. It afterwards turned out that she was an Irishwoman named Rebecca O'Hara, who had lived in England for five years near Red Lion Square. She was found to be hopelessly insane and ordered to be detained during His Majesty's pleasure. In 1780 Thomas Stone, a solicitor from Shaftesbury, wrote a crazy letter to the Queen explaining his infatuation for Princess Augusta Matilda, later Queen of Württemberg. He expressed the hope that if royal approval was given he and the Princess Royal would be a very happy couple. Shortly after writing this letter he appeared personally at St James's Palace asking for a formal introduction on the grounds that as he had received no reply to his letter, presumably his proposal of marriage had been accepted. When he was searched, a number of papers and letters were found on him all addressed to the Princess Royal. One of them contained the following quatrain:

Thrice glad were I to be your willing slave
But not the captive of the fool or knave
When woe on woe you melt my sighing breast
Whilst you reject your humble would-be guest.

After questioning, Stone said that his heart had been stolen from him three years previously, but he did not know who was the robber until he saw the Princess Royal at the theatre looking up at the 2s. gallery where he was sitting. He too was pronounced insane.

A much more dangerous lunatic was Margaret Nicholson of Stockton-on-Tees who tried to murder George III as he was emerging from his carriage at the garden gate of St James's Palace. She had been waiting for him for some time and when he alighted she approached him with a petition. The document was wrapped up and carried the superscription 'For the King's Most Excellent Majesty'. Presenting it with her right hand, she drew a knife with her left hand and aimed straight at his heart as he bent forward to see the document. Not being left-handed, she missed. The King stood back, scarcely believing the testimony of his eyes. Whereupon the woman made a second thrust which just touched his waistcoat before he had time to stop her. At that moment one of the attendants seized the knife from her hand. Said the King, 'Has she cut my waistcoat? Look for I have no time to examine, though nothing could have been softer done, for there was nothing for her to go through but a thin lining and fat.' While the guards surrounded the King, the public tried to lynch the would-be assassin; but the King shouted out, 'The poor creature's mad, do not hurt her. She has not hurt me.' He then walked forward and showed that, truly, he was quite unhurt. Mrs Nicholson was taken into custody but refused to speak and was pronounced hopelessly insane before the Board of Green Cloth. Ordered to be detained during His Majesty's pleasure, she was sent to Bethlehem Hospital where she lived for forty years more.

Another lunatic, a Danish hairdresser named Spang, broke into the apartment of Princess Elizabeth at St James's Palace. The Princess rushed out of the room to call an attendant and the page-in-waiting seized him. Like Margaret Nicholson, he refused to speak and seemed to be quite harmless, though a trifle mad, and he was allowed to leave the palace. Soon afterwards he returned, insisting on an introduction to the Princess, 'that he might lay his adoration at her feet'. This time it was thought advisable to hand him over to the police.

On another occasion, as George III was going in state through the park from St James's Palace to the House of Lords, a lieutenant of the Second Battalion, the Royals, dressed in a scarlet coat, black breeches and a hat adorned with a bright yellow cockade, threw a stone at the royal carriage and was immediately arrested on a charge of high treason. This incident was followed by another involving a lunatic, Thomas Cannon from the Isle of Man, who seized the Colours belonging to the 1st Regiment on Guard in Colour Court and ran off with it before he was seen. Chased by the soldiers, he was finally overpowered but not before he had thrown the Standard to the ground. He was taken to Bow Street where he said that he had always wanted to throw down the Royal Standard of England. As he refused to explain his reasons until he saw the King, the Prince of Wales and the Prime Minister, he was sent to prison.

Shortly afterwards, as the King was riding from the Green Park to St James's Palace, a gentleman in black pulled out from his pocket a paper addressed to the King and stuck it on the park rails. Having done so, he threw his hat on the ground and shot himself dead.

11. Murder most foul

ALL this time, George III and the Queen served as models of domesticity, like George V and Queen Mary a century and a half later. They were both very frugal by contemporary standards. They never had more than a four-course luncheon and they never gave dinner parties. If an occasional guest was asked to a meal he was put at another table. The King's only luxury was fresh fruit. Although not a teetotaller, he was extremely abstemious in an age of hard drinkers, possibly because the Duke of Cumberland had warned him of the family inheritance of obesity.

Altogether, he was a strange character. He would stand for hours at a time talking to William Pitt because of his self-imposed rule that he could never sit down in Pitt's presence. On other occasions he would play practical jokes, rushing up to the bedroom of one of his equerries and routing him out of bed at 5 a.m. for absolutely no reason. He would, too, frequently stop at some cottage while riding, and taste whatever was cooking. He had a rapid staccato method of speaking and frequently repeated whole phrases very fast.

Fanny Burney, who was paid £200 a year with board and lodging by Queen Charlotte as her Keeper of the Robes, was warned that she would probably be unable to understand much of his remarks. As a contemporary historian notes, 'The precipitation of his questions, none of which would wait for an answer, and the hurry of articulation offered to little minds or to malicious observers who only saw him in a Drawing-room at St James's Palace the occasion for calling in question the soundness of his judgment and the strength of his faculties.'

He loved freaks and telescopes and he played the flute quite well, often accompanied by Johann Christian Bach. His favourite composer was Handel and he was delighted when the great composer said of him, 'That young man will preserve my music.' He collected books, accumulating 63,000 volumes at a cost of £135,000. Oddly enough, he thought nothing of Shakespeare. One day he said to Fanny Burney, 'Was there ever such stuff as a great part of Shakespeare? One must not say so, but what do you think? What? What? What? Is there not sad stuff? What? What?'

It was one of the unhappy aspects of his life that he was compelled to employ John Robinson who, based on St James's Palace, spent huge sums of money to bribe electors. In those days parliamentary seats were generally advertised for sale in the newspapers. A seat was reckoned as a saleable asset of a bankrupt and when a defaulting debtor had paid the market price for a seat he was able, under the protection of parliamentary privilege, to escape his creditors by leaving England without arrest. The price rose from £2,000 in 1730 to £6,000 in the 1780's.

Queen Charlotte continued to prove herself an ideal wife. Incidentally, she bore fifteen living children to her husband, twelve of them during the first fifteen years of her marriage. Her favourite child was the Prince of Wales, born in 1762 but regarded by the King as the family black sheep. While the children were young, he loved carrying them about in his arms, his favourite being little Octavius who died after being inoculated against smallpox—to the King's acute grief.

As the children grew older he insisted that the boys had to be out of bed by 7.30 a.m. in winter and then report at 8 a.m. for an hour's instruction before breakfast. Altogether he was a rigid parent.

'I do not believe there is a more unhappy family in the Kingdom,' wrote Sir James Bland Burgess some time later, 'than that of our good King. They have lately passed whole hours together in tears and often they do not meet for half a day, but each remains alone, separately brooding over their misfortunes. The ill-success and disgrace of the Duke of York, the wounds and ill-health of the Princes Ernest and Augustus, and the strange caprices and obstinacy of the Prince of Wales—all these causes are perpetually preying on them and making them miserable. The King sometimes bursts into tears, rises up and walks about the room, then kisses his daughters and thanks God for having given them to him to comfort him, but the Princesses are thereby agitated and sometimes so much so that they go into fits.'

The Prince of Wales alone held aloof from family activities. While he was still seventeen he had become enamoured of Mrs Robinson, an actress, and sent her a number of love letters signed 'Florizel' which his father had to buy back for £5,000. All this, together with the disobedience of Prince William and the Duke of York, brought on another bout of madness, augmented by the impeachment proceedings against Warren Hastings. 'Poor Hastings, poor Hastings,' the King lamented to one of his gardeners. 'They will ruin him, they will ruin him. Poor Hastings. He will be ruined, he will be ruined!'

Once again every attempt was made to conceal his madness from the public although Dr Munro, the head of Bedlam Asylum, was called in. The King tried to delude himself that his illness was in no sense mental and his doctors persuaded him to go to Cheltenham to take the waters. Here he suddenly fell madly in love all over again with the Countess of Pembroke. This was completely out of character. Fanny Burney reports, 'He then ran a race with a horse; and asked Mr Clements if he was the man who ran away with Lady S. Bunbury when he was in love with her . . . he would sit with young women who embroidered, pretending to play on the fiddle.' Another eccentricity was to have a house moved by thirty men from the town to Bay's Hill so that the Duke of York might have comfortable sleeping quarters when he came to stay for one night. Naturally a quick eater, his speed became astonishing: 'The King is so rapid with his meals,' noted Fanny Burney, 'that whoever attends him must be rapid also or follow starving.'

On his return from Cheltenham, he hurried in his coach for a Drawing-room at St James's Palace and suffered extremely from spasms in his stomach and bowels. As a result he was given three doses of the purge, each of which had to be followed by laudanum.

The country was now full of rumours about his health and the Stock Market in consequence started to drop. This was accentuated when Sir George Baker, one of the royal doctors, sold £18,000 worth of stocks in order to take up a mortgage which had been offered to him. This was regarded as highly significant and caused the Funds to fall ten per cent. To retrieve the situation, George III gallantly held a levee at St James's Palace that afternoon. But he was clearly ill and spoke to very few people. Some days later, he developed insomnia. His head was shaved and blistered with a view to 'drawing the noxious substances away from the brain to the skin surfaces' and when Sir George Baker and Dr Heberden, his understudy, visited him, the King repeated in a staccato voice, 'I am nervous. I am not ill. But I am nervous. If you would know what is the matter with me, I am nervous. But I love you both very well, if only you would tell me the truth. I love Dr Heberden best, for he has not told me a lie. Sir George has told me a lie—a white lie, he says. But I hate a white lie. If you will tell me a lie, let it be a black lie.'

Another night he woke up at 1 a.m. and wandered into the bedroom next to his, where the Duke of York among others was resting on a sofa. 'Oh my boy,' he lamented, 'I wish to God I might die, for I am going to be mad.' As a result, on 7 November 1788 the Prince of Wales assumed full charge of his father and sent for the Chancellor to obtain permission to use a strait-jacket if this were necessary. The King had already proved so violent on occasion that it needed four attendants to hold him down. Sometimes they were compelled to sit on him.

* * *

Four days later it was found necessary to have a lord-in-waiting permanently at St James's Palace to answer the daily inquiries regarding the King's health. The first medical bulletin written by Dr Warren was placed on a table. 'His Majesty passed a quiet night,' it read, 'but without any abatement in his complaint.' Hundreds of people went to St James's Palace to sign the book. The Duchess of Devonshire noted in her journal, 'The courtiers pretend it is nothing; and it is a fashion among them to say that they have been all mad; Lord Fauconberg declares everybody must remember his strait-waistcoat; Mr Robinson the same and Lord Salisbury declares that the King has as much understanding as he has.'

Hydrotherapy, well-known to modern psychiatrists, was now used to promote sleep for the royal patient who was kept in a tub at 95° F. for a quarter of an hour and then put into bed. He liked this very much. An additional doctor, Sir Lucas Pepys, contributed the idea of 'carded wool and bootikins and woollen yarn to His Majesty's feet'. Nevertheless, the next day the King talked unceasingly from 1 a.m. to breakfast time. All kinds of quack cures were suggested by laymen. One suggested 'communicating the itch'. Another recommended injecting the blood of a donkey to which the brains of a ram were to be added.

Strangely enough, the King's illness seemed to make him more popular. Bystanders would stop the coaches of the doctors in the street and ask for first-hand reports. If these were gloomy the doctors would be sent on their way with shouts of 'The worse shame for you'. In the meantime, more and more experts were brought in. They included Dr Reynolds, Dr Gisbourne and the Rev. Dr Francis Willis, who had opened a private asylum at Gretford and whose patients paid anything from four guineas to fifty guineas a week.

As Dr Willis entered George III's room for the first time, the King said, 'Sir, your dress and appearance bespeaks you of the Church; you belong to it?'

'I did formerly, but lately I have attended chiefly to physick.'

'I am sorry for that,' was the reply. 'You have quitted a profession I have always loved and you have embraced one I most heartily detest. Alter your line of life; ask what preferment you wish and make me your friend. I recommend to you the parish of Worcester.'

'Our Saviour Himself went about healing the sick,' the reverend doctor objected.

'Yes,' replied the King, 'but he didn't get seven hundred pounds a year for it.'

Dr Willis, in fact, showed great skill with his royal patient. He had come with a kind of strait-jacket, warning the King that he would have to use it if he did not behave himself. At the same

162

time he allowed him to use a knife and fork and even to shave himself, on the grounds that the King was so religious that he was most unlikely to commit suicide. (According to a diagnosis given later in the House of Lords, he came to the conclusion that the madness was attributable to unduly violent exercise, a sparse diet and lack of sleep caused by anxiety about international affairs.)

Slowly the King started to improve but there were still signs of madness, notably his frequent reference to Lady Pembroke. Every now and then he would shout the song,

> I made love to Kate,
> Long I sighed for she
> 'Til I heard of late
> That she'd a mind for me.

His conversation was frequently erotic. Thus, when playing picquet with Dr Willis he addressed the Queen of Hearts as 'dear Elizabeth' and kissed it.

At this point it is interesting to note the annual cost of his illness as later itemized by Sir Herbert Taylor, the King's Secretary to the Lord of the Treasury:

	Per Annum	
	Guineas	Shillings
Attendance of 3 ordinary Physicians @ 30 G. per diem	1828	
Mr Dundas @ 15 G. per diem	9501	10
Dr Robert Willis @ 30 G. per diem 365 days	11497	10
Dr John Willis @ 30 G. per diem 8 months	7056	
Post horses for regular physicians three times a week back & forth	1716	
Post horses for Willis & Dundas	500	
Dr Willis' attendants	600	
Extra attendance of Physicians and Mr Dundas on Council Days—say 12 per annum	1300	
	33990	

It was now becoming evident that a Regency would have to be

created unless the King recovered very rapidly; mercifully he did, thanks to the ministrations of Dr Willis.

London at once became immensely gay, perhaps in direct defiance of the looming shadows foreboding the French Revolution in Paris. Admittedly, the first Drawing-room at St James's Palace was not attended by the King, but a tremendous number of people were present.

The climax of the celebrations connected with the royal recovery was a Thanksgiving Service at St Paul's on St George's Day. Throughout it the royal princes chattered to one another with a disgraceful lack of decorum, though the King behaved magnificently. Only for a moment did he forget himself, stretching his arms upwards and fixing his eyes on the ceiling for at least a minute. He then clutched his breast and burst into loud sobs, recovering himself, however, very quickly.

In spite of the increase in his popularity, there were those who jibed, such as Peter Pindar, who wrote:

> If blisters on his head applied
> Some little sense bestow,
> What pity 'tis they were not tried
> Some twenty years ago.

Nevertheless, a vast part of the population were delighted with the signs of George III's recovery and 'God save the King', originally written by Dr Bull in 1605 for King James after the discovery of the Gunpowder Plot, now became the official national anthem, instead of being merely a piece of patriotic music without any official connotation. Fanny Burney records that the slogan 'God save the King' was seen everywhere in Weymouth where George III had gone to convalesce. 'They have dressed out every street with labels of God save the King; all shops have it over the doors, and the sailors never approach the house without shouting it aloud. The bathing machines make it their motto over all their windows. Much to the surprise of His Majesty, the first time he was bathing, he had no sooner popped his royal head under the water than a band of music concealed in a neighbouring machine struck up "God save great George our King".'

Convalescence at Weymouth was so rapid that George III

was able to hold a Drawing-room at St James's Palace for the first time since his illness.

The next year, St James's was the scene of a ball, given in celebration of the King's birthday, which subsequently resulted in one of the King's sons being challenged by one of his subjects—certainly an historic occasion.

'This memorable incident occurred on May 26,' wrote Sir John Fielding. 'The Duke of York was then in his twenty-sixth year, and his opponent about the same age. The dispute originated in the following circumstance: At a dinner party given by the Prince of Wales, Colonel Lennox, who happened to be one of the guests, proposed, in a moment of excitement, the health of Mr Pitt, the great leader of the political party then arrayed against the Heir Apparent. Angry words arose; but the good sense of the company so far prevailed that the matter was immediately settled. The following day, however, a report circulated that the Duke of York had in the public room of his Club commented somewhat too harshly on the conduct of Colonel Lennox, and had asserted that terms had been applied to that officer to which no gentleman ought to submit. These observations being repeated to the Colonel, he took an opportunity, while the Duke of York was on parade, to address him, desiring to know what were the words and by whom they were spoken. To this H.R.H. gave no other reply than ordering the Lieut-Colonel to his post. The Parade being over, the Duke went into the Orderly-room, and sent for Colonel Lennox, where by all accounts, an angry and animated discussion took place. Eventually the Duke consented to give Colonel Lennox the meeting required. Lord Rawdon accompanied the Duke of York, and Lord Winchelsea was the second of Colonel Lennox.'

They met on the traditional duelling ground on Wimbledon Common. The distance between the two men was measured at twelve paces and both parties were to fire at a signal agreed upon. The signal being given, Colonel Lennox fired and the ball grazed His Royal Highness's curl. The Duke of York did not fire in return. When Colonel Lennox commented on this somewhat naïvely, Lord Rawdon declared 'that it had never been the intention of the Duke of York to fire, H.R.H. had come out upon Colonel Lennox's desire to give him satisfaction but had no animosity against him'.

This was the first instance of a Prince of the Blood in England being challenged by a subject. The King appeared to think it a matter of etiquette to overlook the offence; but the Prince of Wales was unable to restrain his feelings, and at the first meeting with Colonel Lennox at Court, he expressed his displeasure in the most pointed manner, consistent with the presence of Royalty.

The newspapers of the day refer to the circumstance as follows: Colonel Lennox, to the surprise of everyone, had appeared at the Ball given at St James's on the King's Birthday, 1789. The Colonel stood up with Lady Catherine Barnard. The Prince, who danced with his sister the Princess Royal, was so far down the set that the Colonel and Lady Catherine were the next couple. The Prince paused, looked at the Colonel, took his partner's hand, and led her to the bottom of the dance. The Duke of Clarence followed his example, but the Duke of York made no distinction between the Colonel and the other gentlemen of the party. When the Colonel and his partner had danced down the set, the Prince again took his sister's hand and led her to a seat. Observing this, the Queen approached and said to the Prince, 'You are heated, Sir, and tired. I had better leave the apartment and put an end to the dance.' 'I am heated,' replied the Prince, 'and tired, not with the dancing, but with a portion of the company;' and emphatically added, 'I certainly never will countenance an insult offered to my family, however it may be regarded by others.'

Meanwhile, the Prince of Wales's association with Beau Brummell cannot have been any pleasure to his father. He had a great deal to do with the debts which the Prince of Wales accumulated over the years. Beau Brummell was the son of a rich father who gave each of his children nearly £30,000 and bought him a commission in the 10th Hussars when he was only sixteen. However, when the regiment was ordered to Manchester the shock proved too much for Mr Brummell and he promptly resigned his commission.

In those days, Brummell was living in Chesterfield Street where the Prince would visit him and spend hours discussing

life in general and fashion in particular. The evenings usually
ended in some kind of orgy. Beau Brummell was such a fop that
he insisted on two different craftsmen making his gloves; one—
the fingers and hands and the other—the thumbs, on the grounds
that a particular cut was necessary for each. He claimed that
'with strict economy' dressing might be done on £800 a year,
and he always went home after the opera to change his cravat
for succeeding parties. Like Count d'Orsay, a later dandy, he
carried about with him an enormous chest full of every toilet
requisite, all of silver. He justified this by saying that it was
impossible to spit in earthenware.

In some ways he was a predecessor of Oscar Wilde. A typical
remark of his, when asked whether he had heard anything about
a young couple who had married a week before was, 'No, no,
I have heard nothing, but I believe they are still living together.' On another occasion he was asked whether he had helped
a young man who had been given an introduction to him. 'Yes,
indeed,' was the reply. 'I did my best for the young man. I
once gave him my arm all the way from White's to Watier's.'
(All the way from St James's Street to Bruton Street.)

There are several versions of the occasion when Beau Brummell finally lost the friendship of the Prince of Wales. One is
Captain Gronow's, who reported, 'Brummell was asked one
night at White's to take a hand at whist, when he won from
George Harley Drummond twenty thousand pounds. This
circumstance having been related by the Duke of York to the
Prince of Wales, the Beau was again invited to Carlton House.
At the commencement of dinner, matters went off smoothly;
but Brummell in his joy at finding himself with his old friend,
became excited and drank too much wine. His Royal Highness—
who wanted to pay off Brummell for an insult he had received
at Lady Cholmondeley's ball, when the Beau, turning towards
the Prince, said to Lady Worcester: "Who is your fat friend?"—
had invited him to dinner merely out of a desire for revenge.
The Prince therefore pretended to be affronted with Brummell's
hilarity and said to his brother the Duke of York, who was
present: "I think we had better order Mr Brummell's carriage
before he gets drunk." Whereupon he rang the bell and Brummell left the royal presence.'

Lord Houghton, in another version, says, 'The tradition of his impertinence rests on certain stories which are often told without the circumstances that explain or excuse them. An example of this may be given. Mr Brummell was one of the committee of the fete given by the three most fashionable clubs to the Allied sovereigns. The scene was Burlington House, or rather the garden behind it, where a monster marquee was erected. The committee lined the passage through the house and each royal personage, as he passed, shook hands with the members alternately from side to side. Mr Brummell was standing opposite Sir Henry Mildmay with whom the Regent shook hands and who, instead of taking him in his natural turn, passed over him and saluted the next opposite member, thus presenting the reverse of his portly figure to Mr Brummell, who leaning over it, said to Sir Henry in a loud aside, "Henry, who is our fat friend?"

'Considering the old intimacy, indeed, as far as the difference of state permitted the friendship between the Prince and the playfellow, this was felt at the time to be rather a witty retort to a provocation than an unmannerly insult.'

Whatever the cause of the rift, Beau Brummell was a tremendous gambler, his favourite game being Macao. This was a predecessor of Vingt-et-un, but face cards and tens counted zero and a nine on the first card immediately trebled the bet, while an eight doubled it. One evening at Watier's, the biggest gaming club in London at the time, he won £1,500 in less than ten minutes.

Finally his luck ran out and he was compelled to flee to Calais. Later he was consul at Caen, a post from which he resigned and was promptly jailed, ending his days in a French lunatic asylum.

For the next twelve years, the King enjoyed good health and showed no signs of insanity despite many trying circumstances. In 1791 there were several celebrations in England to mark the Fall of the Bastille, and revolutionary societies sprang up all over the country. Furthermore, the French declared war on England and the English forces suffered under the disastrous generalship of the King's favourite son, the Duke of York, always remembered for the lines:

The noble Duke of York,
He had ten thousand men,
He marched them up to the top of the hill
And marched them down again.
And when they were up, they were up,
And when they were down, they were down,
And when they were only half way up
They were neither up nor down.

Another awkward period for George III was when the Prince of Wales married Caroline of Brunswick although he had already married Mrs Fitzherbert morganatically. Princess Caroline was a niece of George III and certainly no beauty. Yet this scarcely excused England's First Gentleman being so drunk at the wedding that he had to be held up. As for the bridal night, his wife recorded that he passed the greatest part of it in the grate, 'Where he fell and I left him.'

Maria Fitzherbert had been married twice before she met the Prince and was six years older than he. She was a staunch Roman Catholic and soon made it clear that she would never become merely his mistress. She told the Prince that he must forget her, but he said that this was impossible and staged an attempted suicide, stabbing himself in his side. Maria Fitzherbert nevertheless refused to see him unless chaperoned by the Duchess of Devonshire.

The Prince declared on her arrival that he would definitely commit suicide unless she married him and actually persuaded her to let him put a ring on her finger; but when she returned home, she decided she could not go through with the liaison and went abroad next day. All the British Embassies on the Continent were alerted to track her down. She was finally located and returned to England and the couple were married secretly on 15 December 1784 in Park Street, London, W.1., by the Rev. R. Burt, the sole clergyman of the Church of England who was prepared to risk the penalties of praemunire. The only witnesses were Maria Fitzherbert's uncle and brother.

Mrs Fitzherbert now became uniquely the wife masquerading as a mistress, instead of the other way round. In view of the Royal Marriage Act, of course, the marriage was not legal and the Prince was able to deny to Charles James Fox that he was in fact married. He knew that Maria would never betray him.

George III continued to show no signs of loss of composure even when the Royal Navy mutinied at Spithead and the Nore; not even when the country was so nearly bankrupt that the Bank of England suspended cash payments. Ireland, too, was difficult. The only method of curbing its growing independence was to buy eighty-four Irish pocket boroughs at a cost of over a million pounds and raise fifty-six Irishmen to the peerage. After this it was possible for Pitt to persuade the Irish Parliament to vote for its own extinction and effect a union with England.

What finally drove George III literally to distraction was the resignation of Pitt on the subject of the Bill for Catholic Toleration. One day he went to a service at the chapel at St James's Palace and suddenly in the middle of it raised himself to his feet and cried, 'Forty years long was I grieved with this generation and said, "This is a people that do err in their hearts for they have not known my ways." '

Within a week the Court at St James's was once again alarmed by his behaviour—his garrulity, his jumping from topic to topic and his highly indiscreet remarks. Dr Willis (Junior) was called in and immediately asked that his father should also be summoned. He found that the royal pulse was 144 and bulletins had again to be issued regularly at St James's Palace. After very large doses of opiates, the King slept eleven hours and seemed to be almost entirely recovered. But, in spite of the briefness of the attack, convalescence was long drawn out with various interruptions. True, he forgot his former infatuation for Lady Pembroke but he now wished to act as knight errant for his niece Caroline, discarded wife of the Prince of Wales—to fight for her against him. Also, he took an immense dislike to the three Dr Willises. He himself thought he was almost completely recovered and held a levee on his birthday at St James's Palace where he received the congratulations of the foreign ambassadors. (It is, incidentally, George III's birthday which is celebrated at Eton on every 4 June.)

Once again he went to Weymouth where the sea-bathing did him a great deal of good. By this time, Henry Addington had been presented with the seals of the Treasury, at which one of his former colleagues at the House of Commons 'had such a fit of laughter that he laughed the whole way from the Horse Guards to the Stable Yard and was obliged to sit down on a bench in St James's Park to rest'. Addington was an insignificant character and as Canning put it:

> Pitt is to Addington
> As London is to Paddington.

George III, by contrast, was delighted with him.

In 1803 there was once again war with France, and Napoleon collected an army of nearly 100,000 troops at Calais and Boulogne.

In reply, George III with his sons took the salute as 12,000 men of the Volunteer Corps of London marched past in Hyde Park. These national preoccupations kept him so busy that his mind was taken off the appalling behaviour of the Prince of Wales, until the latter published his private correspondence with his father in the *Morning Chronicle*, the Opposition daily newspaper. This abominable trick caused the King to refuse to see or correspond with him.

Realizing that he had overplayed his hand, the Prince of Wales endeavoured to reconcile himself with his father who, not surprisingly, would have nothing to do with him. They did, however, have one common link—Princess Charlotte, the eight-year-old daughter of the Prince of Wales, and at the time, the King's only grandchild, with whom he spent some of his happiest hours while she sat on his knee singing 'Hearts of Oak' to him. He knew that her father, who spent most of his time with his various mistresses, was neglecting her; he therefore wanted her to come and live with him.

The Prince of Wales presumed that if he agreed he would regain favour. George III however wrote to Lord Eldon, the Lord Chancellor, 'Undoubtedly the Prince of Wales's making the offer of having dear little Charlotte's education and principles attended to, is the best earnest he can give for returning to a sense of what he owes to his father, indeed to the country, and may to a degree mollify the feelings of an injured father; but it will require some reflection before the King can bring himself to receive the publisher of his letters.'

Once more the King went to Weymouth where the abnormally accelerated tempo of his daily life is described by Lady Harriet Hesketh.

You will feel a very mixed sensation when I tell you their Majesties travelled all night after travelling all day; and arrived here some time after 6 in the morning! To me and perhaps to you this sort of Evolution may appear to have required Rest and Repose but our gracious Sovereign thought very differently, for at 7 and 8 he was walking about the town! At 10 he got on horseback and rode two hours after which he and the Queen walked on the Esplanade! After which he went out of Town and employed himself in marking out the Camp, and giving the proper directions —after dinner 'till quite dark, he saw all the troops pass before him; and in particular the Hanoverian Horse, very fine troops indeed, as I am told, for I did not see them. In honour of them, he mounted a very spirited Hanoverian Charger which he rode and exercised as if he had been a man of thirty and certainly galloped as hard! What he did afterward I know not, but had a card party I conclude, and talked to all the world; this morning I saw him walking before breakfast and the moment Church was over the royal family embarked at the pierhead and went aboard the new Yacht, the Royal Sovereign.

A few weeks later Sir Robert Wilson recorded another of the King's visits to the royal yacht where, while taking some papers out of a green box, he observed to Mrs Deas who was sitting on the sofa with the three Princesses, 'Mrs Deas, you look very well, very well indeed, dear lovely Mrs Deas. What a pretty arse you have got. How I should like to pat such a pretty arse.' This was said twice in the same quaint manner in a voice that reached every part of the ship. The confusion of the Princesses, ladies and gentlemen, officers and sailors was indescribable. Some of the sailors tumbled over one another into the hatchway unable to restrain their fits of laughter. Actually, this outburst from the King had resulted from his overhearing Mrs Deas saying that morning to a donkey, 'Dear pretty little ass, come here that I may pat you. How I should like to pat you, dear pretty ass.'

In November 1804 a formal reconciliation was effected between the King and his eldest son. The King was already complaining about his failing eyesight—he was suffering from cataract and dreaded the operation—so he appointed Lieut.-Colonel Herbert Taylor to help him with his correspondence. He was in fact one of the most voluminous letter-writers in history, writing with the same tremendous speed and energy as he talked.

Eighteen months later, Pitt died. This deeply affected the King, who was compelled to allow Fox and Grenville to take over the Government. Fox, however, died within six months. A further blow was the public rumours about the immorality of Princess Caroline, the discarded wife of the Prince of Wales.

Although he had been devoted to her, the King agreed to an official inquiry into her behaviour. It was known as 'The Delicate Investigation'. The result was the verdict that her adopted son William Austin was not her illegitimate child, but that she had slept with at least three men, including Sir Thomas Lawrence, the royal portrait painter.

By 1808, George III was totally blind. This made it all the more unfortunate for him when one of the Duke of York's mistresses, Mary Anne Clarke, the wife of a stonemason, exposed her protector when he deserted her for another mistress. The Duke of York at that time was Commander-in-Chief. Mary Anne Clarke employed a former colonel of the Royal Welch Fusiliers, Colonel Wardle, by now a Member of Parliament, to spread stories of corruption about him. Colonel Wardle raised the matter in the House of Commons. The King, unable to read the documents, refused to believe the stories and agreed to a public investigation. After seven weeks it became only too clear that Mary Anne Clarke, supported by her royal lover, had conducted a successful business in army promotions. There were set prices: to become a major with full pay cost £2,600, with half pay £900; a captain with full pay cost £1,500, with half pay £700; she also sold a number of bishoprics. Mary Anne Clarke was a very attractive, clever woman. When she appeared before the House of Commons she was asked, 'Pray, madam, under whose protection are you now?' With downcast eyes she turned to the chairman and said demurely, 'At present, sir, I believe I am under yours.'

The House of Commons, strangely enough, acquitted the

Duke of personal corruption, but he was compelled to resign from the army.

Fortunately, in view of his blindness, the King was not, at the time, staying in St James's Palace in January 1809 when a fire broke out, the second in two years. One of the sentries in the palace yard heard a dog barking violently and noticed heavy smoke emerging. The alarm was immediately given and several fire engines arrived. Some time elapsed, however, before the necessary supply of water from the canal in St James's Park, nearly a thousand yards away, could be pumped up.

The fire had broken out in the apartments between the armoury and the King's private entrance into the palace from St James's Park. The flames soon spread to the whole east wing of the inner courtyard on the side which housed the Queen's private drawing-room, bedroom and other rooms. At the end of this wing were other apartments belonging to the Duke of Cambridge, the whole of which were burned down. Luckily, the Queen's German Chapel was not affected and was used for depositing those treasures which could be saved from the flames. This wing, incidentally the one which had been the scene of the famous warming-pan incident, has never been entirely rebuilt although the rooms were partly repaired ten years later.

* * *

The following year a gruesome murder took place at St James's Palace in the royal apartments of the Duke of Cumberland, the most hated man of his day. A graphic description is given by a man named Yew who was at that time one of his retainers:

> I was in the Duke's household, in May, 1810, and on the evening of the 31st I attended his Royal Highness to the Opera. That night it was my turn to undress his Royal Highness. On our arriving at St James's, I found Sellis had retired for the night, as he had to prepare his master's apparel, etc., and to accompany him on a journey early in the morning.
>
> I slept that night in my own room, but Neale, another valet to the Duke, slept in an apartment very slightly divided from that occupied by his Royal Highness. A few days previous to this date I was commanded by my master to lay a sword upon one of the sofas in his bedchamber, and I did so.

MRS FITZHERBERT

GEORGE IV WHO WAS ADDICTED TO CHERRY BRANDY

FIELD MARSHAL BLÜCHER

QUEEN CAROLINE AND PRINCESS CHARLOTTE

WILLIAM IV

THE DUCHESS OF KENT AND PRINCESS VICTORIA

QUEEN VICTORIA'S WEDDING IN ST JAMES'S PALACE

After undressing his Royal Highness, I retired to bed. I had not long been asleep when I was disturbed by Neale, who told me to get up immediately as my master, the Duke, was nearly murdered. I lost no time, and very soon entered his Royal Highness's bedroom. His Royal Highness was then standing nearly in the middle of the chamber, apparently quite cool and composed. His shirt was bloody, and he commanded me to fetch Sir Henry Hulford, saying 'I am severely wounded'. The sword which, a few days before, I had laid upon the sofa, was then lying on the floor, and was very bloody. I went with all possible haste for Sir Henry, and soon returned with him. I stood by when the wounds were examined, none of which were of a serious nature or appearance. That in his hand was the most considerable.

During this period, which was nearly two hours, neither Neale nor Sellis had been in the Duke's room which appeared to me a very unaccountable circumstance. At length, when all the bustle of dressing the wounds (which was very considerable) was over, and the room arranged, the Duke said, 'Call Sellis'. I went to Sellis's door, and, upon opening it, the most terrific scene presented itself. Sellis was lying perfectly straight in the bed, the head raised up against the headboard, and nearly severed from the body; his hands were lying quite straight on each side of him, and upon examination I saw him weltering in blood, it having covered the under part of the body. He had on his shirt, his waistcoat, and his stockings; the inside of his hands were perfectly clean, but on the outside were smears of blood. His watch was hanging up over his head, wound up. His coat was carefully folded inside out, and laid over the back of the chair. A razor, covered with blood, was lying at a distance from his body, but too far off to have been used by himself or to have been thrown there by him in such a mutilated condition, as it was very apparent, death must have been immediate after such an act. The washbasin was in the stand but was half full of bloody water. Upon examining Sellis's cravat, it was found to be cut. The padding which he usually wore was covered with silk and quilted, but, what was most remarkable, both the padding and the cravat were cut, as if some person had made an attempt to cut the throat with the cravat on, then, finding the woollen or cotton stuffing to impede the razor, took it off in order more readily to effect the purpose.

The coroner's verdict was that Sellis had tried to murder the Duke of Cumberland and committed suicide when he failed to do so. This was generally disbelieved. It was certainly impossible for Sellis to have practically hacked off his own head and the Duke of Cumberland was perfectly capable of having committed the murder. The verdict was still more improbable in view of the fact that Sellis was a meek little man and apparently on good terms with the Duke. It is of course possible that Neale committed the murder. . . .

The newspapers, like everyone else, hated the Duke of Cumberland and when some time later he nearly rode down two girls at Hammersmith, *The Times* published Tom Moore's poem on the subject:

> The Duke is the lad to frighten a lass
>   Galloping dreary Duke.
> The Duke is the lad to frighten a lass,
> He's an ogre to meet and the Devil to pass;
>   With his charger prancing,
>   Grim eye glancing
>   Chin like a mufti,
>   Grizzled and tufty,
>   Galloping dreary Duke.
>
> Ye Misses, beware of the neighbourhood
>   Of this galloping dreary Duke
> Avoid him all who see no good
> In being run o'er by a Prince of the Blood.
>   And as no nymph is
>   Fond of a grim phiz,
>   Fly, ye new married,
>   For crowds have miscarried
> At the sight of this dreary Duke.

* * *

This year (1810) marked the jubilee of George III's reign, an unhappy anniversary particularly since his daughter the Princess Amelia was dying of a broken heart because she was not allowed to marry General Charles Fitzroy owing to the Royal Marriage Act.

Queen Charlotte, in spite of everything, was determined to prove that her husband was quite fit and arranged a gala celebration at St James's Palace.

I shall never forget (wrote one of the Princesses' attendants), the last evening of my seeing him. It was the anniversary of his Accession. The whole family except the Queen of Württemberg and my dear Princess Amelia were present when he entered the room, the Queen holding his arm. He called to each of his sons separately, and said things to them equally sublime and instructive but very unlike what he would have said before so many people, had he been conscious of his circumstances. As he went around the Circle as usual, it was easy to perceive the dreadful excitement in his countenance. As he could not distinguish persons, it was the custom to speak to him as he approached that he might recognize by the voice whom he was about to address. I forget what I said to him, but shall ever remember what he said to me: 'You are not easy, I am sure, about Amelia. You are not to be deceived, but you know she is in no danger.' At that same time, he squeezed my hand with such force that I could scarcely help crying out. The Queen, however, dragged him away.

As Dr Manfred Guttmacher says in *America's Last King*, 'Here was tragedy in its purest form. The last public appearance of King George III; the mighty monarch of Great Britain on the gala night of his Jubilee—a blind old man struggling manfully to preserve his reason, as his beloved child was sinking to her death.'

12. *Madness at the palace*

THE Regency finally began on 6 February 1811 and, thereafter, encouraging health bulletins about George III were regularly posted at St James's Palace. The secret progress of the symptoms of the King's illness makes pathetic reading:

March 2.   The delusions abated, but being alone with a Page, a former confidant, he talked of his attachment (Lady Pembroke).
March 8.   Much in adjusting his bed clothes.
March 12.   This morning in too high spirits.
March 21.   There is a nervousness and anxiety to be declared well; and a distrust of physicians. Slept 4 hours. Occupied when awake in adjusting bed clothes by rolling them down and then up again.
March 30.   The delusions on going to bed implied an expectation of being with the object of his wishes. It appears that when with the Pages, he acts according to his feelings; when with the physicians is in restraint and conceals them.
March 31.   In the presence of Sir Henry Holford said he had sworn five times on the Bible to be faithful to his dear Eliza who had been faithful to him for fifty-five years. Sir Henry also heard that he had drunk the health of 'Sanctissima mea uxor Elizabetha' and formed the idea of becoming a Lutheran which was necessary to the lefthand marriage and which connected itself with the whole scheme of Hanover.

Dr Willis was now completely in charge of the case and he called in other doctors only if he thought it desirable.

Still more pathetic are the clinical notes from the doctors during July and August, thus:

July 6.   Provoked to anger with slight causes. Gross and indecent allusions.

July 11.   At dinner declared the operation upon his eye should not be performed without Eliza's command.

July 16.   Throughout the day constantly talking or imitating the sounds of instruments.

July 18.   Required restraint. Fits of violence. Pulse 88.

July 26.   Is under the impression of his being attended by persons not now in existence; only at the moment distinguishes the voices of Physicians but immediately relapses into confusion and error. Pulse 88. Refuses food, seems that some notion respecting Eliza is the cause of his refusal.

August 1.   Full of power, he professes to raise the dead and assimilate different ages. All his favourites are to remain seventeen. It being necessary to take Physic, restraint was necessary to get it down.

August 2.   Wildness and languor in his look. Pulse 94.

August 4.   Slept 7 hours without opium, remains irascible and when they wanted to feel his pulse, was so violent that all the Physicians left the room.

August 5.   Was under restraint, either furious or sullen while up.

August 18.   Before the physicians in high spirits. Pulse 64. Sung several songs. Played on the flute and harpsichord.

August 26.   Proposed sinking a part of England, marrying living persons with those dead, and Eliza much dwelt upon. This morning enquired about Royal Family for the first time in a long while.

Still later that year, there was little or no change in the pathetic royal patient, thus:

September 9.   This morning too violent to receive the Physicians.

September 13.   The late King was alive and had commanded him to take the name of George Augustus, Prince of Wales; Prince Octavius was alive and married to a daughter of the Duke of Montrose. He had signed death warrants for six of his sons.

September 17.   In the afternoon restraint required on account of Exposing his Person.

September 19.   Detailed the effect of an Act of Parliament just passed, and read in all the Churches for the Dissolution of all Marriages before the first of August. Also his power of bringing people to life and making them young again.

October 27.   At six in the evening threw off wig and neck cloth; when replaced, threatened if not allowed to bed, he would befoul himself, and did so and required restraint; then wetted himself and was put to bed. Slept 3 hours and then required restraint.

October 31. Said one of the Princes had been executed and he had only one son left.

November 2. No sleep, in restraint all night.

November 10. Gave Princess Amelia a minute account of her own funeral. Told Doctor Baillie he was in the Queen's Lodge.

December 1. Longer ceremony before dinner mixed with Hunting Song and threw down the table without eating.

December 12. This morning in a violent burst of passion against Sir Henry Halford for not allowing that the Prince Regent had thrown overboard one of his sisters, and drowned his brother in a passage to France.

For the last nine years of the blind, mad, old King, there was at least a respite from the outside world. He was no longer harassed by the thoughts of government or the behaviour of his children and he was almost entirely forgotten by the general public in spite of the bulletins published at St James's Palace. The Princess Elizabeth described her father's condition during his last seven years by saying that Dr Willis assured her that he was perfectly happy—probably never so happy, for he had no cares and enjoyed his music and his army. Here are further clinical notes made by the royal physicians during this period:

January 3, 1813. Reviewing troops.

June 9. Became nervous, laughing and shedding tears. Chattering his teeth.

July 8. Full of schemes of building, journeys, and giving appointments, cheerful, silent, good-humoured but has hardly time to dress and eat his meals.

February 16, 1814. No hour passes without proofs of mental derangement, but quiet.

April 14. Impatient of help necessary to direct his steps in walking from room to room. His anger is momentary; his good humour remarkable.

June 1. Though he had dined, apprehended he had not and became irritable.

June 29. His malady furnishing such scenes of amusement as delighted him when he was well.

Perhaps not surprisingly, his physical health continued to be remarkably good right up to the last minute, as he died only two days after he finally took to his bed.

In the meantime, following the apparently decisive defeat of Napoleon at Leipzig and his expulsion to Elba, St James's Palace witnessed the arrival of the Czar, the King of Prussia and more importantly, Field-Marshal Blücher. The Prince Regent had spent large sums of money in redecorating the apartments of the Duke of Cumberland for the Emperor Alexander. To his consternation, Alexander arrived in London without a single attendant and drove at once to the Pulteney Hotel where his sister, the Grand Duchess of Oldenburg, was staying with her children. This was all very disappointing. A guard of honour had been drawn up in the courtyard opposite St James's Palace throughout the day and was not dismissed until 7 p.m. when it was clear that the Emperor was not coming.

The King of Prussia, by contrast, drove straight to Clarence House as arranged. Marshal Blücher, after paying his respects to the Prince Regent at Carlton House, drove to St James's Palace, where the crowd remained in the courtyard until after dark cheering him each time he went to the window to let them see him. His quarters were the brick house on the west side of Ambassadors Court where he sat in the first-floor window puffing away at his pipe and bowing to the passers-by, obviously delighted with his popularity. It is said that when he did not feel like going to the window once more he put his dog there to represent him.

A series of anonymous letters written at the time by 'F.R.' provide a pleasant account of the excitement caused by Blücher:

> This London is in a complete bustle. Two millions of people run about in a state of frenzy. England has never before witnessed so noble a scene, and ever since the arrival of the Emperor and King, the Princes and Marshals, by whose assisting prowess Europe has been delivered, Great Britain seems to be in an uproar. And now that our German heroes are on English shore, Blücher is the soul of London, the idol of England. . . .
>
> The Kitchen Court of the King's palace where Blücher had his apartments was the focus of London and here it was hardly possible to enter. Although I am not an intruder, I regret much that

I delayed my visit of respect, because every day, even every hour, afforded some interesting circumstance respecting the touchstone of his feelings; and his sympathy for the object of the tale of woe afforded the key of success to his ever ready presence. In consequence services were required of him, and both noble and ridiculous applications assailed his generosity. Everybody seemed to have a claim upon Blücher, but particularly the fair sex; and an old soldier of 70 years of age seemed to have enveloped the faculties and turned the brains of the ladies of England. Thousands of them flock to see him, and tens of thousands appear as if their hearts could melt for Blücher. It became fashionable for ladies to intrude themselves into his parlour, to shake hands with him, to kiss his moustachios, and then retire. Neither Blücher nor his aides-de-camp understand a word of the English language. Being intimate with one of them, Count Hostisch, some years ago at Rome, I used to be frequently employed as an interpreter to Blücher, and this gave me the most pleasing opportunities of witnessing many an extraordinary occurrence and I have frequently had the happiness to observe that when the feelings of an English lady's heart are roused, they arrive to a degree of sensibility of which the nature of any other individual is scarcely susceptible. . . .

One morning, soon after his arrival in London, he called for his faithful attendant, William. 'Your Highness's pleasure?' said William, on approaching the Marshal. 'Highness, Highness,' said Blücher. 'God damn your Highness, you shall call me General,' said the hero of Leipzig, 'or I will send you to wait upon the Emperor at Elba!' Very good, thought I, there are many great warriors and heroes, who are not Highnesses, and some of those, Highnesses whose actions disgrace the name of a great man.

A certain tooth-drawer wrote to Blücher begging permission to take the appellation of Prince Blücher's dentist. 'What the devil use could that be to him?' said the Marshal, 'the fellow must be an Irishman! Tell him I have scarcely a tooth left in my mouth, therefore I cannot want a dentist; yet, if it gives him pleasure or profit, he may call himself my dentist, or whatever else he pleases'. . . .

Prince Blücher becomes quite domesticated in London. He sits and smokes his pipe several hours in the day, showing himself at intervals to the populace, who constantly surround the entrance to 'Wahlstadd Palace'. The King of Prussia resides near to Blücher, in the mansion of the Duke of Clarence, and hence public curiosity had made the Kitchen Court at St James's the focus of London.

Blücher, the Sovereigns, the Princes, Count Platoff, and the whole illustrious people have left England, and millions of English people have returned to their different occupations. A grand Jubilee took place a few days since in St James's Park, the Green Park, and in Hyde Park. The fireworks were splendid beyond example, and the whole affair was arranged and conducted upon the most magnificent scale. . . . A finer night could not have been bestowed from heaven, and a more delightful scene never presented itself to the enraptured souls of these noble-minded English. For a week afterwards the Parks, the numerous tents and booths were kept open, and honest John Bull could be daily seen in all his native pride, from the most respectable to the poorest ranks of society . . . which came to my knowledge. I will come to the facts at once: Blücher's regimental coat, the identical dress he wore and conquered in at the battle of Leipzig, has been exhibited in a Gallery in London, at 1 shilling admittance for the sight to each person.

One of the Marshal's aides-de-camp, who was fonder of pelf than his fair fame, deposited the Prince's coat, sword, hat, and his full dress apparel at the disposal of a person to exhibit after his departure. A thousand crowns were paid by the aide-de-camp into the German banker's hands (Mr S. of Mansion House St) to defray the first expenses of placing the costume of 'the hero of Leipzig' upon a machine and wooden head for public exhibition. The figure was got up in great style and placed in a picture gallery in Pall Mall, where the public were invited, by means of circular letters, hand and posting bills, to repair and behold 'Prince Marshal Blücher'. Some of the placards intimated these words, 'Blücher is yet in London!'

The newspapers and Sunday journals were paid for puffing off the artifices and every means used by the agent of the aide-de-camp, who satisfied himself, on his leaving London, that he should accumulate a mountain of gold by this mean device. But John Bull 'was not to be had' on this occasion; too many of the brave English had seen the living figure, and had shaken the hands of the Marshal, and preserved sufficient reason not to be caught by a sight of his coat and hat, at the expense, perhaps, to many an idle fellow, of his last shilling.

In fact, this shabby scheme wholly failed, as it should do, and the grand material of the hollow figure was consigned for sale to a hatter and hosier in St James's Street, who had a claim upon the machinery for rent and ornaments, and who absolutely sold the same to a Jew, with all the engraved certificates and signatures of the aide-de-camp, for the sum of one hundred guineas, to be exhibited again in the country towns of England.

*　　*　　*

The death of the Regent's only legitimate child, the Princess Charlotte, in childbirth two years after the Battle of Waterloo, now confronted the Government with the problem of the succession. The Prince Regent was comparatively fit in spite of his gross way of life, but it was highly improbable that he would get himself an heir, especially as he was unable to obtain a divorce. There was, of course, the Duke of Clarence, his brother (later William IV), but he had no legitimate children. It looked therefore as though in due course the thirteen-year-old Duke of Brunswick might come to the throne. He had paid only one visit to London, staying at St James's Palace, but one glimpse of him showed that he was a weedy, undesirable child. So it became quite clear that one or other of the Regent's brothers should do their duty and produce an heir. The Duke of York's marriage had proved barren. This left the Duke of Kent, the Duke of Cambridge and the Duke of Clarence. The Duke of Kent had lived for twenty-seven years with Madame de St Laurent. Nevertheless it was suggested to him that he should get rid of her, make a legitimate marriage and produce an heir. Similarly it was suggested to the Duke of Clarence that he should give up Mrs Jordan and also marry with this object in view. So the following year, he married Princess Adelaide of Saxe-Meiningen. The Duke of Cambridge meanwhile married Princess Augusta of Hesse-Cassel. The Duke of Kent, in turn, pensioned off Madame de St Laurent and married the widowed Princess of Leinigen-Dachsbourg-Hadenbourg, whose existing son and daughter were likely evidence that she could produce an heir. It was however by no means certain that she would become Queen because the Duchess of Clarence had in the meantime produced a baby which had died as an infant; but there was always the possibility that another, healthier one, might follow. The Duke and Duchess of Kent, however, felt certain that their baby was destined to become Queen; so, to run no risk of disqualification, they had borrowed just enough money to come to

England. On their arrival at Dover, the Duke was compelled to drive the coach himself because he could not afford a coachman. But to make matters as watertight as possible, he summoned more state officials than ever before to witness the birth. The baby duly born was named Alexandrina Georgiana Augusta, with Victoria almost as an afterthought, on 24 May 1819.

The Duke of Kent, who had expected that all his debts would be paid, together with an annuity of at least £25,000 a year for doing his duty, was furious when he was granted a mere £6,000 a year; but he did not have long to grieve. He died of pneumonia shortly after the birth of his daughter, leaving a mountain of debts.

Once again the Duchess of Clarence became pregnant, but the baby died soon after birth and Prince Leopold, later King of the Belgians, gave the Duchess of Kent £3,000 a year, which enabled her to remain in London with her daughter, Princess Victoria, as the most likely successor to the throne.

* * *

George III finally died on 29 January 1820, but on the day that George IV was proclaimed by ancient custom as King at St James's Palace, he was desperately ill at Brighton. He had already lost eighty ounces of blood and it was not until another seventy ounces were taken from him that he showed signs of recovery. Three weeks later he returned to London and refused to allow the Queen's name to be included in the prayers when alterations were made to the Liturgy as a result of the death of his father.

Barely a fortnight elapsed before the Cato Street conspiracy was discovered. Arthur Thistlewood, leader of the conspirators, was planning to kill all the members of the Cabinet at a dinner party given by Lord Harrowby. Royal agents got wind of the plot, however, and the conspirators were soon discovered.

Such was the disaffection at this time that even the regiments of foot-guards whose primary job was to protect Carlton House, St James's Palace and other royal residences were suspect. The arrival of the Queen in London added to the tension.

Queen Caroline had left England in 1817 with a considerable retinue, which included Sir William Gell. Having first visited

Brunswick to see her brother, she drove to Naples by way of the
Simplon Pass. There, at a ball given specially for her, she arrived, according to Sir William Gell, 'dressed en Vénus or
rather not dressed further than the waist. I was, as she used to
say herself, "all over shock". A more injudicious costume cannot
be imagined. When she began to waltz, the terrae motus was
terrible to see. I was infinitely grieved to see her make herself
so utterly ridiculous.' In the course of her subsequent travels
she visited Jerusalem, where she founded the Order of 'St
Caroline' and then set up residence at Villa d'Este on Lake
Como, where she appointed Louis Bergami as major-domo. It
was here that adultery was supposed to have taken place. Yet,
in spite of her reputation for extreme immorality, she was received in London by the populace with tremendous enthusiasm.
Women waved pocket handkerchiefs and men cheered when she
passed them in an open landau. As she drove past White's,
where enormous sums had been won and lost on the question of
whether or not she would return, she bowed and smiled to the
members in the windows. She became a real sensation: the
question was what the King would do. The windows of his
mistress, Lady Hertford, were broken by the mob and a few
days later the Scots Guards refused to give up their ball cart-
ridges when they came off duty at St James's Palace. In consequence, they were ordered to Plymouth, leaving at 4 a.m. But
by the time they reached Brentford, many were drunk and shouting 'God save Queen Caroline'.

Soon afterwards, the Queen's trial for adultery, which took
the form of a Bill of Pains and Penalties, was conducted in the
House of Lords with speeches by Counsel and examination of
witnesses. The Bill passed the three readings with such dimi-
nishing majorities that when, on the third occasion, it obtained
a majority of only nine, it was abandoned by the Government.
When George IV went to Drury Lane for the first time after
his accession, a man in the gallery called out, 'Where's your
wife, George?'

A year later, on the death of Napoleon in May 1821, a
courtier announced dramatically, 'Sire, your greatest enemy is
dead.'

'Is she, by God!' the King exclaimed. Actually, Queen Caroline did not die until three months later when he was at Holy-head on his way to Ireland.

The memoirs of Charles Greville, who became racing manager to the Duke of York, now assume great historical interest. It appears that George IV held his annual Jockey Club dinner at St James's Palace towards the end of each June. Writes Greville,

> There were about thirty people, several not being invited whom he did not fancy. The Duke of Leeds told me a much greater list had been made out, but he had scratched several out of it. We assembled in the Throne Room, and found him already there looking very well and walking about. He soon, however, sat down, and desired everybody to do so. Nobody spoke and he laughed and said, 'This is more like a Quaker than a Jockey Club meeting.'
>
> We soon went to dinner, which was in the Great Supper Room and very magnificent. He sat in the middle, with the Dukes of Richmond and Grafton on each side of him. I sat opposite to him, and he was particularly gracious to me, talking across to me and recommending all the good things; he made me (after eating a quantity of turtle) cat a dish of crawfish soup, till I thought I should have burst.
>
> After dinner the Duke of Leeds who sat at the head of the table gave 'the King'. We all stood up when his Majesty thanked us, and said he hoped this would be the first of annual meetings of the sort to take place, there or elsewhere under his roof. He then ordered paper, pens, etc. and they began making matches and stakes; the most perfect ease was established, just as much as if we had been dining with the Duke of York, and he seemed delighted. He made one or two little speeches, one recommending that a stop should be put to the exportation of horses. He twice gave 'the Turf' and at the end the Duke of Richmond asked his leave to give a toast and again gave 'the King'. He got up at half-past twelve and wished us goodnight. Nothing could go off better and Mount Charles told me he was sure he was delighted.

A few months later, Greville notes:

> The King complains he is tired to death of all the people about him. He is less violent about the Catholic question, tired of that too, and does not wish to hear any more about it. He leads a most extraordinary life—never gets up till six in the afternoon. They

come to him and open the window curtains at six or seven in the morning; he breakfasts in bed, does whatever business he can be brought to transact in bed too, he reads every newspaper quite through, dozes three or four hours, gets up in time for dinner and goes to bed between ten and eleven. He sleeps very ill and rings his bell forty times in the night; if he wants to know the hour, though a watch hangs close to him, he will have his *valet de chambre* down rather than turn his head to look at it. The same thing if he wants a drink of water, he won't stretch out his hand to get it. His valets are nearly destroyed and at last Lady Conyngham prevailed on him to agree to an arrangement by which they wait on him on alternate days. The service is still most severe as on the days they are in waiting, their labours are incessant, and they cannot take off their clothes at night, and hardly lie down. He is in good health but irritable and has been horribly annoyed by other matters besides the Catholic affair.

In 1824, the Duke and the Duchess of Clarence were given apartments at St James's Palace but clearly did not like them, to judge by a letter from the Duke to the Lord Chamberlain.

His Majesty having so graciously pleased to listen to my suggestion respecting the alteration for the Hanoverian office at the Palace, I venture once more to trouble you on the point of the building intended for that purpose. To the accommodation of the Duchess this additional slip at the back of the present apartment would be most to be wished and desired and never can make a complete Hanoverian office without our kitchen, which the King has so kindly allowed us to keep. Under this perfect conviction I venture to apply for this slip of building which was intended for the Hanoverian office. I am confident His Majesty is fully aware of the inconvenience and unfitness of our present apartments here. They were arranged for me in 1809 when I was a bachelor and without an idea at that time of my ever being married, since which, now fifteen years, nothing has been done to them, and you well know the dirt and unfitness for the Duchess of our present abode. Under these circumstances I earnestly request for the sake of the amiable and excellent Duchess, you will, when the King is quite recovered, present the wretched state and dirt of our apartments and the infinite advantage this slip would produce to the convenience and comfort of the Duchess. God bless the King and yourself and ever believe me, etc.,

WILLIAM

* * *

There is a general impression that George IV seldom, if ever, visited St James's Palace except for official ceremonies. There are, however, many letters extant written from St James's Palace, showing that the reverse is true. Thus, the King to Sir William Knighton:

St James's Palace,
Friday, April 6, 1827

Dear Friend,

For God's sake, for all our sakes, pray, pray take care of yourself and do not think, upon any account, of stirring until tomorrow morning. It is true, I am jaded and quite worn out, and writing from my bed, where I have laid down for a little rest; but tomorrow will be quite time enough. Little or no advance, I regret to say has yet been made, amidst, perhaps, almost unravelable perplexities.

Yours affectionately,
G. R.

A letter from him to the Duke of Wellington, dated St James's Palace, 21 May 1827, is also extant. In it George IV wrote to say that he could not fail to tell him that the command of the army was still open and that if he chose to recall his resignation which grieved him so much to receive, he had permission to do so. Two other letters written from St James's Palace to the Duke of Wellington on 25 April 1828 and 25 May 1828 also show that the King was in residence. His annual Jockey Club dinners continued.

On 28 May 1829, George IV gave a dinner at St James's Palace to the Dukes of Orléans and Chartres and in the evening there was a children's ball. 'It was pretty enough,' recorded Charles Greville, 'and I saw for the first time the ten-year-old Queen of Portugal and our little Victoria. The Queen was finely dressed with a riband and Order over her shoulder and she sat by the King. She is good-looking and the King was kind to her. Our little Princess is a short, plain-looking child and not near so good-looking as the Portuguese. However, if nature has not done so much for her, fortune is likely to do a good deal more.'

As time marched on, George IV started to have the same kind of delusions, although to a lesser extent, as his father. All the rooms in the palace were kept at stove temperature and he

189

drank incredible quantities of cherry brandy. It was possibly this addiction which fuddled his brain and caused so much morbid amusement. On various occasions he claimed to have fought at the Battle of Waterloo—as a result of having once visited the battlefield with the Duke of Wellington. On another occasion, talking about Fleur de Lys, which won the Goodwood Cup, he came to believe that he had ridden the horse himself. In addition to this, he had kept all the coats he had ever had for fifty years, three hundred whips, innumerable canes, every sort of uniform, the costumes of all the Orders in Europe, furs, pelisses, hunting coats and breeches. Although he had never paid for them, his memory was so accurate that he recollected every article of clothing, no matter how old, and frequently ordered his valets to produce some particular coat or other which he had acquired previously.

Probably because he had grown so bloated and bulky, he now began to live in seclusion. His favourite spot was the Sandpit near Windsor where his menagerie was maintained. Here he invented a new dress for the Brigade of Guards. One item was an extravagant cap for the Grenadiers which, in a high wind, was apt to overbalance its wearer. Unfortunately, in May 1829 at a military review in honour of the visiting French princes, the Duke of Wellington fell from his horse at the feet of the Duke of Cumberland on account of this tall hat. Another invention was a new method of folding an envelope of a letter in which shape he insisted all papers should be sent to him.

He now became more and more languid and it was not long before the Duke of Wellington and Sir Robert Peel started taking precautions about the succession. The truth was that he was suffering from a combination of dropsy and a heart condition, but kept on rallying until finally on 25 May 1830 he fell asleep leaning on a table, his forehead resting on one hand, the other being held by Sir Wathan Waller, who was sitting up with him. He woke up in the small hours of the morning, asked for some clove tea, sat down in his armchair, tried to drink some sal volatile, but failed, and then sent for his physician, Halford. Suddenly, he shouted, 'Watty! What is this? This is death. They have deceived me.' And fell back dead. And indeed this accusation of deception was confirmed by Halford in his *Essays and Orations* published some years later, in which he justified his need of discretion because 'the health or otherwise of the King was an object of anxiety to the nation; and therefore he had a duty to perform not only to the Royal patient but also to the public'.

Another version of George IV's last remarks is that, looking at Sir Wathan Waller with a strange expression, he said, 'My boy, this is death', a phrase which has an awful and original ghastliness.

At least it can be said for him that during the previous twenty-four hours he thought of Maria Fitzherbert, who had sent a letter offering to come and soothe his last moments. Years previously George IV had given her a large diamond which was cut in half and placed into two lockets. When their morganatic marriage broke up, she sent back his to him, but he did not return hers. When he was dying, he asked the Duke of Wellington to see that he was buried as he lay, without his nightdress being undone. When he was dead, the Duke could not resist looking for the reason for this request and found the jewel round his neck attached to a dirty piece of black ribbon.

George IV in retrospect was a shifty, self-indulgent libertine with, however, many epicurean tastes and on occasion spasms of generosity, although his gifts were never large. He gave £200 to Beethoven when he was in need of money, together with £1,000 a year to the Royal Society of Literature. He also began to collect Dutch and Flemish Masters at a time when they were not appreciated. Nor can one forget his commissioning Nash to transform Regent Street, Oxford Street and Regent's Park. Another of his protégés, if that is the word, was Sir Walter Scott, who in return paid him the famous compliment that 'He was the First Gentleman he had seen, certainly the First Gentleman of his day', adding, however, 'As to his abilities as distinct from his charming manners, how can anyone form a fair judgment of that man who introduces what subject he chooses, discusses it just as long as he chooses and dismisses it when he chooses?'

His extravagances were sensational. More than £250,000 was spent on his Coronation and the value of the snuff-boxes he gave to various ambassadors to the Court of St James was no less than £22,000. There was also the little matter of the Pavilion at Brighton and the money he lavished on Carlton House and Buckingham Palace.

Nevertheless, after his death it was soon discovered that he had been a real miser. Over £10,000 was found in various boxes and despatch cases, together with 500 pocket-books with money in all of them, mostly guineas and pound notes. Remarkable quantities of trinkets and trash were also revealed. He never gave anything away. There was a prodigious amount of women's hair of all colours and great heaps of women's gloves, *gages d'amour* which had been given to him at Court balls, with the perspiration still marked on the fingers.

His death was regretted by nobody and the accession of William IV was received with great relief by the public—although the new King's life had until then been spent in obscurity, surrounded by numerous bastards, and he himself was generally regarded as ridiculous in his grotesque ways and meddling curiosity. The great point was that his accession was bound to be a change for the better.

13. Virtue triumphant

THE new King had taken a long, early drive from Bushey Park to St James's Palace when he heard the news, dressed in deep mourning, the ribbon of the Garter being the only colour to relieve his black clothes. As might be expected, enormous crowds lined the street both in carriages and on foot and were standing even in the courtyard of the palace itself. In those days, Marlborough House Road had not been constructed and Friary Court was walled in. Some of the Court officials became angry at finding the courtyard full of crowds who, although obviously loyal and orderly, were, to say the least, miscellaneous. As a result, they not only ordered the Life Guards to disperse the spectators and clear the courtyard, but also to close the gates. Thereupon the Heralds took up their historic positions overlooking Friary Court.

William, on his arrival, was surprised to see that none of the loyal subjects he had expected were waiting to receive him. As soon as he heard what had happened, he ordered the gates to be opened immediately and the delighted crowds rushed in again. The proclamation was then read by Garter King of Arms under the windows of the palace. Drums sounded and the King was so affected by the cheers of the crowds that tears poured down his cheeks.

A few weeks previously, while George IV was slowly dying, the one-legged Marquess of Anglesey had an interview with the future King, arranged by Lord Erroll, his son-in-law. Among the Marquess's papers is a memorandum of what took place:

'In the course of May, Lord Erroll called upon me and told me how much the Duke of Clarence talked of me and how much

he respected me. . . . He told me the Duke often complained he
had no one to consult & advise with & so forth. This induced me
to express myself pretty fully as to the line of policy & of general
conduct H.R.H. ought to pursue. Lrd E. forcibly struck with
my remarks asked me should H.R.H. wish to see me, if I would
call upon him.'

When they met, the Marquess wrote,

The conversation was at first rather constrained and neither
chose to begin upon serious matter. The Duke (I really believe
for shyness) got into some very mild, light & frivolous subjects
which, as they were by no means what I came to discuss, I con-
trived to stop & at once entering into grave matter, I craved his
permission to express myself fairly & openly. I would speak
out, if I was to speak at all, & in this H.R.H. having encouraged
me, I proceeded thus:

'The public looks with considerable alarm to your ascending
the Throne—people think you will be wild, unmanageable, full
of prejudices and arbitrary. Now I have always maintained a contrary opinion and I now assert that if Y.R.Hss is surrounded by
proper persons & honest men, you are about to enter a career that
will enable you to be the most popular and the most constitutional
Sovereign that ever filled the Throne. You will commence under
every advantage & if you profit by it your reign will be a prosperous & a brilliant one.

'You follow a Court the most sombre & melancholy that ever
was known, for the King with all his love of pomp, and his taste
for magnificence—for the Arts—for brilliant society, together
with his powers for shining under such circumstances has shut
himself up and withdrawn himself from the Public Eye, and that
too at a time when the most profuse expenditure has been carrying
on, by which the Public have in no respect profited and for which
ample grounds have been laid for the most heavy and just com-
plaints on the score of extravagance.

'Your R. Hss must bear this in mind. You must keep a brilliant
Court, you must have regular periodical Levees and Drawing
Rooms—you must go not infrequently to the Theatre—without
making yourself too common; you must nevertheless frequently
show yourself amongst your subjects. Your habits of life have been
economical and with these habits you will have ample funds for
a splendid Court—for creditable acts of liberality, without preying upon the pockets of the people. The People are truly loyal.

They love their Kings. They are really Monarchical & will be ever ready to maintain the fair splendour of a Court. They will never refuse reasonable demands to uphold the dignity of their Kings, but they will always grumble & resist profusion and extravagance.

'Let it be a fixed rule, when anything is wanted for Palaces or for any legitimate expences to lay the claim fairly before the public. . . .

'Your R. Hss stands in a very peculiar situation on account of your children. It will require much discretion to provide fairly and handsomely by them, without bringing them too prominently before the public eye—but with your economical habits & ample means you will easily provide for them without burdening the public, yet in time & by degrees, they may attain situations of trust and respectability, to which no objection will be made.' But (looking at a picture of Charles II which was in the room) I observed that we were not living in times when that Monarch could be taken as a Model with impunity.

I said that he was most fortunate in his consort—that she was universally well spoken of & that the advantages of a female Court after so long an absence of anything of the sort were incalculable.

Apart from these matters, the Marquess advised his future King also on the peerage, the army, his choice of ministers, how he should go about forming a new Cabinet and expressed his opinion upon the Government. The present Marquess of Anglesey, commenting on this memorandum which he quotes in his biography of his ancestor, 'One Leg', says, 'It goes a long way to explain why George IV and his brother both feared and respected him. Here is a subject-to-be giving advice to his prospective sovereign with complete frankness, without the smallest reservations and not without wisdom and common-sense.'

Perhaps as a result of this advice one of William IV's first actions was to continue to live in St James's Palace instead of moving to Buckingham Palace on which his brother had spent so much money.

Like George I, William IV had no particular wish to become King. Certainly his wife Adelaide did not wish to be Queen (she said so in so many words) and having spent all his service career at sea, he presented a somewhat ludicrous appearance when he wore military uniform for the first time in his life. When he inspected the Coldstream Guards at St James's Palace, he wore a huge pair of gold spurs halfway up his legs like a game-cock, although he was unable to ride.

Soon, as a result of his attitude towards the Reform Bill, the King was hooted and pelted on his way back to St James's Palace from the theatre, and a stone smashed through the window of his coach, falling into the lap of Prince George of Cumberland. Not surprisingly, the King was exceedingly annoyed.

Two or three months later, the programme for the Coronation was brought to him for approval at St James's Palace. According to precedent, each bishop was supposed to kiss his cheek in succession, followed by the peers. William IV at first refused to be kissed by the bishops and ordered this part to be taken out of the programme; but the Archbishop of Canterbury insisted and the King had to accept the situation.

Ultimately, the Coronation went off well but the real talk of the town was about the toast he gave at a banquet that night at St James's Palace. Over ninety guests, Cabinet Ministers, leading peers and peeresses and foreign ambassadors and their wives were present. After dinner, he made a long rambling speech in French and ended by giving his 'sentiment' as he called it—'The Land we Live in'. This was before the ladies left the room. After they had gone, he made another speech in French during which he discussed every topic under the sun and ended with a very coarse toast and the words, 'Honi soit qui mal y pense'. It was altogether very shaming but everyone, of course, laughed. Lord Sefton, who sat next to the great Talleyrand, said, 'Eh bien, que pensez vous de cela?' To which Talleyrand replied without any expression on his face, 'C'est bien remarquable.'

Later, when the Duke of Wellington agreed to become Prime Minister and called at St James's Palace he was cheered as he left, although the King was hissed. In the meantime, William IV became furious at the public appearances of the Duchess of Kent with the future Queen Victoria, particularly when they went to Cowes and salutes were fired in their honour by the Royal Navy. He told the First Sea Lord and the Commander-in-Chief of the army that this practice was to cease.

Their reaction was to contact the Duchess of Kent; to persuade her of her own free will to waive the salutes and to say that when she went to the Isle of Wight she was there on a private visit and did not want any public recognition of her. The Duchess refused; so the regulations were altered by an Order-in-Council and from then onwards the Royal Standard could only be saluted when King William IV or Queen Adelaide was present.

The Duchess of Kent continued to aggravate William IV. In September he went to Kensington Palace after Parliament was prorogued and found to his fury that she had appropriated to her own use a huge suite of apartments which he had refused to allow her the previous year. That night at Windsor he went up to Princess Victoria, took her by the hand and expressed his pleasure at seeing her there. He then turned to the Duchess of Kent, made her a low bow and shouted that a most unwarrantable liberty had been taken by her at Kensington Palace and that he could never understand or endure such disrespectful conduct.

On the following day—his birthday—he delivered a long speech after his health was drunk in the course of which he said, 'I trust in God that my life may be spared for nine months longer—after which period in the event of my death, no Regency would take place. I should then have the satisfaction of leaving the royal authority to the personal exercise of that young lady (pointing to Princess Victoria) the heiress presumptive of the Crown, and not in the hands of a person now near me who is surrounded by evil advisers and who is herself incompetent to act with propriety in the station in which she would be placed. I have no hesitation in saying that I have been insulted—grossly and continually insulted—by that person, but I am determined to endure no longer a course of behaviour so disrespectful to me. Amongst other things I have particularly to complain of the way in which that young lady has been kept from my Drawing-rooms at which she ought always to have been present, but I am fully resolved that this shall not happen again. I would have her know that I am King, and I am determined to make my authority respected and for the future I shall insist and command that the Princess do upon all occasions appear at my court as it is her duty to do.'

He ended his speech with a polite allusion to the Princess, who burst into tears—although her mother said nothing.

In April 1834 came the first procession of the Trades Unions. London was alive with troops and police, and the sentries at St James's Palace were doubled. As events proved, nothing could have gone off more quietly. There were about 25,000 Trade Unionists, mostly well-dressed, who created no disturbances. They represented 250,000 members of the movement—the slang name for those who did not belong to them being 'dungs', not 'blacklegs'.

The King's domestic habits at this time were revealed to Charles Greville by Adolphus Fitzclarence, one of the royal bastards. Apparently the King slept in the same room at the palace as the Queen, but in a separate bed. At 7.45 a.m. his valet knocked at the door. Five minutes later the King got out of bed, put on a flannel dressing-gown and walked into the dressing-room where he spent an hour and a half washing and putting on his clothes. At 9.30 he breakfasted with the Queen, the ladies and any of his family, off a couple of biscuits and a cup of coffee. After breakfast he read *The Times* and the *Morning Post*, commenting loudly on what he read—'That's a damned lie' being a typical remark. After this he devoted himself to business with his personal secretary, Sir Herbert Taylor, until 2 p.m., when he usually lunched off two cutlets washed down by two glasses of sherry. He would then go out for a drive until dinner when he ate moderately and drank a bottle of his favourite sherry before going to bed at 11 p.m.

At this stage he was in very low spirits, hating all his ministers and refusing to invite them to St James's Palace.

On 17 November of that year, William IV was in residence at the palace where Lord Melbourne and the other Cabinet Ministers handed over their seals after being summarily dismissed. Charles Greville describes the scene. In the outer room he found the Duke of Wellington and other members of the Privy Council. The ex-Cabinet met in the Throne Room. As they passed their successors it was interesting to see how they all showed some civility to each other except Lord Brougham, who stalked through, looking as black as thunder and taking no notice of anybody. The King then said: 'Having thought proper to make a change in my Government, at the present moment I have directed a new commission to be issued for executing the office of Lord High Treasurer at the head of which I have placed the Duke of Wellington and his Grace has kissed hands accordingly upon that appointment. As by the Constitution of this country the King can do no wrong but those persons responsible for his acts in whom he places his confidence—as I do in the Lords now present—it is necessary to place the seals of the Secretary of State for the Home Department in those hands in which I can best confide and I have therefore thought proper to confer that office likewise on his Grace, who will be sworn in accordingly.' Here the Duke came round and after much fumbling for his spectacles took the oath of Secretary of State. The King then resumed. 'It is likewise necessary for me to dispose of the seals of the other two Secretaries of State, and I therefore place them likewise for the present in the same hands, as he is already First Lord of the Treasury and Secretary of State for the Home Office.'

On 18 May 1837, the King, then in his seventy-third year, held his ultimate Drawing-room at St James's Palace when for the first time he sat down while presentations were made to him. Everybody noticed that he was looking very tired and worn and as soon as the ceremony was over he headed for Windsor.

The old King was now sinking fast. On 18 June he remembered it was the anniversary of the Battle of Waterloo. 'Let me but live over this memorable day,' he said to his physician, 'I shall never live to see another sunset.'

In fact he died on the morning of 20 June.

*　　*　　*

A few hours later Lord Conyngham and the Archbishop of Canterbury rushed off to Kensington Palace to tell the new Sovereign of her accession. Arriving at 5 a.m. they had some difficulty in waking anyone up. Finally, the Duchess of Kent roused her daughter, who hurried downstairs wrapped in a shawl over her dressing-gown to see the visitors. At 11 a.m. the young Queen met her Council. The following day she drove to St James's Palace for the proclamation, with the Duchess of Kent sitting beside her. All the approaches to St James's

Palace were thronged, as well as the quadrangle of the palace nearest Marlborough House and underneath the windows of the Privy Council Chamber; prominent among the throng there being Daniel O'Connell, who waved his hat and cheered vociferously.

A salute fired in St James's Park announced her approach and soon after the heralds, with the Duke of Norfolk as Earl Marshal of England at their head, proclaimed the accession of 'Her Royal Majesty Alexandrina Victoria, Queen of the United Kingdom'—the style and title in which the Sovereign was spoken of in all the official documents until at her wish they were changed, the first name being omitted and the second, which up to then had found no favour in her subjects' eyes, being retained. At the same time as she was proclaimed, the Queen appeared at the window of the Privy Council Chamber, surrounded by her ministers, with her mother in the background.

> Never shall I forget [said one of the crowd, a youth who afterwards became Lord Albemarle], the enthusiastic cheers which greeted the slight girlish figure of the illustrious young lady, nor the thrill of chivalrous loyalty that ran through the assembled multitude. At the sound of the first shouts, the colour faded from the Queen's cheeks and her eyes filled with tears. The emotion thus called forth imparted an additional charm to the winning courtesy with which the girl Sovereign accepted the proffered homage.
>
> At twelve o'clock the same day, she presided at a Council with as much ease as if she had been doing it all her life; after which she received the archbishops and bishops to who she said nothing, but showed an extreme dignity and gracefulness of manner. This ceremony finished and the duties of the day at an end, she retired with slow stateliness; but forgetful that the door through which she had passed had glass panels which allowed her departure to be seen, she had no sooner left the Chamber than she scampered light-heartedly away like a child released from school.

At this time neither the general public, nor indeed the Court, knew anything about her character or intentions. She had been kept in such jealous seclusion by her mother that she had never slept out of her own bedroom nor been alone with anyone but herself and the Baroness Lehzen. None of her acquaintances, not even the Duchess of Northumberland, her governess, had any idea how she was likely to turn out.

Her first act on becoming Queen was to stop this continuous supervision of her every moment. Going to her mother she said, with no apparent guile, 'Now Mama, am I really and truly Queen?'

'Yes, my dear, that is so.'

'Then dear Mama, I hope you will grant my first request I make to you as Queen. Let me be by myself for an hour.'

Sixty minutes later, she ordered her bed to be moved out of her mother's room and so, on the night of her accession, she slept in a bedroom alone for the first time in her life.

Charles Greville was quick to report well of the young Queen, mentioning the remarkable speed with which she had 'slid' into her high situation and discharged its duties without any assistance from the Duchess of Kent but in full co-operation with Lord Melbourne.

The question of Queen Victoria's marriage to Prince Albert had already been mooted; indeed he had visited London the previous year, although nothing had been said openly. However, when Prince Albert went to stay with King Leopold of the Belgians (Queen Victoria's uncle) in 1837 and again in 1838, tongues began to wag.

At this point Baron Stockmar comes into prominence as the plenipotentiary of King Leopold. He received a letter from the latter pointing out that he had a long talk with Prince Albert, who did not like the idea of waiting for two or three years while Queen Victoria decided whether or not to marry him, as it would 'place him in a very ridiculous position and would to a certain extent ruin all the prospects of his future life'.

In December 1838, Stockmar accompanied the Prince to Italy and on his return to England was largely responsible for the marriage. Prince Albert was determined to tell Queen Victoria that if she did not make up her mind immediately, he would not be able to wait any longer. However, the betrothal took place and the Queen wrote to all the members of her family to announce the fact.

When she saw the Duchess of Gloucester in London and told her that she was going to make her declaration public, the

Duchess asked her if it was not a somewhat nervous thing to do. Said the Queen,

'Yes, but I did a much more nervous thing a little while ago.'

'What was that?'

'I proposed to Prince Albert.'

The wedding took place at St James's Palace in February 1840. The Queen's dressing-room was behind the Throne Room. It was here that she waited with the train-bearers until she received the Lord Chamberlain's summons to proceed to the chapel. The ceremony was of no great interest but the little Queen (she was barely five feet tall) was dwarfed by the huge procession. Lady Lyttelton—lady-of-the-bedchamber—said that she was prevented by the bulky forms and finery of the Duchess of Bedford and Lady Normanby, who walked in front of her, from seeing the Queen at all.

The Queen's own account of the ceremony is not very revealing for she was so obviously in love that she had no eyes for anyone but the Prince.

According to Charles Greville, the wedding went off 'tolerably well'. On the actual wedding day there were torrents of rain and violent gusts of wind. In spite of this there were tremendous crowds although there was no cheering. (He made the same comment on her arrival at St James's Palace to be proclaimed three years earlier.) According to the *Morning Chronicle*, the Queen appeared rather pale when she approached the chapel, but looked very flushed after the ceremony, while Prince Albert remained inscrutable.

* * *

At that time, no fewer than 174 people were living in St James's Palace—almost exactly double the number of those in Windsor Castle and Buckingham Palace combined. The residents of St James's Palace consisted mostly of people who had grace and favour apartments and actual courtiers such as the Lord Chamberlain—at that time the Earl of Uxbridge (son of the Lord Anglesey who had expressed himself so freely to William IV).

In those days, the post of Lord Chamberlain was a political appointment; indeed, it was not until 1924 when the first

Labour Government under Ramsay MacDonald came into power that it became non-political, the Lord Chamberlain being thereafter chosen by the Sovereign.

It is now time to give details of this all-important post. The Lord Chamberlain was and is in charge of Court ceremonial, Court mourning, the Chapels Royal, the royal swans, precedence at Court, Foreign State visits, all royal weddings and funerals except that of the Sovereign, which is the responsibility of the Duke of Norfolk as Earl Marshal; Courts and presentation parties, Levees and garden parties, most state invitations and the censorship of stage plays. Under him come the Ecclesiastical Household, the Medical Household, the Gentlemen at Arms, the Yeomen of the Guard, the Gentlemen Ushers, Sergeants-at-Arms, and the Marshal of the Diplomatic Corps. The Lord Chamberlain's office also comprises the central Chancellery of the Orders of Knighthood and is responsible for the maintenance of the royal residences and the Crown Jewels.

The Lord Chamberlain advises the Sovereign as to who should be invited to Court and who should not. (In Queen Victoria's reign, people who had been divorced, whether they were the innocent or the guilty parties, were banned.)

A perusal of the records of the Lord Chamberlain's office in Victorian times provides fascinating reading. The cost of the ceremonial christening of the Prince of Wales, later Edward VII, is shown to have been £4,991 16s. 5d. Some years later one finds that the cost of the funeral of the Duke of Wellington which was also the responsibility of the Lord Chamberlain's department, was over £27,000, of which £23,000 was due to a couple of undertakers who were not paid for nearly three years.

Another odd entry was concerned with the arrival of a tiger sent to Queen Victoria by King William, alias Denny of Bonny on the west coast of Africa. Lord Palmerston as Foreign Secretary asked the Lord Chamberlain what was to be done about it. At the same time he enclosed a copy of the letter from the would-be donor:

To her Most Gracious Majesty Queen Victoria of Great Britain and Ireland: King William, (alias Denny) of Gaboon, will be highly gratified if Her Majesty will accept the present of a tiger as a token of his great respect.

King William has in his possession the very handsome medal that Her Majesty was pleased to send him in 1838.

I wish to tell her Most gracious Majesty that I have received a medal (the Legion of Honour) from the French King, also a French uniform.

I am most desirous to wear Her Majesty's medal but I have not a suitable dress on which to place such a very handsome orna-ment.

I should also like a crown after English manufacture together with some cloth and beads my Queen may wear on State occasions.

I am also anxious that my brother should go to England for instruction for the language and customs.

his
Signed: King x William
mark.

Alias Denny of the Gaboons, 5th December 1850. Off Ganga Tanga, West Coast of Africa.

The Lord Chamberlain duly forwarded the letter and the enclosure to the Queen who ultimately presented the tiger to the Zoo.

Almost simultaneously there was trouble with one of the royal swans which was being exposed for sale in a shop in Gracechurch Street. The owners of the shop did their best to excuse themselves by saying that the man from whom they had bought it did not know of its royal character.

In the middle of the Crimean War, the Czar Nicholas of Russia died. This put the Queen in a dilemma, for it was the custom of the Court to go into mourning for any foreign sovereign. On this occasion, of course, Great Britain was at war with Russia and it was the unfortunate Lord Chamberlain's job to find a solution. On his advice, the Queen decided not to wear black. The war over, it was again the Lord Chamberlain's duty to issue the exact protocol for the proclamation of peace—at Charing Cross and Temple Bar.

Another problem was that of Dr Dakins, one of the Priests in Ordinary to the Queen who pleaded immunity from imprison-ment as one of the Queen's chaplains. He had run into debt as a result of drink and it was shown that in six months he had consumed eight dozen bottles of port, three dozen of sherry, five gallons of gin, three gallons of brandy and four dozen bottles of marsala. Dr Dakins was removed from his post and summarily jailed.

Baron Stockmar now reappears on the scene with a memorandum on the Royal Household. He pointed out that there was no proper system of co-ordination between the Lord Chamberlain's office, the Woods and Forests and the Lord Steward. It seems that the housekeepers, pages and housemaids were under the authority of the Lord Chamberlain; the footmen, liveried porters and under-butlers under the Master of the Horse; while the cooks and porters were under the jurisdiction of the Lord Steward. Still more ludicrously, the Lord Steward's department provided fuel and laid the grates while the Lord Chamberlain's department lit the fires. (The restrictive practices of modern trades unionists pale into insignificance in comparison.) In the same way, the Lord Chamberlain's department provided all the lamps, but the Lord Steward's department had to clean, trim and light them.

If a pane of glass broke or the door of a cupboard needed mending in the scullery at St James's Palace, it had to be done as follows: a requisition was prepared and signed by the chief cook, countersigned by the Clerk of the Kitchen, and taken to be signed by the Master of the Household. Only when the Lord Chamberlain's office authorized it, was it laid before the Clerk of the Works in the Woods and Forests Department. In consequence, many a window and cupboard remained broken for months at a time.

As for Buckingham Palace—since neither the Lord Chamberlain nor the Master of Horse had a regular deputy living there, the servants could come off duty as they chose, with nobody to reprimand them. When guests arrived, there was no one to see them to their apartments; no one who even knew which apartments they had been assigned. On one occasion, a youth named Jones made his way into the palace and was found at 1 a.m. under the sofa in the room adjoining Queen Victoria's bedroom.

It was left to the Prince Consort to undertake these reforms, nor was this easy so long as the Lord Chamberlain was a political appointment. There were no fewer than nine of them between 1837 and 1859.

This was one of the last acts of the Prince Consort who, like the Duchess of Kent, died in 1861. The Queen was too upset to give any instructions as to the formalities for his funeral and it was left to the Lord Chamberlain's office at St James's Palace to carry it out. Nor was this an easy matter, because there was a shortage of black drugget and the funeral was due to take place nine days later. Fortunately the 'electric telegraph' had recently been established and it was possible to secure sufficient quantities just in time.

Queen Victoria remained so grief-stricken that public mourning for the Prince Consort was the longest in modern times (three months) while none of the Household was allowed to appear in public out of mourning for less than a year. The Queen herself remained in mourning for the rest of her life. Furthermore, she closed Buckingham Palace and it was not until the next June that the Queen's direct influence was felt again by the Lord Chamberlain when Princess Alice married Prince Louis of Hesse.

The following year St James's Palace, or rather the Lord Chamberlain's office, was kept exceedingly busy with the plans for the marriage of the Prince of Wales and Princess Alexandra of Denmark; but it was not until 1864 that Drawing-rooms at Buckingham Palace and Levees at St James's Palace were revived.

Then came the visit of the Sultan of Turkey, who insisted on shooting a few of the tame stags at Windsor before attending a naval review—which incidentally made him very seasick and caused his rapid departure.

Among the residents of St James's Palace at this time was the Queen's private secretary, General the Hon. Sir Charles Grey. When he died in 1870, the Queen gave permission for his widow to remain there for another five years.

A private and confidential letter from the Lord Chamberlain at St James's Palace dated 24 March 1871 concerned the presentation of Lady Stanley of Alderley at Court. It appears that rumours had been in circulation that she had been living with Lord Stanley for some years before her marriage and Viscount

ABOVE: MOUNTING GUARD AT THE PALACE, 1841
BELOW: THE COLOUR COURT, ST. JAMES'S, 1851

THE
CONFERENCE
ROOM,
ST JAMES'S
PALACE

ABOVE: CONFERENCE OF IMPERIAL AND ALLIED STATESMEN
AT THE PALACE IN 1941. *BELOW:* BOMB DAMAGE AT THE PALACE

THE CLOCK TOWER, ST JAMES'S

Sydney, as Lord Chamberlain, was compelled to write to Lady Sheffield, who had offered to present her, to discover whether the stories were true. Lady Sheffield replied that they had been previously married in Algiers before remarrying in England; so all was well.

Perhaps the most awkward duty of the Lord Chamberlain concerned the arrival of the Shah of Persia. The Foreign Office having heard that the Shah was liable to bring three wives with him, the Lord Chamberlain was instructed to find out, if this were true, what was to be done with them. Another problem was whether he would bring any horses and, if so, how many Persian grooms. Other questions were whether he was an early riser and whether there was anything he could not eat, whether he would drink wines, sleep on the floor or on a bed, sit on sofas or on the carpet. Letters were promptly despatched to the British Embassy at St Petersburg, where the Shah was a guest of the Czar. The reply came that he wanted to visit Woolwich Arsenal and the Dockyards and wished for a naval review because the Sultan had been accorded one. He also required a firework show at the Crystal Palace. As for his wives, they had all been returned to store from Moscow. Further information was that the Shah was quite prepared to sleep in a bed and sit on a chair instead of using the floor, out of politeness to the British.

When the news of his impending visit was made public, the proprietor of the Jermyn Street Turkish Baths sent a book of tickets for his use. This situation was handled without difficulty, but the real problem was providing Persian flags and discovering the correct national anthem, both of which required a great deal of research.

Worse and later news from Berlin, which he had visited after leaving St Petersburg, showed that the free and easy manners of the Shah, who was not yet accustomed to the behaviour of European women, had given great offence to the German royal family. The Shah himself was most unpunctual, sat down to dinner before the Empress, took her by the elbow to make her get up, put his fingers into the dishes, took food out of his mouth to look at it after it had been chewed and sometimes threw it under the table if he did not like the taste. The Court was also shocked by the manner in which the Shah consoled himself for the absence of his harem.

Worst of all, it was revealed that the Shah had telegraphed his minister at Constantinople to buy him a Georgian slave girl or two and send them on to him in London. No wonder Queen Victoria decided to lodge her guest at Buckingham Palace and to receive him for only a few hours at Windsor where she was staying.

Information from Brussels where he was expected from Berlin revealed that when the Shah dined alone he preferred to have his meals on the floor. For this purpose a movable carpet was needed, so that the Persian servants could put the dishes on it when they had been brought to the door by the English servants. It was also announced that he did not like his meat cut up and that he liked rice, lamb, mutton and chicken.

The finishing touch to his visit was his desire to see English prize-fighting. The Marquess of Queensberry duly produced fifteen men at very short notice and they gave a display of boxing for his benefit in St James's Park.

Meantime, a committee was set up to report on the sanitary conditions of the royal palaces, notably Buckingham Palace and St James's Palace, where one of the residents complained bitterly of the appalling smells arising from defective drainage. (It is strange that only the Prince Consort, of all the royal family, died of typhoid in the nineteenth century.)

Among the residents of St James's Palace in 1875 was the Duchess of Cambridge. Previously she had lived at Kew but insisted on moving to the rather gloomy apartments which were afterwards given to King George V when he was Duke of York and had just married Princess May, later Queen Mary. This section of St James's Palace had no name at the time and was only dubbed York House when the future George V went to live there.

The old Duchess of Cambridge grew more and more bent as the years went by—to the extent that people who wished to speak to her as she sat in a chair had to kneel down on the floor. One of her eccentricities was to keep her cap and wig on a stand by her chair and slap them on her head, often askew, when anyone came to call. One of the Battenberg princesses, however, met her at Clarence House wearing neither cap nor wig 'and her absolutely bald head looked like a very big egg'.

As a result of her moving to London, the Duchess of Cambridge's Teck grandchildren, Princess May, the Marquess of Cambridge and the Earl of Athlone, saw a great deal of St James's Palace, especially on Sundays. They used to gather round the invalid's chair and sing hymns, rather scared by her decrepit appearance. Nevertheless, the Duchess lingered on for several more years and the future Queen Mary and her mother, the Duchess of Teck, were allowed to use two of her rooms during the London season. When the Duchess of Cambridge finally died at the age of ninety-one Queen Victoria hurried up from Windsor to see her corpse and wrote, 'I saw dear old aunt in the same place where we last saw her, looking so peaceful and at rest and very free of suffering! She looked so nice with a white cap tucked under her chin, her head a little turned to one side—her hands folded over her breast and a little crucifix in her hands . . . May did not show very much grief . . . but later she will feel what she has lost. . . .' Although Queen Victoria was morbidly interested in death, she did not usually attend funerals. But she made an exception for her Aunt Cambridge.

Two years later, the future Queen Mary was once again at St James's Palace, this time choosing wallpapers. She had become engaged to the Duke of Clarence and the Duchess of Cambridge's apartments had been allotted to them by the Queen.

With the Duke of Clarence's unexpected death, the apartments remained unoccupied. However, within two years she married the future George V in the Chapel Royal at St James's Palace. It was a tremendous affair, attended by most of the royalty of Europe, and there was only one slight hitch. The Lord Chamberlain had forgotten that since the Queen would be taking the short route down the Mall to St James's Palace, she would arrive before the rest of the procession, which proceeded up Constitution Hill and then by way of Piccadilly to St James's Palace. In consequence of this there was only one Gentleman Usher to receive her. The Duchess of Teck diplomatically stepped into the breach. She suggested that the Queen should wait in the room on the left of the chapel while she herself walked imperiously up the aisle to take her place by the altar as mother of the bride. Behind her came a lady-in-waiting, Miss Thesiger, who suddenly felt a tug at her skirt, followed by the words, 'I am going first', and the little old lady leaning heavily on a stick brushed past the Duchess of Teck—looking to her right and left, with a white lace bonnet nodding on her head. Later, she said she was glad this had happened because it was amusing to see everyone arriving. 'Dear May looked so pretty and quiet and dignified', she wrote in her diary. '. . . Prince George gave his answers distinctly while May, though quite self-possessed, spoke very low.'

Once again, after the honeymoon, the future Queen Mary was shopping for wallpapers for York House and this time she finally moved in. That year, she was painted three times by different artists and later by Edward Hughes, whose portrait was hung over the mantelpiece in the future George V's study. It was so big that the cornice had to be cut away and since his desk was in the middle, facing the fireplace, he was able to look at it every day. Access to this study on the ground floor was through the room in which his consort dealt with her correspondence at her own desk.

By now, the young couple had equerries and ladies-in-waiting, the first of whom was Lady Eva Dugdale, only daughter of the fourth Earl of Warwick. The Duke of York's first equerry was Colonel Derek Keppel. He and Lady Eva always took luncheon and dinner with their royal employers which meant that later, the royal children were scarcely ever alone with their parents.

'So now you are installed at St James's, dear old St James's!' wrote the Grand Duchess Augusta to her niece. 'I always have it before my mind's eye since I know you are housed there. Shall I ever be able to come there again? If so, you must take me there. I am sure dearest Mama would be glad to know you are in her old rooms.'

The Duke of York was not so happy about it. 'This is a beastly house and I think very unhealthy,' he wrote to his wife, during a temporary absence, after they had been there two years. Later on he was recorded as saying, 'I hate this house more than ever when you are away.' The truth of the matter is that York House has always been dark and awkward. It has no fewer than seventy-five rooms, but the only large ones face due north. The entrance is remarkably small; at least, however, the ceilings are high.

The dining-room in those days had painted panels, with niches holding oriental vases and brass lamps in the shape of formal figures, supporting frosted white globes. In addition, there was a glass fire-screen and a circular mahogany dining-table with heavy mahogany chairs. There were two further sitting-rooms on the ground floor, with, upstairs, three fine rooms which opened into one another, all lit by heavy crystal chandeliers and wall sconces. In addition to this there were potted palms and various flowers on small tables, ottomans and sofas covered in striped silk. Opening out of one of the drawing-rooms was the future Queen Mary's bedroom with its polished brass bedstead, white painted furniture, crucifix, religious figures and a quantity of family photographs, including one of the Duke of Clarence which hung high up beside the bed.

The rest of York House was full of passages, with unexpected flights of stairs leading to small rooms all crammed with furniture. It is quite possible this was the part where Queen Caroline proved to Lord Grantham that she could reach a particular room without passing by the back stairs. These passages were really quite dangerous. 'I know how distressed you will be when you hear that I fell down full length from the night nursery into the passage, arriving on my hands and knees,' wrote the Duchess of Teck to her daughter. The retort of the future King George V was that there was a perfectly good electric light at the top of the stairs and it ought to have been turned on because, aided by Maples, he had repaired York House in a very thorough way.

As time went on, the royal couple took a better view of York House, where they gave a number of grand dinners and received further additions such as satin sofas and screens in the form of Christmas presents and birthday presents.

14. *Modern times at St James's*

FOLLOWING the death of Queen Victoria in 1901, Edward VII moved from Marlborough House to Buckingham Palace and the Duke and Duchess of York in turn moved to Marlborough House, but not for a couple of years. For one thing, Queen Alexandra refused at first to go to Buckingham Palace which, in any event, needed a great deal of modernization.

From 1903 York House was empty and between that date and 1914 was only used for the accommodation of sovereigns and heads of state paying official visits to this country. Among them were President Poincaré of France and the King of the Belgians.

The list of other Edwardian occupants of residential apartments at St James's Palace recalls the names of the best-known courtiers, such as Sir Francis Knollys, Private Secretary to Edward VII; Sir John McNeill, Sir Arthur Bigge, Sir Harry Stonor, Sir Seymour Fortescue, Sir Thomas Biddulph, Sir Godfrey Thomas, Sir Sidney Greville and Sir Frederick Ponsonby, who was created Lord Sysonby just before his death.

Sir Frederick and, later, his daughter, Loelia, Duchess of Westminster, wrote fascinating autobiographies. True, Sir Frederick made few references to his long occupation of apartments in St James's Palace, preferring to tell anecdotes of his intimate association with Queen Victoria, Edward VII and King George V. In each case, he travelled abroad with the reigning monarch and from his *Recollections of Three Reigns* rather gives the impression that he personally carried out all the duties of the Lord Chamberlain's office in connexion with State Visits abroad, in addition to his other duties. He began by being junior equerry to Queen Victoria and ended up as Keeper of the Privy Purse to George V. He does, however, tell a couple of stories about Levees at St James's Palace. Incidentally, Levees were discontinued in 1939 and have never been revived.

The first occasion was when Lord Milner, having been given the Order of the Garter, decided to wear it like the Order of the Bath at a St James's Palace Levee—over the right shoulder instead of over the left. Quite unconscious that he was wearing it incorrectly, he appeared in the Ante-chamber at the palace. Here he met Lord Curzon, who was so scandalized at his ignorance that he later wrote him a letter to say that it was almost inconceivable that anyone who had been given this Ancient Order, the highest in the land, should not have taken the trouble to find out how it should be worn.

Some months later, there was another Levee at St James's Palace on a Collar day. Collar days are certain Saints' days and Festivals on which the Knights of the various Orders of Chivalry wear the Collar of their Orders and on these occasions the ribands are not worn because the badge is attached to the Collar. Lord Curzon came rather late to the Levee and arrived in the Throne Room only just ahead of King George V; so it was not noticed that he had committed the heinous offence of wearing the riband as well as the Collar. King George V observed this at once and chaffed Curzon about his mistake. Lord Milner, overhearing this, promptly wrote to Curzon repeating word for word that 'it was almost inconceivable that anyone who had been given this Ancient Order. . . .'

Sir Frederick gives a close-up account of the accident to King George V in 1915. He had left St James's Palace to accompany the Monarch on his tour of the Front. Among his other official engagements, George V inspected fifty men of the Royal Flying Corps.

> Having ridden down the line, the King spoke to the Commanding Officer and asked him about the new machines. Seeing his superior engaged in conversation with the King, it occurred to the second-in-command, who apparently was ignorant of the instructions issued on the subject, that it devolved on him to call for three cheers; he promptly did so, while the King's horse was not more than a few yards off. The animal quivered with terror and

crouched down upon its haunches. Then suddenly springing up, it reared straight up in the air and, its hind legs slipping, it fell back right on top of the King. Now the whole point of my riding immediately behind the King was that I might be of some use if anything of the sort happened; but all this took place so quickly that I never had time to reach His Majesty.

I at once jumped off and flung the reins to the nearest man. I ran up and knelt down by the King, who had had all the wind knocked out of him. For two or three minutes he lay quite still, and then opened his eyes.

My first thought was that he had probably broken his pelvis, but he suddenly expressed a wish to stand up and we supported him on each side. I then came to the conclusion that nothing could be broken—a conclusion which I afterwards learned was absolutely wrong.

He also reveals what few people must have known at the time, that Edward VII had a golf-course laid out at Windsor and rather fancied his short game. Today, the Duke of Windsor is the only member of the royal family who enables golf justifiably to be called 'The Royal and Ancient Game'.

Loelia, Duchess of Westminster, recalls that her family's apartments in St James's Palace were at Marlborough Gate, looking partly up St James's Street, partly up Pall Mall and partly up to Marlborough House. This was originally a section of what was known as Queen Anne's Bower and gave her mother plenty of scope for interior decoration. Among other drastic changes, she pulled out the original staircase, installed an antique one with barley-sugar banisters, and boldly painted the panelling in the drawing-room. Between this drawing-room and her father's bedroom lay a 'haunted' passage. The ghost was supposed to be Sellis, the Duke of Cumberland's valet who, it will be remembered, was found murdered. Sir Frederick Ponsonby pooh-poohed the idea of a ghost; but according to his daughter, the corridor had an eerie atmosphere and strange noises could be heard at night. At least one of her friends slept there and swore that she would never spend another night there—she had been so frightened. She herself lived on the second floor. In the attics above was a mound of papers, including a box of documents all concerned with John Brown, Queen

Victoria's Scottish attendant who was so impertinent that many people believed he had been morganatically married to her. Queen Victoria wanted to write his biography but had been finally dissuaded. No doubt these documents were part of her research.

An advantage of the attic was that the Ponsonby children could squeeze through the sky-light and roam up and down the roofs of the palace. One of their childish tricks was to fill their bath-sponges with water and drip them on to the sentries below to make them think that it was raining. The object of the exercise was to make them retire into their sentry-boxes. This was often achieved.

* * *

At the outbreak of the 1914 War, Queen Mary was given permission by the King to use the vast State Apartments at St James's Palace for her Relief Clothing Guild. The officials of the National Relief Fund had also been given quarters in York House for this fund. The Prince of Wales and Queen Mary issued an appeal which raised £250,000 in the first twenty-four hours. Every day, the Queen and her lady-in-waiting, Lady Bertha Dawkins, spent their time working on the scheme and helping women who were out of work because of the war. In contrast with World War II, no bombs fell on St James's Palace, although Zeppelin raids were comparatively frequent; a wire-mesh net was stretched across the top of Buckingham Palace and air-raid precautions were drawn up for the palace staff.

On the day that peace was signed, Queen Mary spent the morning inspecting York House, which was being made ready for the Prince of Wales. (Lord Kitchener had lived there briefly during the war, until he sailed for Russia and was drowned en route. He was followed at York House by General Sir William Robertson.)

The Prince of Wales finally settled in just before leaving for Canada in 1919. His major-domo was Finch, who had originally been his nursery footman and who had once spanked him for invading Princess Mary's nursery. The advantage of York House was the extra space available for the Prince of Wales's staff which now automatically included equerries and a Private Secretary. The next addition to his retinue was Major 'Fruity' Metcalfe, whom he had met on his Indian tour and whom he immediately liked because he had arranged for him to play polo, which was outside the official programme.

'Fruity' was in those days a young captain in Skinner's Horse. He was given a room at York House and whenever there were no public functions to perform, he accompanied the Prince of Wales into the West End of London.

The evenings usually began with cocktails at York House which, according to the Prince of Wales, were much too strong at first, because Finch refused to put ice into them on the grounds that it would bruise the gin. Thereafter, the royal party would dine at the Embassy Club or perhaps see a show and end up at the Café de Paris. Sometimes they would end the evening at York House, when Fred and Adele Astaire, then performing in *Stop Flirting* at the Shaftesbury Theatre, would come and give a special exhibition of dancing to the gramophone.

Another sign of the times was that the Prince of Wales departed from the usual royal protocol of having his clothes fitted for him at home—York House. Instead of sending for Scholte, his tailor, he nearly always went to see him at his shop.

In this connexion, there was the time at York House when the Prince of Wales accoutred himself with considerable care on the first occasion when he was on duty in full dress. Having mounted his horse and ridden to Clarence House to fetch the Duke of Connaught and accompany him to Buckingham Palace, the Duke informed him tersely that he was improperly dressed. In consequence he had to turn his horse round and trot all the way back to St James's Palace where, without dismounting, the prescribed gold and crimson net sash and the gold lace sword slings and knot were put around him.

By now, the Prince of Wales was undertaking more and more tours both at home and abroad. In York House, he kept a full-scale map of the British Isles with flags marking the places which he had visited. Every now and then he would arrange for his Private Secretary to write to the Lord-Lieutenant of some county which he had not visited and ask whether it would be a good plan if he paid a visit. The answer was always in the affirmative.

During King George V's illness in 1928, the Prince of Wales deputized at each of the Levees which invariably took place at 11.30 a.m. in the Throne Room at St James's Palace. Another of his duties was to act as escort to Queen Mary when she had to hold a Court. At the Court of St James, it was routine for all the men to wear black velvet knee-breeches over black silk stockings, black pumps and a black velvet tail coat. This caused a real Anglo-American incident when Mr Charles Dawes, the new American Ambassador, announced that he would not in any circumstances wear knee-breeches—or knickers, as he called them. There were tremendous repercussions at Court and the King, then convalescing at Windsor, was most indignant. At the time, the Prince of Wales was on a trip to Northern Ireland but as soon as he returned to St James's Palace, the Lord Chamberlain (Lord Cromer) telephoned to say that Mr Dawes was determined not to wear knee-breeches, and suggested that he should come to York House to see the Prince of Wales immediately. This he did, told the Prince that the King was extremely upset and put it to him that he should call on Mr Dawes himself. The Prince refused. It was finally hoped that the American Ambassador would put on knee-breeches under the black evening trousers he had sworn he would wear and then remove the latter in a private room at the palace. The moment of truth came when Mr Dawes appeared wearing trousers.

In 1930, the Prince of Wales decided that York House was more an office than a home and received permission from King George V to take over Fort Belvedere, originally built for the Duke of Cumberland. Having renovated it most successfully, he now decided to do the same for York House. Its Victorian gloom positively demanded some kind of redecoration. A further reason for this was that, as he was taking over more and more of his father's work, the Prince was obliged to give many more formal dinners at York House, which necessitated a more dignified setting and the rearrangement and refurnishing of the reception rooms. In addition, since Prince George (later the Duke of Kent) had just left the Royal Navy, the Prince of Wales

217

decided to give him a bachelor apartment so that he could come and live with him. (It was not until 1934 when he married Princess Marina that Prince George moved away.)

One of the more important dinner parties held at York House during this period was the occasion when the Prince of Wales invited Ramsay MacDonald, Neville Chamberlain, Sir Hylton Young and Lord Derby. The talk went on until midnight on the subject of better housing conditions and slum clearance.

As Duke of Cornwall, the Prince of Wales was particularly interested in the eighty acres of real estate in London (at Kennington) of which he was technically the administrator. Hundreds of houses on the estate had been sold to the London County Council, which tore them down but did not rebuild on the site. The Prince of Wales persuaded Herbert Morrison, the LCC's Socialist leader, to meet a financial syndicate which was prepared to turn this section of Kennington into a model housing estate. Herbert Morrison arrived one afternoon at York House with, among other officials, the architect and surveyor. The meeting came to nothing (Herbert Morrison decided that it was more warehousing than housing) but it had an amusing sequel. The Prince (as he writes in *A King's Story*) had hardly escorted Mr Morrison to the door when he returned to ask for his brief-case which he had left in the dining-room. Finch handed it over. 'Ha!' exclaimed Mr Morrison, tucking it under his arm. 'It would never have done to leave the secrets of the Socialist Party at York House, would it, Sir?' 'Mr Morrison,' the Prince replied, 'It would be hard to imagine a safer place.'

In 1930, the first Levee was held at Buckingham Palace because St James's Palace was the setting of the famous Naval Treaty of London which involved the United States, Japan, France, Italy and Great Britain. Three hundred reporters 'covered' the event, dozens of extra telephones had to be installed and the vast apartment which had previously been Queen Anne's drawing-room was the centre-piece of the discussions.

That same year, the Prince of Wales threw three rooms on the ground floor of York House into one. (This was particularly useful for showing the films he had personally taken on his

African safari just previously.) Also, apartments formerly occupied by the Master of Ceremonies and later by Princess Marie Louise, which lay between it and the old archway leading from Pall Mall into Ambassadors Court, were incorporated into York House.

Rumours that it was to be turned into a royal guest house were, of course, incorrect. As a bachelor, the Prince of Wales preferred it to Marlborough House, which was essentially for a married man and, incidentally, costly to maintain.

* * *

On the death of George V, the Prince of Wales, according to protocol, entered the Banqueting Hall at St James's Palace, where all the available Privy Councillors had assembled to swear allegiance. He had, in fact, come by aeroplane from Sandringham, which was undoubtedly a precedent. The actual proclamation read by Sir Maurice Hankey, the Clerk of the Council, went as follows: '. . . We, therefore, the Lords Spiritual and Temporal of this realm do now hereby with one voice and consent of tongue and heart publish and proclaim that the High and Mighty Prince Edward Albert Christian George Andrew Patrick David is now by the death of our late sovereign of happy memory become our only lawful and rightful liege Lord, Edward VIII by the Grace of God of Great Britain, Ireland and the British Dominions beyond the seas—King, Defender of the Faith, Emperor of India. . . .'

That night the new King slept at York House, knowing that his accession would have to be publicly proclaimed at four different points in London, the first by the Garter King of Arms at St James's Palace. By this time, of course, he had fallen deeply in love with Mrs Simpson and he arranged for her and a few other friends to watch the ceremony from the grand room overlooking Friary Court. Just before the ceremony (somewhat bungled by Garter King, to the evident annoyance of the Earl Marshal, the Duke of Norfolk) took place, Edward VIII, having decided to watch the Proclamation himself, hurried across Ambassadors Court and joined them. As the Proclamation was read, Edward VIII in his own words 'realized that my relations with Wallis had suddenly entered a more significant phase', adding her comment, 'It was all very moving but it has also made me realize how different your life is going to be.'

There is one more small note on the actual ceremony. Garter King was not the only person who did not carry out his duties to everyone's satisfaction. There was a troop of the Household Cavalry drawn up in Pall Mall and the long wait which is inevitable on ceremonial occasions made the horses restless. Out of irritation the one on the right flank leant against his neighbour, who in turn leant, and the whole troop leaned over like a line of toy soldiers. The horse on the left flank could not support the weight placed upon him, crossed his legs and fell over; his rider landed in the road with a clank of body armour which resembled the proverbial kitchen stove. At the end of the ceremony a company sergeant-major in Pall Mall ordered the platoon of Foot Guards drawn up in open order facing the courtyard to turn to the right, whereupon half turned to the right and half to the left—no doubt confused by the babble of noise which had broken out from the huge crowd as soon as the proclamation had ended. On the order 'Quick march' half the guardsmen marched towards Pall Mall while the other half headed away for Wellington Barracks. The last man of the retreating body finally broke discipline when he could hear no heavy footsteps behind him and looked round; seeing what had happened, he let out a wild cry of 'Oi!' and with military precision they turned about and headed back towards Pall Mall. The CSM in an endeavour to make his voice heard above the crowd and in fury at this humiliating gaffe had turned a deep and rich mulberry hue.

Edward VIII continued to live in York House, if only because Queen Mary did not wish to leave Buckingham Palace at once. He merely transferred his office to a small waiting-room decorated in oriental style, on the ground floor, while the Royal Standard flew from the Clock Tower of St James's Palace, proving that his more carefree days as Heir Apparent were ended.

During the first six months of his reign, Edward VIII reinforced George V's household with his own York House staff. Many of his father's officials were, however, ready to retire. In addition, there were necessary changes in the appointments of the Treasurer of the Household, the Captain of the Gentlemen at Arms and the Captain of the Yeomen of the Guard.

During Court mourning, Edward VIII had few social engagements. But he gave a number of official dinner parties at York House, including two at which Mrs Simpson was present at the same time as the Prime Minister and Mrs Baldwin, Mr and Mrs Winston Churchill and Colonel and Mrs Charles Lindbergh.

Then came the famous departure from York House for the yachting trip in the *Nahlin* to the Ægean, as a result of which photographs of Mrs Simpson first appeared in the newspapers, notably one when the yacht was going through the Gulf of Corinth. Immediately on his return to York House, Edward VIII changed and dined with Queen Mary at Buckingham Palace, where she was in the middle of moving her accumulated treasures to Marlborough House to make room for him. In the meantime he was in the process of handing over York House to the Duke and Duchess of Gloucester, who have made it their London headquarters ever since.

Came 1 December 1936—the day that the Bishop of Bradford made an indirect but obvious reference to Edward VIII's private life and the need for divine guidance in the discharge of his high office. British newspapers which, until then, had loyally refused to comment on the royal liaison in spite of widespread reports in American and Continental newspapers, at last broke their silence and in a matter of days, Mrs Simpson hurried off to the South of France on a circuitous route to avoid the press. To confuse any eavesdroppers who might be listening to her telephone conversations with him, Edward VIII arranged a code whereby Lord Beaverbrook was called Tornado; Mr Stanley Baldwin was Crutch; Mr Churchill was W.S.C. (from his initials) and he himself was simply Mr James, after St James's Palace. That was his last association with it. The Abdication followed almost immediately.

* * *

With World War II looming, the Duke and Duchess of Gloucester decided to close York House and move to their new home, Barnwell Castle in Northamptonshire. This was a wise decision.

St James's Palace was hit four times in eighteen months. On 15 October 1940, a land-mine dropped near the railings in St James's Park, damaged the windows of the State Apartments and Clarence House and all the apartments in Ambassadors Court, Engine Court and Friary Court. On 10/11 November 1940, a bomb fell in Cleveland Row causing damage to York House and the palace generally.

On 8 March 1941, an incendiary bomb fell on the Guard Room, Engine Court, and another on the roof of York House, but both were quickly dealt with and no fire resulted. On the night of 10/11 May 1941, eight servants' rooms in Friary Court, belonging to the apartment of Lady Helena Gleichen, were destroyed by high explosive bombs and much superficial damage was done to the palace generally. This included the damage done to the famous clock which faces up St James's Street—the same clock which had caused trouble in the days of William IV. Two guardsmen who were on sentry duty below it were killed.

Lady Helena Gleichen, in spite of her age, was the originator of the Home Guard. It was on a bright spring afternoon in March 1940 that, having left St James's Palace, she called at the Battalion Headquarters of the K.S.L.I. stationed at Ross-on-Wye, saying that she was alarmed at the possibility of German Parachute troops landing in the thinly populated areas of Herefordshire and the Welsh border. She had, therefore, organized her staff and tenantry to the number of eighty in bands of watchers whom she had stationed on the high ground in the neighbourhood of Much Marcle. These men went on duty every night and each had an arm-band stencilled 'Much Marcle Watchers'. She asked for the loan of eighty rifles and ammunition 'with a couple of machine-guns if you have any'. Naturally, the Battalion Commander could not comply with her wishes, but there, two months before the Local Defence Volunteers were formed, was the first Home Guard with brassards and organization—even to the lack of arms.

In January 1946, St James's Palace was the scene of a unique banquet attended by the Cabinet and the United Nations Secretariat and presided over by King George VI, who sat beneath the portrait of William IV. It must have been a wonderful sight with the tall candles in solid gold candelabra and gold vases filled with chrysanthemums and pink and white orchids. The knives, forks and spoons were also of gold and the guests left their hats in the Guard Room where Charles I spent his last night.

In view of the austerities of the day, it was fortunate that the King could provide pheasants from Sandringham and that lobsters were also available. Among the guests were King Feisal II, Mr Byrnes, the U.S. Secretary of State, and Mr Ernest Bevin, the Foreign Secretary.

In the course of his speech, George VI said that it was in their hands to make or mar the happiness of millions and that, in the long course of history, it was the most important meeting ever held in London.

Later that year, the clock was put in order again.

Today there are twenty residential apartments at St James's Palace, ranging from two rooms to York House. The occupants include the Duke and Duchess of Gloucester; the Princess Royal, who has the second largest set of apartments with an entrance between Friary Court and Engine Court; the Rev. Maurice Foxell, Sub-dean of the Chapels Royal: Sir Mark Milbank, Master of the Household; Sir Norman Gwatkin, Comptroller of the Lord Chamberlain's office; Lord Cairns, Marshal of the Diplomatic Corps; Sir Michael Adeane, the Queen's Private Secretary; Sir Edward Ford, Assistant Private Secretary to the Queen; Mr Michael Watts, Page of the Back-stairs; Sir Frank Evans, Chief Accountant to the Privy Purse; Mr A. J. Galpin, Secretary to the Lord Chamberlain's office; Lord Tryon, Keeper of the Privy Purse; Mr W. Buckell, Sergeant of the Vestry (in other words, head verger); and Major Michael Hawkins, Private Secretary to the Duke of Gloucester.

Although he had a town house, Lord Cobbold, who succeeded Lord Scarbrough as Lord Chamberlain, decided to move into the apartments which Lord Scarbrough occupied in his official capacity.

It is one of the conditions of the occupancy of these apartments that the cost of interior alterations made by new tenants has to be met by them and not by the Crown. The occupants must also agree to spend at least part of the year in the apartments and, if absent, must leave domestic servants in charge. The reason for this was primarily that when the Duke of Cumberland became King of Hanover and failed to return for some years, he refused to give up his right to the apartments, although Queen Victoria badly wanted them for her mother, the Duchess of Kent.

As the standard of comfort increases, more and more changes are made by the incoming tenants. New bathrooms are installed and small rooms are knocked into large ones, but the palace continues to resemble an assortment of college buildings clustered around a number of courtyards, its rather shabby appearance being a legacy from the old days when castles were becoming homes rather than fortresses. Indeed, St James's Palace today looks more like a secondary Cambridge college than a palace, in spite of the Clock Tower and the guardsmen on sentry duty.

Like undergraduates and dons, the occupants are continuously coming and going—in the latter case as a result of the death or retirement of Court officials, this eventuality being frequently determined by the change in the monarchy.

* * *

A present-day personal tour of York House is fascinating. The numbers of winding staircases, the nooks and crannies, the really—in the best sense of the word—homely atmosphere; the elderly oil paintings of former members of the royal family contrasting with the sporting prints of the present occupants; the private flat of Amos the butler who was left behind by the Duke of Windsor; the Jubilee Room (once the nerve centre of the King George V Jubilee Trust Fund, earlier the bedroom and sitting-room of the Duke of Kent when he was Prince George and now the office and bedroom of the current lady-in-waiting to the Duchess of Gloucester); the Kitchener chair, sole relic of the Field Marshal's occupancy in World War I; the peeling pseudo-panelling on the first flight of the main staircase; the Duke's study dominated by its magnificent bookcase; the Duchess's sitting-room dominated in turn by a king-size writing desk; the splendid ballroom which is, however, officially unsafe for dancing; the dining-room with its picture of

Adonis (the white charger of George III); Prince William's suite of bedroom, bathroom and sitting-room; the former nursery now available as a spare bedroom; the profusion of Chinese screens; the writing table in the Jubilee Room constructed from all the woods of Australia—walnut, tulip, jarrah and blackwood; the hollow pillars in the main entrance; the inner hall with its comfortable red sofas and Chinese wallpaper; the green drawing-room and salon, the six bathrooms, the series of servants' bedrooms on the top floor; the distinguished furniture and the countless references to the 10th Hussars, with whom the Duke of Gloucester served as a younger man— all add up to a really comfortable home, rather than a part of the most historic palace in Great Britain, if not in the world.

To run it requires a Private Secretary, a Comptroller, two equerries and two ladies-in-waiting, who alternate each month (there are four extra equerries and two extra ladies-in-waiting when the occasion demands), the Duchess's secretary, a secretary each for the Private Secretary and the Comptroller, a butler, a valet, a personal maid, two footmen, an odd-job man, a cook, two kitchen-maids, a head housemaid, two ordinary housemaids, two daily helps and finally two chauffeurs who have flats in the Mews at the back of Marlborough House.

In tremendous contrast are the State Apartments, mostly overlooking the Mall or Friary Court. On the ground floor is the Lower Corridor with its scarlet carpets and portraits of Charles I and Prince Rupert as a boy. This is used as a cloak-room for the men, when the occasion demands, and leads to the double Grand Staircase which ascends left and right to the actual State Rooms. The first on the left is the Guard Room with its green walls and badge of the Garter on the ceiling. This is where Charles I spent his last night before his execution and from where Edward VIII and, later, Queen Elizabeth II watched themselves being proclaimed as Monarch from the low balcony of Friary Court. Normally it is used as a powder room for the ladies, although its walls are covered with mediaeval pistols, pikes and swords. Next to it is the Armoury, also with green walls and still more old-time methods of destruction in the form of blunderbusses, cutlasses, dirks and lances. This leads into the Tapestry Room—red-carpeted and with an ancient fireplace on the left-hand side of which one can still see the entwined initials of H and A (for Henry VIII and Anne Boleyn) although the A on the right-hand side has been cut off. The walls are covered with the priceless Mortlake tapestries, faded but still beautiful. The Tapestry Room leads into a vast chamber with a white ceiling, gold scroll-work in the corners, a massive chandelier and tired portraits by Sir Joshua Reynolds of the Marquess of Granby (immortalized by so many public-houses) and William, Count of Lippe-Buckburg. Both pictures badly need cleaning.

The Queen Anne Drawing-room, another most impressive chamber, used as an entrée room, finally leads to the Throne Room, with its gilded Grinling Gibbons carvings and its flattering portrait of George IV by Sir Thomas Lawrence. At the far end is the actual throne—a golden armchair with a crown picked out in pearls and the initials of Queen Elizabeth II, although the backcloth still bears the Victorian cipher. Today it is only used on State Visits, when the worthies of the City and elsewhere are presented to visiting royalty.

When in 1960 Mr Peregrine Bertie married Miss Susan Wills, the daughter of Major Wills, who was related to the Queen Mother through his marriage to the Hon. Jean Buller-Fullerton-Elphinstone, almost the whole royal family was present at the wedding reception which was held in the Queen Anne Room and the Throne Room at St James's Palace. The occasion was enlivened by Prince Charles, who was one of the pages, doing somersaults in his Royal Stuart kilt until he was removed by the flunkeys.

Behind the Throne Room is the Council Chamber with its silk and nylon wall coverings (used by the Privy Council on very special occasions) and the Sovereign's Staircase for the use of the Monarch when coming over from Buckingham Palace. Close to this is the Ascot office of the Duke of Norfolk. In one corner is a door connecting, since 1960, with Clarence House; for the benefit of the Queen Mother, a covered passage was constructed over an open area so that she could enter St James's Palace without going outside. To make this possible, a toilet-room had to be demolished.

Also on the first floor is the Picture Gallery, its walls covered with poorly kept pictures of the various sovereigns down to

Queen Victoria, all dominated at one end by the copy of Holbein's famous portrait of Henry VIII standing with his feet well apart.

This room is frequently used for charity purposes, like the vast Banqueting Hall which was not completely restored, after its bomb damage in 1941, until 1962. Nearby is the so-called Matted Hall (a small ante-room) and the passage leading to the Chapel Royal along which Charles I walked a few minutes before his death.

The Chapel Royal, which holds 170 people, is all scarlet and gold except for its original Holbein ceiling and the panelled organ installed by George V.

The only picture of all those in the State Rooms which does not seem to need restoring is the one of Charles II, said to be the first state portrait specially painted for the accession of a Monarch. (Presumably the Holbein portrait of Henry VIII does not come into this category.) The reason for this particular picture being restored is that it was lent to the Royal Academy and cleaned for a special exhibition.

So much, briefly, for the State Rooms. Above the Armoury is the room where officers dine when on Guard. On one side of the mantelpiece is the short sword worn by George II at the Battle of Dettingen in 1742. It is in a glass case, carefully locked since 1949 when there was an unfortunate incident. An American dining on Guard as a guest of the Irish Guards was sitting on the padded fireplace when his attention was attracted to the sword. Taking it out of the glass case, he placed it under his foot and, to test the temper of the steel, which he doubted, proceeded to bend it. The end snapped off. Before his horrified host and fellow-guests could prevent him, he did it again, causing a second break. The consequence was that a senior expert of the firm holding the Royal Warrant for looking after and providing swords for the palace had to be brought back hastily from a fishing holiday in Scotland to mend it. This was done and the bill of £90 or thereabouts was footed by the American.

Elsewhere in the acre of royal apartments are, among others, the Duke of Gloucester's offices, the Yeomen of the Guard, the Clarence House offices, the Gentlemen at Arms, the Ministry of Works stores, and above all, the Lord Chamberlain's office. This is still the centre of communications for royal movements and almost everything else which is not connected with the funeral arrangements of the current sovereign. (If, for example, the Queen's aircraft is delayed in flight, it is the business of the Lord Chamberlain's office to warn by telephone or telegram all kinds of notables from the Prime Minister downwards about the late arrival.)

Until 1962, it was the Lord Chamberlain's office which was responsible for the safe-keeping overnight of the Imperial Crown after it had been brought from the Tower of London and before it was taken to Buckingham Palace for the Monarch to wear on the occasion of the Royal Speech in the House of Lords.

His offices are small, dark and at first sight riddled with untidy little staircases leading up and down. In addition to his duties described earlier, another responsibility is, of course, the censoring of plays—a duty going back centuries. Lord Morrison of Lambeth, the head of the Film Censors Board, hinted more than once that the broadmindedness of the Lord Chamberlain's office caused him some concern, particularly in relation to homosexual themes. This is in startling contrast to the theory generally held by the theatre critics that present-day censoring of plays is far too strict and quite anachronistic. Incidentally, the Lord Chamberlain has no control over the censorship of music-hall jokes and patter, so that official references to Heads of State at a Royal Command Variety performance are entirely at the discretion of the individual comedian.

The palace was twice used in 1963 for royal parties. The first was a cocktail dance in the State Rooms given by the Duke of Gloucester for Prince William's twenty-first birthday, following some time after a private dinner party given at York House which all the Royal Family attended.

The wedding reception given with the Queen's permission by Princess Marina for Princess Alexandra and the Hon. Angus Ogilvy was attended by five hundred guests. Of these, one hundred were members of the British or foreign royal families, headed by the King of Norway, the Queens of Sweden and Greece and ex-Queen Ena of Spain. The reception was given in the Queen Anne Room and the ante-room; the Throne Room being democratically used for the equipment of the television cameras. The number of guests was matched by the five hundred dark red baccarat roses which formed a screen behind the five-tiered wedding cake. When Princess Alexandra cut it, she had to be helped by her husband to penetrate the very thick icing. There was the traditional good-humoured advice from various members of the Royal Family, including the Duke of Kent. Mr Ogilvy, turning to his wife, said smilingly after the first incision, 'Go on, do the lot.'

The Duke of Kent gave the toast of 'the bride and bridegroom', to which the bridegroom replied, 'Ladies and gentlemen, thank you very much, and thank you all for coming.'

It needed all the dexterity of Lady Moyra Hamilton, who carried the enormous train of the bride, to enable her to circulate around the guests. They included one hundred and fifty tenants and staff from Kensington Palace, Coppins, the Castle of Airlie and Cortachie Castle. Also among the guests were the Archbishop of Canterbury and a sergeant from the Wellington, West Coast and Taranaki Regiment who had come from the other side of the world for the occasion.

Having gone through the covered passage to Clarence House to change into their going-away clothes, the bride and bridegroom returned to St James's Palace and heralded by pipers of the Scots Guards walked down the grand staircase to Friary Court, which was the setting for their farewell and where they were seen off by the Queen and other members of the Royal Family, including Prince Charles, who thoroughly enjoyed himself showering rice on them and anyone else in the neighbourhood.

Space forbids a recapitulation of the many famous ambassadors accredited to the Court of St James. But room must be made for Monsieur de Fleuriau, the French Ambassador just before World War II. He was granted an audience by the Empress Eugénie on the same day as the eighty-year-old Duchesse de Richelieu. The latter, in conversation with the Empress, observed casually in French to her, 'Yes, as my husband was telling Louis XIV. . . .'

Princess Marie Louise, herself a former occupant of one of the grace and favour apartments at St James's Palace, repeated the story in her memoirs published shortly before her death and explained that the Duke, who had been a page of Louis XIV's at the age of nine, had married the Duchess as his third wife when he was over eighty.

Such are the personal links with the past. Even more exciting are those of the Palace Extraordinary still very much in excistence, bursting with activity and as lively as ever it was in the days when Henry VIII lived there so passionately with Anne Boleyn.

Bibliography

Churchill, Randolph. *They serve the Queen*. London, 1953.

Graeme, Bruce. *The Story of St James's Palace*. London, 1929.

Leaves from the Greville Diary, ed. P. Morrell. London, 1929.

Guttmacher, M. S. *America's Last King*. New York, 1941.

Hennessy, James Pope. *Queen Mary, 1867–1953*. London, 1959.

Love Letters of Henry VIII, ed. H. Savage. London, 1949.

Lord Hervey. *Memoirs of the Reign of George II*. 2 vols. London, 1848.

McCormick, Donald. *The Hellfire Club*. London, 1958.

Marie Louise, Princess. *My Memories of six Reigns*. London, 1956.

Millar, A. *The Life of Prince Henry, Prince of Wales*. London, 1760.

Molloy, Joseph Fitzgerald. *The Sailor King: William IV, his Court and his Subjects*. London, 1903.

Montagu, Lady Mary Wortley. *Letters and Memoirs*.

Pearson, Hesketh. *Charles II*. London, 1960.

Ponsonby, Sir Frederick. *Recollections of three Reigns*. London, 1951.

Powell, S. *The Life and Uncommon Adventures of Captain Dudley Bradstreet*. Dublin, 1775.

Public Record Office.

Sheppard, J. Edgar. *Memorials of St James's Palace*. 2 vols. London, 1894.

Sidney, Thomas. *Heirs Apparent*. London, 1957.

Memoirs of Baron Stockmar, ed. F. Max Müller. 2 vols. London, 1872.

Strickland, Agnes. *Lives of the Queens of England*. 12 vols. London, 1840–8.

Swift, Jonathan. *Journal to Stella*. ed. G. A. Aitken, London, 1901.

BIBLIOGRAPHY

Turner, E. S. *The Court of St James*. London, 1959.

Watson, Vera. *A Queen at Home*. London, 1952.

Westminster, Loelia, Duchess of. *Grace and Favour*. London, 1961.

Wilkins, W. H. *Caroline the Illustrious, Queen Consort of George II*. 2 vols. London, 1901.

Williams, Charles. *James I*. London, 1934.

Windsor, H.R.H. the Duke of. *A King's Story*. London, 1951.
A Family Album. London, 1960.

Wood, Edward J. *Giants and Dwarfs*. London, 1868.

Index

Index

238

INDEX

Pitt, William (Earl of Chatham), 145, 147, 149, 152, 158
Pitt, William, the younger, 165, 170, 173
Play censorship, 228
Plymouth, Charles Fitzcharles, Earl of, 61
Poincaré, Raymond, 212
Polly (Gay), 123
Ponsonby, Sir Frederick, 212–14
Pope, Alexander, 118, 120–1
Portland, Lady, 110
Portsmouth, Louise de Kérouaille, Duchess of, 61–2, 69, 70, 71, 97, 141
Price, Goditha, 62
Princess Royal, 223
Privy Council, 12, 17, 74, 78, 101–2, 151, 198–9, 200, 226
Pultency, William, 120
Purcell, Henry, 95
Purcell, Mrs, 125–6

Queen's Chapel, 36, 54, 64, 65, 66, 72, 81
Queen Anne Drawing-room, 226
Queen Anne's Bower, 214
Queensberry, 8th Marquess of, 208
Queensberry, Duchess of, 123

Raleigh, Sir Walter, 28, 31, 34
Recollections of Three Reigns (Ponsonby), 212–14
Reform Bill (1831), 196
Reynolds, Sir Joshua, 226
Reynolds, Dr Henry Revell, 162
Richelieu, Duc de, 228–9
Richmond, 32, 33, 113
Richmond, Henry Fitzroy, 1st Duke of, 1, 6, 11
Richmond, Charles Stuart, 3rd Duke of, 59–60
Robartes, Lady, 62
Roberts, Jane, 60
Robertson, General Sir William, 215

Robinson, John, 159
Robinson, Perdita, 160
Rochester, Earl of, 71
Rochford, George, Viscount, 9, 10, 11
Rochford, Lady, 9, 10
Romney, George, 110
Rosamond's Pond, 73
Rose, John, 53
Ross, Thomas, 53
Royal Marriage Act (1772), 151, 169, 176
Royal Society of Literature, 191
Rupert, Prince, 63, 225
Russell, Lady Caroline, 142

St Albans, Charles Beauclerk, Duke of, 61
St Albans, Duchess of, 98
St George, Madame, 37
St James's Chapel, 79, 86, 93, 117, 170
St James's Fair, 24, 63–4, 89–91, 93
St James's Park, 3, 21, 36, 53, 56, 58, 64, 96, 119, 174, 183; Evelyn's description of, 65; increase of, 73; Queen Anne's regulations for, 87–9
St. John, Lady, 110
St John's College, Oxford, 63
St Laurent, Madame de, 184
St Thomas's Hospital, 14–15
Sandpit, Windsor, 190
Sandwich, Edward Montagu, 1st Earl of, 55
Sanitation, 3–4, 24, 32, 208
Sawston Hall, 17
Sayes Court, Deptford, 82
Schulenburg, Countess of, 99–100, 101, 102, 104
Scott, Sir Walter, 191
Scrope, Lady, 27
Sedley, Catharine (Countess of Dorchester), 67, 72, 75, 97
Sefton, Lord, 196

243